SNOWDON

For my grandchildren,
Charles, Lucinda, Theodore,
Rose and Phoebe

SNOWDON

Public Figure, Private Man

Brian Hoey

SUTTON PUBLISHING

First published in 2005 by
Sutton Publishing Limited · Phoenix Mill
Thrupp · Stroud · Gloucestershire · GL5 2BU

British Library Cataloguing in Publication Data
A catalogue record for this book is available from the British
Library

ISBN 0-7509-3867-6

Typeset in 11/14.5pt Sabon.
Typesetting and origination by
Sutton Publishing Limited.
Printed and bound in England by
J.H. Haynes & Co. Ltd, Sparkford.

Contents

List of Illustrations   vii
Author's Note   ix

1   Snowdon at Home   1
2   Public Figure, Private Man   11
3   Early Days   25
4   A Photographer in the Making   47
5   Royalty Revealed   57
6   An Engagement is Announced   67
7   A Royal Wedding   75
8   Honeymoon Afloat   89
9   Tony & Margaret   97
10   Tony & the Royal Household   113
11   The Reluctant Royal   119
12   The Royal Impresario   133
13   A Parting of the Ways   145
14   Tony & Diana   163
15   Life after Margaret   177
16   The Snowdon Children   189
17   Tony Today   205
18   Two Royal Deaths   213
19   Still Searching for Happiness?   223

Appendix I: Snowdon the Craftsman   231
Appendix 2: Snowdon Family Tree   236
Select Bibliography   237
Index   239

List of Illustrations

Black and white plates, between pages 118 and 119

On the balcony of Buckingham Palace after their wedding, 6 May
    1969
After a Beatles première
With David and Sarah, Kensington Palace garden
Arriving back in Britain from Australia
On the Isle of Man TT course
Arriving at Caernarvon Castle for the Investiture of the Prince of
    Wales
Leaving Pant Glas Junior School, Aberfan
With Lucy Lindsay-Hogg, Kensington and Chelsea Register Office
Greetings at the Dunhill Party
With David Linley and Sarah Chatto at the National Theatre
Viscount Linley and Lady Frances Armstrong-Jones
Lucy, Countess Snowdon, and Sarah Chatto
At the wedding of Sarah to Daniel Chatto
With the Queen at the reopening of the Albert Memorial
En route to the Queen's golden wedding anniversary lunch
Melanie Cable-Alexander and son Jasper
At Princess Margaret's funeral

Author's Note

I originally started to write this book more than five years ago when Lord Snowdon gave me a number of interviews during which we recorded several hours of his comments about his life and work. He also provided me with access to his vast personal collection of press cuttings and arranged for me to talk to his son, David, and to some of his closest friends who were happy to see me, once they had checked with him. Unfortunately, three of them have since died – Sir Harry Secombe, Quentin Crewe and David Hicks – but their words live on through the tape recordings I made with them. I also discussed Lord Snowdon with the late Diana, Princess of Wales just a few weeks before she died, and I feel what she said then is still relevant today.

For a number of reasons I was unable to complete the book at that time. So this year, I returned to the manuscript and rewrote it, also extending the text to bring it up to date. When I told Lord Snowdon of my plans now to publish the book, he invited me to visit him again at his home in Kensington.

Although I have known him on and off for the best part of forty years, we have met only spasmodically in that time, and our meetings have always been for purely professional reasons. So I do not pretend to claim a close friendship with him. But as I subscribe to the theory that it is not necessary for a successful biography to rely on a personal relationship with the subject, this should not be a problem. Indeed, it may even benefit by being more objective because of our admittedly slight acquaintanceship. What follows is, I hope, a fair and balanced account of one of the most interesting and fascinating figures to be associated with the royal family.

Apart from those mentioned above, a number of others have helped me in writing this book. My first and respectful thanks must go to Her Majesty The Queen, who gave her gracious permission for me to visit the Royal Archives at Windsor Castle where all the documents relating to the wedding of Princess Margaret and Lord Snowdon were made available. I have also been able to talk to Gunn Brinson, Lord Snowdon's picture editor on the *Sunday Times Magazine* and the woman who worked more closely with him than almost anyone else during his newspaper days. Among the others to whom I owe a debt of gratitude are: Lord Snowdon's son, Viscount Linley, Lady Myra Secombe, Sir Anthony Hopkins, Richard Goodwin, Lord Brabourne, Ronald Allison, former Press Secretary to the Queen, Pamela Clark, Registrar, Royal Archives, Windsor Castle, Frank Bruno, Margaret Jones, Graham Stark, Thomas Whitaker, Janice Robertson, Simon Weston and Mrs L. Dunn at Lord Snowdon's former home, Plas Dinas, in North Wales. Several members of the royal household, past and present, also contributed, but whose anonymity I am pledged to respect.

At Sutton Publishing, Jeremy Yates-Round commissioned the book, while Jaqueline Mitchell has been the engine that has driven the project from start to finish, Alison Miles has been my editor, Jane Entrican has overseen the selection of illustrations, and Helen Holness has had the responsibility for marketing *Snowdon: Public Figure, Private Man*. My thanks to them all.

As usual, all opinions, unless directly quoted and sourced, are mine and mine alone – as are any errors.

Brian Hoey, August 2004

ONE

Snowdon at Home

On a cold February morning I rang the bell outside the lower ground floor of Lord Snowdon's house in Kensington, practically a stone's throw from his former home at Kensington Palace.

The door was opened by Lord Snowdon's younger daughter, Lady Frances Armstrong-Jones. I was shown into an office-cum-studio, which was the tidiest room I had ever seen for such a busy person. Minimalism was the word that sprang to mind. Three of Lord Snowdon's simple red wooden chairs, which he had designed for the Investiture of the Prince of Wales, lined one wall with a long, low table in front of them. There were filing cabinets, all neatly labelled on two other walls and an assistant's desk, with telephone, fax machine and word processor completing the furnishing. There was nothing to indicate that this was the headquarters of one of the world's top photographers; no pictures of famous personalities, Pirelli calendars or other paraphernalia littered the room.

Lady Frances told me that her father would join me in a moment and that he had left a few books and files for me to look at while I was waiting.

I hadn't seen him for some years, and from press reports I had read I was expecting to see someone half-crippled, wrinkled and stooped. But the years have been kind to Tony Snowdon – in some ways. He is now in his seventies, looks ten years younger and, while he retains a trim body, there is nothing weak or insubstantial about his appearance at all, apart from the fact that he now has great difficulty in walking unaided. As he says, without a hint of self-pity, 'The legs have gone.' But even here he has used his own talents to design the walking stick he now needs. It's good-looking, circular-

1

handled and made of laminated wood. One thing you notice about him when he shakes hands is that he has the strongest grip and workmanlike hands. He has retained a full head of chestnut-coloured hair with barely a hint of grey and now wears glasses all the time. But outwardly, his appearance seems barely to have changed in thirty years.

He is wearing an open-necked shirt over a white T-shirt, tan corduroy trousers and black boots which do not have laces but a simple catch to fasten them. He is also wearing a heavy stainless-steel wristwatch that has a practical, if not very elegant, look about it.

Just before we enter his private domain, he indicates the lavatory in case I need it. The door is decorated with a brass plate bearing the legend, 'Sir Robert Armstrong-Jones', Snowdon's grandfather, and on the wall leading to his office is a large wooden sign with the words 'Wine and Spirits' printed on it.

The studio is equipped with two more of the Investiture chairs, which he says have now become collector's items, changing hands for hundreds of pounds each, and if you can lay your hands on a set of six they will cost you a couple of thousand at least. The antiques expert John Bly actually auctioned one set for charity when it was sold for £35,000.

This room is definitely a working photographer's studio; it couldn't be anything else. And the pictures on his desk give a clue to the identity of the photographer. Family photographs of the Queen and Prince Philip, Prince Charles, the Princess Royal, all with personal greetings and a stunning picture of the late Diana, Princess of Wales, inscribed 'To Dearest Tony . . . Love Diana'. One of the nicest is of his daughter Lady Sarah Chatto, whom he calls 'Ya Ya', and his daughter-in-law, Lady (Serena) Linley, together.

The eye is immediately attracted by a dramatic photograph of Princess Margaret – at her most beautiful – and among those pinned up on the walls are three stunning pictures of Lucy, the present Countess of Snowdon.

The decorations show an eclectic taste. Figures of ancient Japanese warriors stand alongside a table of which the legs are in the form of crossed storks' legs. A sophisticated audio system fills one wall, and his collection of tapes is placed where he can reach them easily, and all in perfect order. His personal assistant says he is the most orderly man she has ever met; he knows where everything is – or should be – and can get very impatient if something is not in its right place.

All in all, his office tells you something, but not much, about Snowdon the man. The neatness perhaps illustrates his own fastidiousness, but there is no hint of the private man or even the public figure he has become since marrying into the royal family in 1960. And nothing that reflects either his orderly mind or his wildly fluctuating moods. There is one clue to his fascination with working with his hands. A cupboard reveals one of the most comprehensive collections of tools imaginable. There is every kind of spanner, ratchet, screwdriver and chisel. And every one shows signs of extensive use.

He is a man of enormous passions and enthusiasms, two of the earliest being riding motorcycles and driving fast cars. Today he no longer drives, his childhood polio having affected his left leg. But as a young man he could handle anything on wheels.

When we spoke about him riding around Caernarvon on his Triumph 500 motorbike and driving his Aston Martin DB5 – the James Bond model – it reminds him that riding motorbikes is one of the most enjoyable pastimes and he recounts the number he has owned and their make and engine capacity. 'I love motorbikes, I always have. The only time I don't like them is when my son, David, rides them. He is like I was at his age, and I get very scared for him sometimes.'

Then he remembers the Aston Martin and how he came to buy it: 'It belonged to Peter Sellers, and he could never hang on to a car for longer than a few months, sometimes only weeks. Anyway, he wanted to get rid of the Aston and offered it to me. I couldn't really afford it at the time. It had only done 5,000 miles; it wasn't even run in properly. But Peter insisted that I buy it, and I got it for a price I couldn't refuse, £3,000. I gave it to David who kept it in pristine condition until he sold it. If we'd sold it at the top of the market it would have fetched around £200,000, but we didn't.'

When we talk about style he sets off about Alec Issigonis, the brilliant Italian who designed the first Mini – the car not the skirt! (He is also friendly with the inventor of the miniskirt, Mary Quant.) Snowdon and Issigonis were close friends for years, and Tony tells about the time he had his first Mini. 'This was in the days when the front windows moved from side to side not up and down. So I had a garage take mine out and replace them with the more modern wind-down sort. The car went back to Birmingham for something or other, and when he returned it the windows had been returned to their original state. I asked why he had done it, and he said, "Because it's very bad for your passenger's hair. It doesn't get blown about with my windows. That was why I made them that way in the first place." And, of course, he was absolutely right.'

After a little over an hour of this we leave for lunch. We are going to an hotel practically next door to Clarence House, but he says he doesn't know it and has never been there before. Because of his legs, getting into the restaurant is a slow and painful business and he relies on a walking stick which he now uses increasingly to help him get along. Eventually we sit down and order drinks; he wants a Bloody Mary 'with a very large helping of vodka'. He may not have been in the hotel before but all the staff and the other diners recognise him. There's a certain amount of elbow nudging as we enter the dining-room. He orders a steak so rare it's practically raw and 'big fat chips'. Throughout the meal, which lasts over two hours, he chats animatedly with the wine waiter, discussing various vintages, and tells me about his latest projects that involved trips to Russia and India. But, as he puts it, 'I'm like Australian wine, I do not travel well.'

He is in the mood for talking, and away he goes on another round of anecdotes. Every subject we raise reminds him of a story, and he obviously enjoys an audience. However, he has such a mercurial mind that within minutes he digresses as something sets him off in a completely different direction. His mind is like a grasshopper, leaping about from place to place. The nervous energy is startling, and the ideas tumble over each other. He's interested in everything.

I left feeling slightly exhausted. He has that effect on many people apparently. He is so enthusiastic himself it transfers to everyone around him, and as a motivator he has few equals. I had been told before this meeting that he could be extremely difficult and that if you got off on the wrong foot with him you might just as well leave because things would not improve. This didn't happen with me. I had also been warned that he had a very short attention span and could not concentrate on any one subject for very long. This was not my experience of him. True, he did give the impression of thinking about several subjects at the same time, but for the four hours I was with him he appeared to give me his undivided attention, and when I asked questions to which he did not have a ready answer, he considered for what seemed to be a number of minutes – actually it was probably no more than thirty seconds – before giving a well-thought out reply. He also has the knack of being a good listener and of asking searching questions of his own. Because he has such perfect manners and a disarming personality, he lulls one into forgetting the strength of his passions: his loathing for the current lack of decent behaviour prevalent in Britain, the way in which his own exquisite taste is offended by some of the so-called arbiters of fashion today and the intolerance of many people towards the elderly and handicapped.

In other ways he reminds me of the Duke of Edinburgh. They both have enquiring minds and an insatiable curiosity. Both have short fuses and neither suffers fools gladly – or even at all. But there the resemblance ends. While Prince Philip blatantly uses his position to get what he wants and never allows anyone to forget for an instant who he is, or the position he holds, Lord Snowdon rarely, to my knowledge, resorts to anything approaching bullying tactics. In fact he seems quite vulnerable. While he gives the impression of being self-confident, he contradicts this when he says he is terrified of not being wanted.

I had been advised that he is a man of sudden extremes, who will embrace you or ignore you as the mood takes him. And I was also told that there is something in his make-up that does not allow him to be ambivalent about anything. Those who know him, and those, far fewer, who know him well, agree on one point – he is dedicated to his cause, whatever that might be at any particular time, and he hates dealing with anyone who doesn't feel the same way.

He doesn't appear to be a man who uses his undoubted royal connections to obtain anything for himself, and yet one of the Queen's most senior aides, a long-serving courtier at Buckingham Palace, told me, 'We handle Snowdon with kid gloves. He can be awkward if he thinks he is not being treated in the proper manner, and he's not above using his position, which is still very influential here, if he wants something we are not too happy about providing.'

In an age when cynicism and arrogance appear to be the norm among celebrities, and when good manners and common courtesy are considered to be old-fashioned and, not only outdated, but unwanted in these days of political correctness, it is refreshing to come across a man who exemplifies some of the old-world qualities. I cannot imagine Tony Snowdon not standing to greet a woman, or not holding a door to allow her to precede him. I think it would be completely foreign to his nature. He may like the odd moan about someone he has met and who he has not got along with, but he is more likely to utter it in private.

I may be totally wrong about him. But if I am, he is one of the finest actors I have come across. I left his house with the feeling that he had been glad to see me and that, on that occasion at least, there was nothing in the world more important that he wanted to do, or no one he would rather have spent the day with. If it's an acquired skill, it's one many politicians would kill for. Perhaps it is because he is completely at ease with himself and so does not feel the need to overcompensate with public displays of temper tantrums. He has spent enough time among theatrical 'luvvies' to recognize the infantile behaviour of many real and so-called stars.

He still enjoys the company of actors and writers and admits to being totally stage-struck even now. He no longer has, if he ever did have, any ambitions in the theatre himself, but one gets the impression that he wouldn't have minded in the least if his career had taken off in a direction other than photography – perhaps light comedy in the David Niven or Dudley Moore mould.

He is always busy with so many different projects, and there is always something new to attract his attention and boundless energy. As several of his colleagues say, 'His enthusiasm can be a bit overpowering sometimes.'

Snowdon's working day starts at about 9.15, when he comes down from upstairs where he lives. The upper floors are the residence; the lower half-basement is strictly for work. His first task is to go through the post, and his one inviolable rule is that letters must be answered immediately. Official ones are dictated to his assistant for her to type, while he prefers to write in his own hand many of the others.

He spends hours on the telephone, but usually speaking only to people he knows. If a stranger rings up, he rarely takes the call. His office provides the protective barricade. One call that he was anxious to take himself some time ago came from his old friend Frank Bruno, the former heavyweight boxing champion. It might seem an unusual friendship, but theirs is a warm relationship that goes back many years. It began when Snowdon photographed Bruno in his heyday and Frank discovered that Tony had also been a talented amateur boxer at school, until he was forced to give up the sport he loved when he contracted polio. Lord Snowdon is one person Frank knows he can trust absolutely. Bruno was having personal problems when he turned to Lord Snowdon. 'Lord Snowdon first photographed me when I was twenty-four, and he became like a father to me over the years,' he says. 'I phoned him out of desperation. He listened, gave me advice and afterwards . . . I put down the phone and cried. I was overcome. I couldn't believe such a great man, a member of the royal family, was helping me. He's from the top of the social scale. His voice is very posh and very proper, but he's the most down-to-earth, honest and kind man I know. He's not too grand to befriend a working-class boy from South London. It's a favour I will never forget.' And although they do not see each other as often as they used to, Frank and Tony remain the best of friends.

Someone else with cause to remember Lord Snowdon's kindness is William Tallon, 'Backstairs Billy', the Queen Mother's former page and closest servant. William found himself virtually cut off from the rest of the royal household after fifty-one years' loyal service, once the Queen Mother had died. He was unceremoniously evicted from his grace-and-favour residence – the bijou Gate House Lodge adjoining Clarence House – with indecent haste, and many of his former colleagues were not so welcoming once he had left his influential post. Lord Snowdon has known William for over half a century and understood his suffering. They now see each other frequently, with William joining Tony for lunch most Sundays.

Once the post and the most urgent phone calls have been dealt with, the day's real work begins. If there is a photographic sitting – he dislikes the word 'shoot' – he will either go to the location or to a studio he uses a short distance from his home. The studio-cum-office that is his headquarters is really too small for all but the most basic work. He cannot arrange any of the large, complicated sets he likes to use here, but if it's a simple portrait he can manage. As the assignments he now accepts are getting fewer each year, he no longer employs a permanent photographic assistant either. He uses a couple of freelance helpers when they are needed. Now well past the official retiring age, he shows little sign of slowing down and none at all of giving up work altogether. He is one of the most sought-after photographers in the world – and one of the most expensive. It is said that he won't even switch on his camera for less than a four-figure fee. But obviously this doesn't put off his international clients, and he turns down more commissions than he accepts.

As the morning progresses an inner clock reminds him it is time for a glass of white wine, and any visitor is invited to join him. Tony is a gregarious man so he enjoys going out to lunch, but these are rarely purely social occasions. He likes to make good use of every hour of the day so, if a journalist wants to interview him about one of his projects, it often takes place as a working lunch.

But on a normal working day with no engagements, he will stay at his desk and perhaps eat a sandwich. Equally though he might forget about lunch altogether and work straight through. He is not a clock-watcher.

Once the business of the day is over, he moves back upstairs to the private part of the house, but not before his assistant has given him a typed sheet of paper listing his engagements for the following day.

Tony never receives callers who do not have an appointment, and his personal assistant vets all incoming calls. There are separate telephone numbers for the office and house, and he uses the latter for all his private calls in the evening.

Television does not play an important role in Lord Snowdon's life unless he is working on a programme. His mind is far too active to allow him to sit for hours watching the latest soaps. But he does enjoy films on television; his favourite is *The Third Man*, which he says he can see over and over again. And most of the films he likes 'have to be in black and white'. This is a reflection of his work where nearly all his most striking photographs are monochrome. However, an annual television 'must see' is the last night of the Proms from the Royal Albert Hall. He says he loves the sense of occasion, the flag waving and obvious enjoyment of the promenaders.

Towards the end of the day, he will usually talk on the telephone to his son, David, or his elder daughter, Sarah, while Frances, his 23-year-old daughter by his second wife, Lucy, often pops in to see that dad is all right. It's not far for her as she occupies the entire top floor of the house as her own flat. He says she comes and goes as she pleases and lives her own life, but it's nice to know she is on hand.

Weekends are reserved for family and friends. He no longer has the use of his house in Sussex so he remains in London. He says this is no hardship as nearly everyone else has gone to the country. So if there is something he particularly wants to see – a film or museum – it is easier to get around because the streets are less crowded and traffic is lighter, and he usually has guests for luncheon on Sundays. These meals are one of the social highlights of the week and have been known to last for four hours or more. He still receives dozens of invitations to parties, gallery openings and society functions, but he declines more than he accepts these days. It is all a far cry from the period when he was married to Princess Margaret and they were required to attend all sorts of engagements on a daily basis. But if he misses those far-off days when he was at the very heart of society he gives no indication of the loss. He still sees the friends he wants to see, and even though he is less mobile than he was ten years ago it doesn't appear to have curbed his enthusiasm for life.

The main difference is that now his daily routine is centred around the home.

There is no sign of any shortage of money in the Snowdon household even though he was not left a fortune by his father. He no longer employs the same number of servants he had when he lived at Kensington Palace with Princess Margaret: there's no valet, butler, chauffeur or string of housemaids, but he manages quite nicely with a personal assistant, a housekeeper, a lady who helps with the cleaning and Christopher, who looks after the garden. He does not exactly plead poverty, but he does admit to worrying about money sometimes, though one suspects that, as with most things in life, it is all relative. He is never going to have to be concerned about answering the door to the rent collector, or paying the gas bill, but his lifestyle demands more money than most of us need. And all his income comes from what he earns with his camera. His photographs of Baroness (Margaret) Thatcher, taken in 2003, and which received a huge amount of press attention, demonstrate that he is still obviously much in demand. He says he will never retire: 'I can't imagine not doing anything.' The fear is, as with all freelancers, that the telephone will stop ringing. That basic insecurity never fully leaves anyone who does not have the protection of a regular salary and pension.

In Lord Snowdon's case, though, the fear is all in his mind. There is little chance of his earning capacity drying up in the foreseeable future – and in reality, he knows it. He's good at his job, he delivers on time and his standards never fall. Still, as he puts it himself, 'It *is* lovely to be wanted.'

TWO

Public Figure, Private Man

'Antony Charles Robert, wilt thou have this woman to thy wedded wife . . .'. Sonorously and solemnly, Dr Geoffrey Fisher, dressed in the richly decorated cope and mitre of the Archbishop of Canterbury, asked the question in a hushed Westminster Abbey. The eyes of two thousand guests, and for the first time an entire nation of television watchers, fixed on the short and slim young man at the altar. Firmly and confidently, Antony Charles Robert, a dandyish figure, artistic, a photographer by trade and a man about town by inclination, pronounced his agreement. 'I will,' he said.

Seconds later, Margaret Rose, Princess of the United Kingdom and younger sister of Her Majesty The Queen, added her assent 'to have this man to thy wedded husband', agreeing in the process that, as well as love and honour him, she would also obey. There had been much debate about this in the days running up to the marriage of Princess Margaret and Antony Armstrong-Jones on a beautiful May morning – 'serene and sunny' the newspapers called it – in 1960. Obedience in marriage was being severely questioned; in many a parish church and register office, young girls were deciding to make no such promise. They defied tradition and ditched a vow that no longer fitted the modern world.

It was a small thing in itself but hugely symbolic of a deeper shift in social attitudes. Subservience, whether in marriage, in social relationships or in politics and constitutional matters, was on the way out. Equality would be the creed of the 1960s and beyond. The wedding of the princess and the photographer took place on the very cusp of that change. It was also indicative of the way this partnership would evolve, with neither party dominating the other.

11

But for now traditional values held sway in Britain's most exclusive family. Here divorce was still a dirty word – and its unacceptability in royal circles had an ironic significance to the occasion itself. It was the very thing that had prevented the Princess from marrying her first love, Group-Captain Peter Townsend, five years earlier. If it had not been for that stricture, Antony Armstrong-Jones would not be marrying his princess at all. And it was a powerful factor in Palace protocol. There was much talk, for example, of what status would be afforded the groom's stepmother. His father, Mr Ronald Armstrong-Jones, QC, had a central role in the proceedings with his ex-wife, Antony's mother, now remarried as the Countess of Rosse. But what about the new Mrs Armstrong-Jones? At the rehearsal, the Dean of Westminster dismissed all knowledge of her whereabouts. She was airbrushed out of the ceremony itself. The small print of Palace life shows that she was allowed to accompany her husband to an eve-of-wedding dinner party at Clarence House hosted by the Queen Mother, but, that apart, officially she did not exist.

But the spectre of divorce could not be so easily exorcised from the newly married couple's life together. They were not immune from the loss-of-love bug that has become so much part of modern life. They lasted eighteen years together before splitting up – not bad, some would say, in today's turbulent times, par for the course even. They tried; they failed. They had good times when it worked and awful times when it didn't. In the end they chose separate ways but had two children who have survived the trauma, and in the last years of Princess Margaret's life they were all good friends. In fact their marriage and subsequent divorce add up to a surprisingly neat summary of the deep changes in the British way of life in the second half of the twentieth century. New attitudes to marriage and its permanence, and also to the sanctity of the family, have been freely adopted. We have also knocked the monarchy off its pedestal, cut it down to size and then been both horrified and fascinated as the royal family turned to soap opera and tragedy before our eyes.

Lord Snowdon (as Armstrong-Jones was to become on the birth of his son, ennobled at the insistence of the Queen, who did not want an unaristocratic nephew in the family but who later surrendered to the wishes of her daughter, Princess Anne, when her two children were born untitled) has viewed all this from a unique position. He was an outsider who became a royal insider, but only up to a point. And to the degree that he rejected a royal way of life he is part of the crucial change to the monarchy that has taken place. He was in many ways a forerunner of Diana, Princess of Wales, whose rebellion revealed much that is wrong with royalty but who in herself embodied much that is right about it. To begin with he brought the same sort of glamour to the party as she did twenty years later. But he was infinitely cleverer than her in the way he handled it; he may have bathed in the spotlight from time to time but he refused to be dazzled by it. Professionally he knew the workings of the press too well ever to think he could toy with it as she did. He would never bare his soul on *Panorama*; on the contrary, he is the master of the interview that reveals nothing. To be fair, she was always in a much more exposed position than he, as the wife (and later ex-wife) of the next king and mother of the one after that. He was far enough down the pecking order to be peripheral if he so chose. She could not escape, even if she wanted to.

The other difference between them is that Snowdon survived the Windsors and refused to succumb to the suffocating embrace of royalty. He may have been forced, by marriage, to become a public figure, but at heart, he was and remains very much a private man. And these are the qualities that combine to make him a significant individual, one to be taken seriously, both personally and historically.

The first time I met Lord Snowdon, we played a small part in history on what was one of the saddest days of my life, and, I believe, his also. The date was 21 October 1966, the day of the Aberfan disaster when a coal tip collapsed, swept down a mountainside and killed 144 people, including 116 children in their school classrooms. I was the first reporter on the scene, having been on duty in the BBC television newsroom in Cardiff when the news came through at just after 9 o'clock in the morning. The nightmare of that horrific day was transmitted to every country in the world, and offers of help and sympathy poured in.

Lord Snowdon was the first of the royals to arrive at the tiny South Wales village to see what comfort he could offer (Prince Philip came a few hours later). Tony hadn't been asked to come to Aberfan; it was a spontaneous gesture on his part, as a fellow Welshman, simply to be there to share in the grief of that moment. At the start of that tragic visit, however, there was one light-hearted, albeit unscheduled, moment when he arrived at Cardiff station from London. A small group of dignitaries, including the Minister of State for Wales and the Lord Lieutenant for Glamorgan, Sir Cenydd Traherne, was waiting to greet him. It was 2 o'clock in the morning of Saturday 22 October. They were standing near the first-class coaches, assuming that Lord Snowdon would naturally be travelling in that category. When he didn't appear they were dismayed at first, and then he surprised them all by emerging from a second-class carriage, alone and without an escort, carrying a small suitcase containing his pyjamas and shaving kit. It was probably the first and only time any member of the royal family travelled in such a modest – and economical – manner.

After driving up to Aberfan, he immediately brushed aside all attempts at protocol, bypassed the civic officials with polite but firm determination, and moved among the bereaved parents, offering a quiet word here, a comforting hug there. He was anxious not to be in the way. All he wanted to do was let them know he cared and that he was there to show them that they were not alone in their sorrow.

When he called at the house of one couple who had lost one of their twin daughters they politely asked him to have a cup of tea. It is the first thing that most Welsh people offer to any visitor. Snowdon said, 'Leave it to me, I'll do it.' He then went into the kitchen, put the kettle on and made the tea for them all. There was no fuss. It wasn't a gimmick. He didn't want any publicity. But by that single gesture he endeared himself to an entire community. Joyce Fudge, the lady of the house, said afterwards that she and her husband, Ken, were deeply touched by his visit: 'I couldn't believe it when he walked in and put his arms around me. He was so informal, just like one of us. Not a bit like you'd expect a royal to be at all.'

Looking back, it seems such an easy and natural thing for anyone to do. But Mrs Fudge was right. This was not what royalty did in those days. Two decades later it was to become Diana's hallmark – she would hug Aids sufferers, landmine victims, those struck down by tragic events and disasters – and we came to accept this laying on of hands, as it were, as one of her roles. Snowdon led the way. His demeanour and behaviour among the bereaved parents of Aberfan showed an understanding and compassion that was light years removed from the normal way the royal family conducted itself in public. Prince Philip, with his ever practical mind, was briefed on the problems facing those involved in the rescue operation (which by now had become a recovery effort), while Lord Snowdon moved among the families offering solace. Both were immensely appreciated by the people of Aberfan; Philip because of his insistence on an absence of protocol and fuss, and Tony because of his obvious compassion and approachability. The two royals complemented each other perfectly.

George Thomas, the Labour MP who was number two at the Welsh Office (later to be Speaker of the House of Commons before being elevated to become Viscount Tonypandy), acknowledged what Snowdon had done. 'Tony's coming here showed his true compassion and feelings for the people of South Wales. It was royalty displaying their practical face at a time when nobody wanted empty gestures. With him they didn't get any.' It was George, an old friend, who introduced me to Snowdon that day. Doing my job as a television reporter, I asked him if he would agree to be interviewed about the tragedy. He declined, saying this was not about him or his feelings. It was a day for remembering the dead and those who had lost children, parents, brothers and sisters. He was, of course, absolutely right, and I respected his wishes and left him to carry on his sad round of duties. He was not curt or dismissive, either to me or any of the other reporters and journalists who surrounded him; but at the same time he was not going to be manipulated into being shown as a celebrity sightseer. He was there to help not to show off.

Not that he was averse to a little showing off when it suited him and the occasion. Three years later we met again when he was organizing the Investiture of Prince Charles as Prince of Wales at Caernarvon Castle (*see* Chapter Fourteen). A few days before the big event, he agreed to my request for a television interview and even dressed up in his special uniform as Constable of Caernarvon Castle. Designed by Snowdon himself, the uniform had caused a certain amount of amused controversy among traditionalists when it was first unveiled. With its high collar and long coat, one report described it as 'a Victorian Euston station porter's outfit', thus making sure that photographs of it appeared in newspapers in practically every country in the world.

Although the ceremony was centuries old, Snowdon was determined that it should not be stuffy and militaristic, which is usually the instinctive way with royal events. Everyone puts on uniform and medals, troops march, bands play, guns salute. He pushed for it to be different and won the argument. Crucially he made it clear that the Investiture was to be an occasion at which television was central to the proceedings, not the intrusive nuisance that some royals perceived it to be. He designed a clear perspex canopy over the throne chairs so that the cameras could see everything that was happening. Garter King of Arms, who was also involved in the planning, didn't care for this modern approach, but his objections were quickly disposed of and he wisely knew when he was beaten.

When we had finished our interview, Lord Snowdon changed out of his formal clothes into jeans and a fringed cowboy jacket. We left the castle, and he offered me a lift in his car, an Aston Martin convertible. As we drove through the town, hundreds of people were standing along the pavements, hoping to catch sight of some of the celebrities who were invading Caernarvon for the Investiture. Snowdon had become a familiar figure to the townspeople and also a very popular one as he never failed to stop and chat or acknowledge their greetings as he came and went. 'Wave back at the people,' he urged me as we drove along, 'they love it.' And they did. It was my one and only experience of being in the public eye in the way the royal family are constantly, and while it was fun, exhilarating even, I knew I could not have lived my life the way I wanted if that was an everyday occurrence – which, by then, it was for him.

He had had to learn to be a royal, catapulted from relative obscurity to an uneasy sort of fame which depended on whom he had married rather than who he was or what he had done.

When Antony Armstrong-Jones joined the royal family in 1960 his background was unconventional in terms of a prospective husband for the sister of the Queen. He was not possessed of an ancient title or great fortune, but at the same time he didn't come from the artisan class. Educated at Eton and Cambridge, and living in some of London's most exclusive areas, he mixed easily and comfortably in the highest levels of society. So he was not in the slightest bit overawed to find himself partnered with Princess Margaret.

His father was a prominent and successful barrister; his mother was Anne Messel, a sister of one of the world's top designers, Oliver Messel, from whom it is said Lord Snowdon inherited his artistic talents. His childhood was spent partly in London's Belgravia, where he was born, but he also moved regularly between several family homes. One was in Ireland, where his mother lived after she divorced his father. Then there was a house in Wales, where his paternal grandparents lived, and the Messels' spacious estate in Sussex owned by his maternal grandfather.

Physically slight in stature, it comes as a surprise to learn that Tony Armstrong-Jones was an enthusiastic, aggressive and more than competent boxer as a schoolboy at Eton before polio ended his ambitions in the ring. But he was already successful in another sport – rowing – having coxed one of the Lower Boats, and when he returned to school after his illness he concentrated on that. His greatest success came in 1950 when he coxed the Cambridge University crew to a 3½-lengths victory over Oxford in the University Boat Race, again showing a natural toughness that was at odds with his outward appearance. The men who row at Oxbridge are heavily muscled, superbly fit specimens who don't hesitate to use expletive-riddled insults to encourage each other. At one point in the Boat Race, the Oxford boat came a little too close for Cambridge's liking. The diminutive cox leaned over to his opposite number in the Oxford boat and shouted, 'Piss off and get your f*****g boat out of my way.' It was remarkably effective – and his finest hour at Cambridge.

Unlike, it must be said, his academic studies. Here there was no finest hour at all. He started with natural sciences but quickly gave that up for architecture, a subject which he loved but to which he gave little enough time. Cambridge in the 1950s must have been a joy for a young man with breeding and money, and a motorbike or car to get him back and fore the 60 miles to and from London society. The meritocratic revolution in education which was to vastly inflate the size of Britain's student population and at the same time demand higher academic standards was some years away. To leave with a third-class degree was no disgrace, even if it was not the sort of thing one usually boasted about. Snowdon, though, did not even get that far, failing to take his degree and going down, theoretically for just a year, on the advice of his tutor.

He never went back to his studies, but he had made invaluable contacts which he was able to capitalize on after university. He had already decided on his future career, photography, and he was soon employed as one of London's most fashionable, and gregarious, photographers. It also provided him with an open sesame to many of the city's top families and, eventually, through the doors of Buckingham Palace itself.

This, remember, was a London that at last was beginning to break out of the drabness and austerity that for too long had been Britain's postwar experience. For the ten years after 1945 rationing and re-trenchment made day-to-day living hard for all but the very well off. Then the prosperity of the Macmillan years of government – when elections were won on the promise of boom, and bust was something for economists to worry about – began to spread the benefits downwards. There was money in people's pockets and leisure activities to spend it on. A teen culture began, picking up on every cool import from the USA. Music, films, entertainment, fashion, all began to take off. This wasn't swinging London yet – though that was just a few years ahead – but the seeds of the sixties were well planted. Photographers were at the centre of it all. They fed the new glossy magazines that in turn were feeding the frenzy for fashion, pop music and an ever busier social life for the young. Youth was the key to the future and anything was possible. Class barriers were melting away. Not only could a cat now look at a queen, but a man with a camera could woo her sister.

The courtship of Tony Armstrong-Jones and Princess Margaret was conducted with such secrecy and discretion, aided and abetted by a close circle of friends and relations, that practically nobody outside their own set had any idea it was going on until their engagement was announced. It is no exaggeration to say that it came as a relief to the nation. This was a time, too, of huge sales for popular newspapers, and the saga of sad Margaret, played out in the gossip columns and society diaries, was nearly as compelling as Diana's story was to be many years later. The engagement to Tony restored a lot of goodwill to the Queen and her family. It is generally forgotten how much ill-feeling there had been over the treatment Princess Margaret was said to have received from her closest relatives at the time of the Peter Townsend affair. Even the Queen's kindest biographers concede that she could have done more to help her sister find a better way out of the dilemma of falling in love with a divorced man. The perceived indifference of the Palace had caused many people in Britain and throughout the Commonwealth to feel disgusted, angry and thoroughly disillusioned with royalty. Such feelings were to become widespread again, but for the moment they were dispersed by the happy outcome of the Tony and Margaret romance.

Much of the credit, though, went not to Tony but to Queen Elizabeth The Queen Mother, who was said to be the one responsible for allowing her younger daughter to find some happiness with a man she, the Queen Mother, thoroughly approved of. The fact that he came not from the traditional royal or aristocratic families that princesses of the blood-royal were expected to marry was an added bonus. It showed clearly that the House of Windsor was a modern, up-to-date institution very much in touch with current opinion in Britain, which demanded that everyone should be judged on their merits alone and not because of an accident of birth.

It was a theme that caught the public imagination. Two days before the wedding, a crowd of 50,000 in The Mall surged forward and stopped the Princess's car, which was taking her, her husband-to-be and the Queen Mother to a reception at Buckingham Palace. Through the cheers and waves, police reinforcements arrived on foot and on horseback to hold back the outbreak of congratulations and good wishes. On the day itself half a million people poured onto the streets of London, despite the fact that the all-day television coverage was giving them a much better view in their own living-rooms. Everyone, it seemed, wanted to join in the pleasure of witnessing the Queen's only sister marrying a commoner.

One publication reassured its readers that the term 'commoner' was not in any way a pejorative description that belittled the bridegroom. Used in its correct context, it 'does not mean plebeian or common person but refers to any person who is not entitled to sit in the House of Lords'. It was a helpful explanation even though there was little chance of the upper-class-accented, Eton-educated and double-barrelled Antony Armstrong-Jones being mistaken for a member of the hoi polloi. Nonetheless, it was recognised by all that an important social change was happening before our eyes. The editor of *Burke's Peerage* summed it up when he wrote. 'The marriage of Princess Margaret and Mr Armstrong-Jones is at once a symptom of the great changes in our royal family in the present generation, and a sign which may be taken as indicating further democratization of the royal ideal.' This was not just a wedding, this was 'the event of the decade', as one commentator put it, and a turning point. The *Daily Mail* gossip columnist of the day had no doubt that a mini-revolution was happening as he listed those who had been at a royal reception to mark the wedding. 'They changed the guard at Buckingham Palace last night,' he wrote. 'In went the new names – the people I feel sure will make up the Princess Margaret set of the future.' There were lots of luvvies – though that expression for theatre folk had yet to be coined. Director Peter Hall was there with actress Leslie Caron, his then wife. Margaret Leighton apologized for the absence of husband Larry (Laurence Harvey), away filming in Hollywood. She had brought Noel Coward instead. Others included Joyce Grenfell, Jeremy Brett and wife Anna Massey, and a 'lanky calypso singer' named Rory McEwan. Joe Loss and his Orchestra provided the music, switching effortlessly from the Palais at Hammersmith to the Palace at the end of The Mall, and playing 'all the pop songs, new and old'. One of them, appropriately, was called 'Fings Ain't Wot They Used to Be', no doubt echoing the sentiments of those wearing traditional white tie, tails and medals who stood out amid the general informality of the thousand guests.

But it was in the forecourt of Buckingham Palace that the reporter spotted the true revolution going on. He wrote: 'The eyebrow-raising feature of the evening was the spectacle of tiny worn-out cars and shooting brakes jostling for position among the gleaming Rolls-Royces and Daimlers. Time and again the police were called to push them into the Palace quadrangle when their engines stalled. One of the guests even arrived in a green-painted van bearing L plates.'

What the two people at the heart of all this were feeling only they can know. Most people go into marriage with some misgivings. In the case of Tony and Margaret we now know that there were friends around them who believed the whole business a complete disaster. Even some who had provided them with 'safe houses' and country weekend parties as cover for their secret romance thought there was no future for them as a married couple. David Hicks, the highly re-garded interior designer whose clients included the Prince of Wales, the Princess Royal, the *QE2* and the White House, knew Lord Snowdon for fifty years. They were friends and confidants, fellow aesthetes, though Snowdon would probably have preferred to see themselves described as craftsmen. Hicks also had a knowledge of the royals not granted to most, having married a daughter of Lord Mountbatten, Prince Philip's uncle. Just before Hicks died of cancer in April 1998, he told the author he believed the marriage was doomed from the start. 'Tony was far too independent a character to simply enjoy living in the shadow of his wife. He needed to work and never really enjoyed the royal role anyway. It wasn't his style. For a time Princess Margaret liked his friends and their bohemian lifestyle, but it quickly wore off. She had been used to a certain lifestyle which was hard to discard. She had her own set and they were very different from Tony's. It was inevitable that they would divorce. They simply grew apart.'

The romance of Lord Snowdon and Princess Margaret was certainly an attraction of opposites. He was used to earning his own living, going wherever he wanted, whenever he chose. Spontaneity was a term frequently applied to his way of life. His wife's could scarcely have been more different. The daughter of a king and sister of a queen, she had been raised in a manner that was thoroughly unnatural and incredibly superior. Throughout her life she accepted as her right the privileges accorded to her rank. She never felt the need to compromise and never did. If the public perception at the time was that the commoner and the Princess would somehow blend and create a more democratic dough and a more accessible type of royal, then a few minutes in the company of Her Royal Highness The Princess Margaret would have put that fantasy to flight. She was a notorious stickler for protocol, protecting the dignity of her station at all times and in all circumstances. Her icy glare for those who crossed the forbidden line of familiarity was both famous and feared.

Educated privately at home, with every moment of every day planned down to its tiniest detail, she would never have dreamt of doing anything on the spur of the moment without advance notice. It wasn't her fault; it was simply the manner in which young royal ladies of her generation had been brought up. Tony introduced her to so many experiences which would have been normal to any other girl but which to her were completely new. Until she began her relationship with him she had never handled money before, and she had certainly never ridden on the pillion of a motorcycle, which she did as he roared around the streets of London's Docklands in the middle of the night. It appeared not to have changed her one jot, however. There never was any chance of her becoming more like him. He was the one who would have to adapt, to become 'one of them'.

He put up stiff resistance by being constantly busy. If he had to be a royal, he would not be an observer of other people's work, a visitor into other people's lives; he would be a doer. While still photography remained his main interest and source of income, he branched out into other forms of picture-making including producing documentary films for BBC television with his close friend Derek Hart. They were brilliantly successful and in 1968 won two Emmy awards in the USA. He also designed the aviary for London Zoo at Regent's Park and then joined the board of the Design Council, where he showed he was not going to be merely a royal name on a letterhead, even if the job was unpaid.

It kept him sane, but it was ultimately all in vain. The royal 'system' is guaranteed to wear down even the most independent spirit, and moving into Kensington Palace after his marriage meant the start of a process that would eventually claim Tony Snowdon as its victim. He tried very hard to maintain his freedom and a lifestyle that would enable him to preserve his dignity while having to walk two steps behind his wife at all times in public. It wasn't to be. They separated in 1976 and divorced two years later.

There had been such high hopes at the beginning. Tony's acceptance into the royal family at the very start of the 1960s had an historic significance, particularly when placed alongside what was happening in other countries at the same time. In the USA they were electing their youngest ever president (John F. Kennedy), who brought a new glamorous dimension to the White House. In the early days of their marriage, Margaret and Tony were seen by some as the British equivalent of the Kennedys; a young, attractive couple who could revive the romantic age at Court that had ceased to exist since the brief reign of Edward VIII. Tony was a dynamic, energetic and popular figure who was seen as a badly needed breath of fresh air in the ultra-stuffy and rigid atmosphere of Buckingham Palace and Windsor Castle. His love of the arts – the theatre in particular – excited prominent figures who imagined that his, and Princess Margaret's, influence could lead to a renaissance in royalty's patronage. They both knew every major actor, actress, writer and director in British theatre and films, and Kensington Palace was forecast as the new centre of artistic social life in London. They were seen as the most exhilarating couple in the country, and they were expected to remove at a stroke, years of hidebound, stultifying tradition. They would thrust the monarchy into the latter half of the twentieth century, invigorated and renewed.

The reality was somewhat different. There is little doubt that Tony did become an important figure in the life of the nation during the sixties and seventies. He was seen everywhere, either alongside Princess Margaret or, increasingly, in his own right, and his contribution to the improved image of the royal family during this period should not be underestimated. But he could not break through their obsession with protocol, their aloofness – nobody could ever accuse any member of the family of being tactile; they hate touching and being touched – and their fear of change. What was lacking, and in the opinion of many, still is, was the common touch, the ability to talk to people and convey care. It is the gift Diana, for all her faults, brought to the royal family, only for it to be misunderstood and for her to be mishandled. Just as they misunderstood Snowdon.

He was not mishandled, however; he would not let that happen, either to himself or to the family for whom he undoubtedly has a great deal of regard. He was allowed to go his own way, and he kept his silence and his secrets.

THREE

Early Days

The 1930s were a time of terrible depression in Britain and throughout the world. There were over 2 million unemployed in the United Kingdom alone, with little prospect of economic recovery in the foreseeable future. For those lucky enough to be in work, the average wage was around £150 a year, or just under £3 a week.

On Friday 7 March 1930, the front page of *The Times* consisted, as usual, of advertisements rather than news, including columns of London properties for sale and to let. At Grosvenor House in Park Lane you could take your pick of service flats at £9 a week, furnished or unfurnished, while for bachelors there was an attractive three-room property for rent in Old Burlington Street, W1, for just under £4 a week. At Highgate a new development was aimed at business and professional women only. The flats had constant hot water, cheap electricity, a restaurant, lounge reading-room and hard tennis courts. All for the princely sum of £4 15s a week.

And while the lower orders eked out an existence on whatever they could pick up, there were many attractions available for those fortunate enough not to have to worry about where the next meal was coming from.

The Union-Castle Shipping Line had four sailings to South Africa that month: the *Kennilworth Castle*, the *Windsor Castle*, the *Kildonan Castle* and the *Balmoral Castle* were all fully booked in first class. While Dean & Dawson of Piccadilly were offering bargain Mediterranean cruises on the sailing yacht *Meteor* at £26 for eighteen days. For the well connected and the rich, the social life of the capital city continued apace. The Court Circular in *The Times* recorded Queen Mary, wife of George V, visiting an Exhibition of

Modern Embroidery and their second son, the Duke of York, being present at the banquet of the British Engineering Standards Association at Grocers' Hall. Meanwhile, the newspaper's society column – the noticeboard that was essential reading for anyone who wanted to pinpoint who was doing what and with whom among the people who mattered – revealed that:

> The German Ambassador has left London for Germany, and will be absent for about a week.
>
> The Duke and Duchess of Abercorn will leave 68 Mount Street on Sunday for Government House, Hillsborough, County Down. Charlotte, Lady Inverclyde will return to 10 Berkeley Square this week-end from the country.
>
> Mr and Mrs Neville Chamberlain and Miss Dorothy Chamberlain will disembark from the *Modasa* today at Marseilles, and will travel overland. They hope to reach London on Saturday evening.
>
> The Hon. Mrs Wilfred Abel-Smith and Mrs Alisdair MacGregor of Cardney will give a dance for their daughters . . . on June 3. The Hon. Mrs Ronald Greville has left London for the Continent.
>
> Lady Cowan will be at home at 215 Ashley Gardens, SW1, on Thursday to meet Sir Ronald and Lady Ross.
>
> Owing to illness, Mrs Herbert Da Costa has left London for New Lodge, Windsor, and will be away several weeks.
>
> Mrs Stanley Baldwin was at home yesterday afternoon at 10 Upper Brook Street.

Dinner dances were being held at the Dorchester, the Savoy, the Ritz and the Berkeley hotels, where fashionable orchestras such as those fronted by Carol Gibbons, Henry Hall and Lou Stone played for the pleasure of their well-to-do patrons. London's West End theatres were playing to full houses with musicals by Ivor Novello and Noel Coward, and stars such as Jack Hulbert and Cicely Courtnidge, Jessie Matthews, Jack Buchanan, and Fred and Adele Astaire were packing them in along The Strand.

And at No. 25 Eaton Square in London's Belgravia, then as now, one of the most auspicious addresses in the capital, the mistress of the house, Anne Armstrong-Jones, was preparing for the arrival of her second baby.

Anne had been described on many occasions as the most beautiful woman in London. Some who had seen her went further and hailed her as the most beautiful in Britain. The Prince of Wales (later Edward VIII) was an admirer who sought her out at dances, and sent her a telegram of congratulation when her son was born. Her husband, Ronald Owen Lloyd Armstrong-Jones, then aged 30, was one of the country's most successful young barristers.

Ronald had met Anne Messel through her brother Linley, who rowed in the same crew as he had at Magdalen College, Oxford, and from the moment he first set eyes on her, he was determined that she was going to become his wife. The attraction was mutual, and within months of their first meeting they became engaged.

The Armstrong-Joneses lived a life of extreme comfort. Their house had been a wedding gift from the bride's father, Lieutenant-Colonel Leonard Messel, so there was no mortgage to find, and the briefs that landed on the desk of Ronald Armstrong-Jones ensured that there was no shortage of money to fund their lifestyle. An astute lawyer, he had discovered a niche in the legal market and proceeded to fill it with great success. He specialized in insurance litigation, pursuing claims through the courts on behalf of his clients and winning the majority of his cases. His fees were extremely high by the standards of the day, and at the time his wife gave birth to their second child his annual income was said to be in excess of £10,000. In today's figures that would be the equivalent of about £500,000 a year, a handsome salary even for the Bar. Eventually to become one of the leading men in his field – he was made a QC in 1954 and, before he died in 1966, was appointed the Lord Chancellor's Legal Visitor – Ronald Armstrong-Jones would continue to earn excellent money throughout his life. He never, however, managed to accumulate great wealth, even though his father had left him £68,717 when he died in 1943, a considerable fortune which would have made him the equal of a multimillionaire today.

His lifestyle was such that nearly everything he made he spent. He enjoyed the good things in life and didn't deny himself – or those around him – any of the luxuries he was used to.

The birth of the baby, a boy, was uncomplicated and accomplished without too much distress on the part of his mother. He was immediately handed over to the care of a full-time nurse and banished to the nursery which had been prepared three years earlier when his sister, Susan Anne, was born. He was subsequently christened at the historic Temple Church in the City, a privilege granted to his father as a barrister and member of the Inner Temple. There the baby was given the names Antony Charles Robert Owen Linley, but was to be known always as Tony. The five Christian names recorded in front of seven godparents as he was blessed at the font were short-lived. For his birth certificate, the last two – Owen Linley – disappeared because, as was explained many years later, 'my father thought they were two too many'. The 'Linley', though, was not forgotten and was to resurface as a family name a generation on.

Tony Armstrong-Jones was a healthy and happy child who was taken for walks in nearby Hyde Park by his nanny, the faithful Miss Laura Gunner, who had worked for the Messel family since Tony's mother was just 12 years old. Nanny Gunner became an important part of Tony's life until he was old enough not to need a nanny, and for years afterwards he kept in touch with her. He had a happy childhood. His parents were affectionate and attentive to both their children, but, in keeping with the accepted attitudes of their class, they had very little to do with the actual rearing of their offspring.

Ronald and Anne Armstrong-Jones were young people of their time and class. Gregarious to a fault, they enjoyed a vigorous social life, dining out most evenings, giving dinner parties and cocktail receptions in return and saw comparatively little of their children by today's standards. Susan and Tony were produced, scrubbed and polished, before they went to bed, and their parents were perfectly happy to allow their nanny and nurse to oversee their welfare. There was never any neglect, and Ronald and Anne were generous parents who denied their son and daughter nothing.

But upper-class mothers and fathers did not expect to be bothered by everyday childhood worries, and their servants were there to make sure they weren't.

It is perhaps surprising that Tony became a much more hands-on type of father when his turn came, wanting to know every detail of his own children's upbringing and involving himself in all their day-to-day activities. Times had changed by then, of course, but the active role he chose to take as a parent may also indicate an underlying feeling that his own childhood, while happy enough, may have lacked that special contentment that might come from having a more attentive father and mother. On the other hand, spending much of his time with Nanny meant he was better prepared to absorb the impact of his parents' separation and divorce.

It happened when he was just 4 years old and was not the traumatic event it might have been if he had been a little older. In fact, Lord Snowdon has very little recollection of the event himself. The welfare of the children was the main concern of both parents, and they appear to have been very successful in making the break-up as painless as possible for all those involved. The divorce was by mutual consent with no acrimony on either side. After nine years together they simply felt that the marriage wasn't working and decided to end it, agreeing to share custody of the children. Susan and Tony remained living with their father in London, but they saw their mother as often as they and she wanted.

Both parents had other interests, including companions of the opposite sex, but nobody was cited as co-respondent on either side and, as was the custom of the day, Ronald Armstrong-Jones allowed his wife to bring the divorce action, which was uncontested. When the final decree was granted there was virtually no comment from any of their friends, even though divorce was not exactly commonplace in their set. And there was certainly no scandal attached to the breakdown of the marriage.

Socially it made little difference to either of them. They continued to move in the same circles as they had when they were married to each other, and in the civilized behaviour that was expected they greeted each other cordially when they met. It really did appear to be an arrangement that suited both parties, with no one side being the injured party. In the 1930s divorce was still comparatively rare in Britain and was generally restricted to those with plenty of money; the working class simply couldn't afford the legal fees – or the alimony. Of course, the fact that both parents were independently wealthy contributed in no small part to their amicable arrangements, and the divorce made little difference to the lifestyle of the Armstrong-Jones children, apart from the fact that they spent a great deal of time travelling. They moved not only between the various homes of their parents but also those of both sets of grandparents. Lord Snowdon puts down his lifelong love of travelling to those early years moving between his family's various properties in England, Wales and Ireland.

Anne Messel had grown up used to the best that money could provide; she had never known poverty, and never would throughout her long and satisfying life. Her grandfather, Ludwig Messel, had come to England from Germany with his brother Rudolph as visitors, but they had liked it so much they stayed and prospered. Ludwig founded the successful Messel stockbroking firm. Rudolph, a distinguished scientist, also made a fortune and left a million pounds to the Royal Society on his death. Later it was claimed that much of Tony's drive and strength came from the Jewish side of the family.

As a result of her grandparents' wealth, Anne's mother and father were able to live in great splendour at their country house, Nymans, in Sussex. Tony, a frequent visitor, loved it there as a boy, and as a man was eventually to convert a house on the estate for his own use during his marriage to Princess Margaret (much to her dismay).

From his mother's side of the family he was heir to a talented artistic tradition. His great-grandfather, Linley Sambourne (1844–1910), was for over forty years political cartoonist for *Punch* magazine and a prolific illustrator of books. His most famous work, and his best, were the pictures he drew for Charles Kingsley's *Water Babies* in 1885. His wife, Marion, whom he married in 1874, was the daughter of Spencer Herapath FRS, and they had two children, a son, Mawdley, and a daughter, Maud Frances, who became

Mrs L.R.C. Messel, Tony's grandmother. Another talented member of the Messel clan was Alfred, a distinguished and wealthy German architect, who designed the Berlin National Gallery and who had streets in the German capital, Messelplatz and Messelstrasse, named after him. But perhaps the greatest artistic influence on Tony's life was Anne's brother, Oliver Messel, the well-known theatrical designer. Even today Lord Snowdon holds a biannual lunch in the Oliver Messel Suite at the Dorchester Hotel in honour of his famous uncle, to which he invites an eclectic but invariably fascinating group of guests.

From the Armstrong-Jones side of the family came two important traditions for the future Earl of Snowdon: a love of Wales and a strong sense of public duty. Tony's father's family home was in North Wales, the impressive Plas Dinas in Caernarvonshire, looking up at the bulk of Mount Snowdon itself, from where Tony would one day take his title. Plas Dinas is an historic sixteenth-century manor-house which has been associated with the Armstrong-Jones family since the seventeenth century.

At one time the house was surrounded by a large estate and several farms, but by the time Tony was born it had become just a large and very comfortable country house with several outbuildings, where Tony eventually kept his bicycle, and later his motorbike. There were, and still are, fairly extensive grounds covering 14 acres of parkland, which were kept in immaculate condition by a local gardener, and the staff who looked after the house all spoke only Welsh among themselves. The main house is approached via a winding drive with the entrance guarded by a gatekeeper's lodge.

Plas Dinas, which Tony's father inherited on the death of Sir Robert in 1943, remained in the family until recently but it never become the property of Tony. It was left to his younger half-brother, Peregrine (the son of Ronald Armstrong-Jones and his third wife, Jennifer), with the full agreement of Tony, and it was subsequently leased for use as a residential home for the elderly. The Armstrong-Jones furniture and fittings remained. The drawing-room contains a magnificent and ornate grand piano and an authentic Welsh harp now in need of restringing, while in the hall there is a centuries-old chest full of Armstrong-Jones family documents and official papers. Peregrine has kept for his own use a cottage in the grounds overlooking the Menai Straits, which was once the personal hideaway of his and Tony's father when he wanted somewhere peaceful away from the main house.

In what used to be the Gun Room, Ronald Armstrong-Jones's oar, from the days when he rowed for Magdalen College, Oxford, is displayed, while paintings throughout the house are a constant reminder of the history of the family who once lived there. The Armstrong-Jones family motto in Welsh, 'A Noddo Duw A Noddir' (He whom God protects is indeed protected), still sits below the family's coat of arms. The ancient family Bible reveals that it was in 1893 that Dr Robert Jones married Miss Roberts and that in 1930 Antony Charles Robert Owen Linley Armstrong-Jones was christened at Temple Church in London. Today Plas Dinas is a luxurious country house hotel, still containing many of the original artefacts and furnishings, where guests can enjoy the comforts of the Armstrong-Joneses' former home for up to £165 a night for a suite.

The Armstrong-Joneses were well known and respected in the community, and among their neighbours was another prominent North Wales landowner, Sir Michael Duff, the Lord Lieutenant of Caernarvonshire and Tony's godfather. For the first ten years of his life, Tony and his sister, Susan, spent most of their summer holidays in North Wales and almost every Christmas. Tony remembers with affection the long, hot summers: 'My father had a motor cruiser, looked after by a local boatman who helped us to catch salmon. And we used to take the boat over to the Isle of Anglesey for lovely picnics.' It was in North Wales that they spent many happy hours with their grandfather, the redoubtable Lieutenant-Colonel Sir Robert Armstrong-Jones CBE, MD, DSc, FRCS, FRCP, FSA, JP, DL, an eminent surgeon and distinguished physician. It was he who had double-barrelled the family name. In his early days he was plain Dr Robert Jones but was constantly confused with another Dr Jones. He adopted the surname of his mother's mother, Jane Armstrong of Northumberland, to make himself Dr Robert Armstrong Jones and then added a hyphen when he was knighted to make it Armstrong-

Jones. Retired and in his eighties, Sir Robert enjoyed the company of his grandchildren when they came to stay at Plas Dinas and instilled in Tony the deep affection for Wales he has never lost. Sir Robert had married Margaret Elizabeth, the daughter of another notable figure in North Wales society, Sir Owen Roberts. A barrister and at one time Clerk of the Clothworkers Livery Company, he was one of the founders of Somerville College, Oxford. Both sides of the family had been involved in public duties for over a century.

A year after his parents divorced, Tony's mother married again. Her new husband was an old boyfriend, Michael Parsons, who by the time of the wedding had succeeded to the Irish earldom of Rosse and vast estates that included Birr Castle, set in 26,000 acres in County Offaly, and Wormesley Park in West Yorkshire, where his family fortune had been founded on coal (and where Tony and Susan were taken to live by their mother for a time during the worst part of the London Blitz in the Second World War). The marriage was a true meeting of beautiful people. Anne's looks were legendary while her new husband enjoyed the reputation of being the handsomest aristocrat in Ireland.

Tony and his sister were welcomed by their stepfather from the moment he married their mother. Tony never lost the love he felt throughout his life for his own father, but there was also a great deal of respect and genuine affection for Michael Rosse, which was reciprocated in full. The remarriage of his mother was also to give Tony two maternal half-brothers, Lord Oxmanton, who was born in 1936 and the Hon. Desmond Oliver Martin Parsons, born in 1938.

It was in 1935, when Tony was 5 years old, that he saw Birr Castle for the first time. And if, when he married Princess Margaret, he was expected to be overawed by the splendour of the royal residences she had lived in, those who felt he would be out of place obviously knew little of the style his mother and stepfather enjoyed in Ireland.

Birr Castle, with its sixty rooms, vast kitchens, turrets and dungeons, stood at the end of the main street of Birr but as far as the local people were concerned it might just as well have been on the moon. The earls of Rosse had occupied the estate for 300 years and in that time had become prominent in many aspects of Irish life ranging from politics to science. They were great benefactors to the townspeople, and although the family were Protestants, they were equally philanthropic to the Catholic community, providing land for a church to be built and financing factories where men and women of both denominations were offered work in order to try and stop mass migration to the cities and, more importantly, overseas.

Tony's new stepfather continued the tradition of public service, acting as Vice-Chancellor of Dublin University and sitting on the board of the Irish Arts Council. He was on first-name terms with the country's president, Mr De Valéra, who was a frequent visitor to Birr Castle.

The Rosses were true aristocrats who moved from home to home as the seasons changed. They were benevolent landlords but, until the outbreak of the Second World War, no member of the family had ever been seen to drink in any of the local public houses, buy anything personally in one of the town's shops or even to visit the town's single cinema. They kept to the castle and its grounds, and when the Earl made an appearance in the town it attracted the sort of excitement that normally only accompanies royalty in Britain.

At the time of Tony's first visit, the castle employed twelve indoor servants, including liveried footmen, and more than twenty in the grounds. There was a long-serving butler who had been with the family all his life. So the later charges levelled at Tony when he married into the Windsors that he was unsuited to Palace life and didn't know how to deal with servants was patently untrue. He may not have had much experience of hiring and firing them himself, but throughout his childhood he was used to being waited on by household staff, both male and female. His own father always had a manservant who acted as butler and valet, and his grandparents on both sides were surrounded by servants to fetch and carry and anticipate their every need.

One of the estate workers at Birr, William Eades, became an influential figure in the young Tony's life and also a lifelong friend. Eades was the estate carpenter, and it was through him that Tony learned to love woodwork. Eades would spend hours showing Tony how to shape and fashion pieces of wood into articles of furniture and toys, and it was a craft that the young Armstrong-Jones found so fascinating that he never lost the skill or the enjoyment for the rest of his life. Twenty-five years after that first meeting, when Tony married Princess Margaret, one of the guests in Westminster Abbey was Mr William Eades.

Neither did Tony's father remain a single parent for long. Just two years after being divorced by Anne, Ronald Armstrong-Jones remarried. His bride was fourteen years younger than him, 22-year-old Carol Coombe, an Australian actress, whose father was Sir Thomas Melrose Coombe of Perth, Western Australia. They were married on 18 June 1936. As a stepmother Carol Armstrong-Jones was perfect. She never once tried to take the place of the children's own mother, yet she managed to give them an affection few others might have done.

The second marriage lasted for twenty years, the most formative period in young Tony's life, and then that, too, ended in the divorce court, enabling Tony's father to embark on his third marriage, to an air hostess, Jennifer Unite. Meanwhile, Tony had started his education at Sandroyd preparatory school in Wiltshire (where his father had also been) when he was 8 years old. In 1943 he passed his common entrance examination and was accepted at Eton, for which his name had been entered at birth. He entered Mr J.D. Upcott's house.

In going to Eton, the world's most famous school, he was following in his father's and grandfather's footsteps. Eton, with its unique system of twenty-five self-governing houses, each run by a housemaster who has complete freedom in choosing the boys he will accept, was an ideal choice for Tony. The compact independence of each house, although they all combine for schoolwork and sports, provides the perfect environment for individual development. There is a wealth of societies at Eton catering for practically every interest, including a Film Unit, and with his enquiring mind Tony found there just weren't enough hours in the day for all he wanted to do. He used the school as it was intended to be used, for his own devices.

And in this he was encouraged, as were all his fellow scholars. That was how a boy's particular talents were discovered, and Eton's reputation as a centre of excellence has been founded on the nurturing of individual skills no matter how unusual or non-academic those skills may be.

In 1943, when he started school, Eton, like everywhere else in Britain, was still in the grip of wartime austerity. Food was severely rationed and school meals, which had never been very appetizing to start with, were even more revolting. Powdered egg and dried milk were used, as they were elsewhere in Britain, and the diet consisted of the most basic of foods, served day after day with monotonous regularity. Not that this bothered Tony too much, as even then he paid little attention to what he ate. 'I never noticed what they put in front of me,' he remembers. Today he still prefers the simplest of meals, and he puts this down to his schooldays, when there was no option but to eat what was offered. His favourite food, then and now, was fishcakes, and this earned him the nickname of 'Fishface', a sobriquet his contemporaries from Eton still use when writing to him.

The wartime restrictions also meant that social life in the college was curtailed; strict blackout precautions were enforced in all the school buildings and there were no lights permitted in Eton High Street. During the summer months this didn't matter so much, but in the long dark winter days Eton was a gloomy and fearsomely cold place to be.

In spite of all this, Tony enjoyed Eton, particularly the independence it encouraged in its pupils. It suited him to be able to indulge his hobbies without having someone looking over his shoulder all the time. He says: 'I loved Eton. It was easily the best time of my life. I was useless at games like cricket and soccer because I've never been a team player. So they let me carry on the buns and lemonade at half-time.' He was also good enough to box for the school.

Tony possessed an enquiring mind and an insatiable curiosity about all things mechanical. He loved to take bits of machinery apart to find out how they worked. He still does. Had he been born into a different class, he would, no doubt, have become a skilled tradesman, perhaps a carpenter or welder; certainly something that would have involved him in using his hands. (This is where his son, David, has inherited his own talents as a furniture maker and craftsman in wood.) Tony was still in his early teens when he discovered a love of both architecture and photography. He was 14 when he was given a camera and started to take pictures of his fellow scholars at school and, when he was on holiday, of just about anyone else who would stand still for him.

He soon learned to do his own processing, even building from scratch an enlarger. It was also at school that his business acumen began to show itself. He supplemented his pocket money by selling his photographs to his fellow pupils, and they were not always satisfied customers.

His first efforts were not entirely successful, but he was never someone to be put off by initial failure and as soon as he felt a camera in his hands he realized that this was what he wanted to do as a profession. His family were not impressed, either then or later, at Cambridge, when he had failed his architecture examinations. His mother's reaction when he wrote to tell her of his plans was singularly unencouraging. She sent him a telegram saying, 'On no account consider changing to photography.' But as Lord Snowdon later pointed out, 'My uncle Oliver Messel's mother was just as discouraging to him when he wanted to become a designer – until he became the most successful one in the world.'

It was while he was at Eton that Tony was given his first motorcycle:

My father knew I was desperate to have my own transport so he bought me a Royal Enfield 125. It was my pride and joy. It was black and didn't have a pillion. The driving test was a bit of a farce; all you had to do was ride around the block while the examiner stood and watched. Everyone passed first time. We weren't allowed to keep motorbikes or cars at school; I kept mine in the town so that at the end of term I could ride it home. The war had ended but there was still petrol rationing in force so a motorbike was ideal; you could go for miles on a single gallon. And this was in the days when sophisticated protective clothing hadn't been invented so I stuffed newspapers around my legs which I tied with string. It was remarkably effective and certainly kept the wind out of strategic places.

But on other fronts Tony was clearly not up to speed. Academically he was not particularly interested in any special subject and, as is the case even today, if something did not grab his interest immediately, he did not try to master it. Consequently he languished in the lower reaches of his form; not that there is any evidence that this bothered him too much. One thing became clear: he was obviously not going to follow his father into the legal profession, or his grandfather Sir Robert Armstrong-Jones into a distinguished medical career.

He had, though, established himself as a good athlete and become an excellent flyweight boxer and school champion at his weight. One of his sports masters said later that he could have gone a lot further in the sport because 'he was not afraid to take a punch and had all the guts in the world'.

Then the event took place that was to change his way of life for ever. He was struck down by polio when he was 16, a terrible blow to a young man who had been so devoted to sport. Tony was staying at his father's Welsh home, Plas Dinas, in Caernarvonshire, when the illness struck with lightning force. He remembers the very moment when the first symptoms appeared: 'I had another motorbike at home in North Wales – a 250cc BSA. I got it out of the garage and couldn't start it. I remember kicking and kicking it to try and get it started. I was very fit, boxing for the school and all that, and suddenly I had this agonizing pain shoot up my back. My first thought was that I had just strained it. But I went to bed and I was in agony with a very high temperature. The pain didn't go away and that's when the doctor began to be anxious and suspect it was something more serious. But polio was the furthest thought from my, or anyone's, mind.' At first meningitis was suspected, but then a leading neurologist diagnosed polio. Tony was rushed to hospital in Liverpool some 50 miles from Plas Dinas, and his mother, summoned by a telegram sent by his stepmother, came immediately from Ireland to be with her son.

Normally Tony would have been with his mother but special circumstances had kept them apart that summer. During the war, his stepfather, the Earl of Rosse, had been with his regiment, the Irish Guards, while Tony's mother and her two other children moved from Ireland to live on the Rosse family estates in Yorkshire. With the end of the war, they had been able to move back home and had just done so, but Tony was unable to join them there. British people, including schoolboys, had needed a visa to visit neutral Ireland and, even though this was 1946 and hostilities had been over for a year, the wartime restrictions had still not been fully lifted.

There was a certain amount of relief among the family when meningitis was ruled out as polio was not considered to be life-threatening, but the prospects for the promising young athlete and boxer were far from healthy. He wasn't going to die from the disease but he might have had to face the fact that he was going to be crippled for the rest of his life. The treatment of polio then usually meant at least a year lying in bed, and the outcome often meant that the patient could never walk unaided again. Tony decided, with the bloody-mindedness that has served him well all his life, that, whatever the official medical diagnosis, he was going to recover and walk without a stick. He was unable to do anything about the early treatment – he did stay in bed in hospital – but having a natural inquisitiveness and an aptitude for using his hands, he set about building models of just about everything, the more complicated the better. He also exercised his brain by learning sign language and carried on an extensive correspondence with his favourite uncle, Oliver Messel, without whose encouragement he says he might never have recovered so quickly and so completely.

The physiotherapy treatment for polio is painful and prolonged; wasted muscles have to be exercised diligently even when the patient is in obvious distress. But Tony didn't complain. He was determined to prove the experts wrong and that he was going to recover. Neither did he spend a year in bed. He resolved to be on his feet far sooner than the experts predicted, and within a couple of months he was out of bed, at first in a wheelchair and later walking with the help of a walking stick, which he soon discarded. One of the promises he made to himself was that he would walk out of hospital without having to rely on a walking stick and he kept that promise. In fact it was not until his late sixties that he was forced to resort to a walking stick once more. One permanent legacy of the illness was that one leg is slightly shorter than the other and thinner than normal.

After nearly a year's absence, Tony was able to return to Eton. He had been given lessons while he was at home but he had fallen a long way behind the rest of his class. Not that it worried him particularly; he had never been very academic and the thought of not being able to keep up with his fellow scholars was not something that concerned him greatly.

What did bother him was that his illness meant an end to his sporting ambitions. No more boxing for his school or running in the college sports. That was when he converted to rowing and became a 'wet bob', coxing his house eight with increasing success.

He remained at Eton for the full term, thoroughly enjoying life in the sixth form with its attendant privileges, and when the time came for him to move to the next stage in his education he decided he wanted to study engineering at one of the most academically demanding colleges in the world, the Massachusetts Institute of Technology. He was argued out of applying as the standards were extremely high and his teachers knew he was not up to it because of the long gap in his schooling. He accepted the decision philosophically, and it cannot have been too great a blow, even though he claimed some years later that, 'I suppose I've always been a failed engineer.'

A much more severe setback in his view was his failure to be accepted for National Service, the two years of military training then compulsory for young men of his age. As a public schoolboy he would have naturally been offered a commission, as were most of his contemporaries, but his polio meant he was medically unfit for any of the services, in any rank. This is something that has troubled him ever since: 'I never escaped the feeling that somehow I missed out on National Service.' This was a perfectly normal reaction of many who were rejected on medical grounds. They often seemed to feel that their friends had experienced something they could never share and belonged to a club from which they were permanently excluded.

In Tony's case there was also the disappointment he thought his father might have felt, though there was never any indication of that. Ronald Armstrong-Jones had fought in both world wars. He was commissioned as a subaltern in the Royal Artillery in the First World War by falsely adding a year to his age, and then, at the outbreak of hostilities in 1939, he volunteered once again. He joined the 60th Rifles, rose to the rank of Major and landed in Normandy shortly after D-Day in 1944. With his legal skills, he was appointed Deputy Judge-Advocate on Field Marshal Montgomery's staff and was invalided out of the army in 1945.

Mr Armstrong-Jones resumed his brilliant career at the Bar and moved to a set of rooms in Albany, in London's Piccadilly. Shortly afterwards he was invited to apply to become a King's Counsel, one of the highest honours in the legal profession, but as his son remembers the invitation was not entirely welcome. 'My father was making so much money as a junior specializing in complicated insurance matters that he felt it was not the right time to take silk.' "I'll become a KC when I'm ready, in a couple of years' time," he used to say. Anyway, when he returned the form he had to fill in, he made an error and accepted when he had intended to decline. So my father really became a King's Counsel by mistake.' It didn't make all that much difference to his earning power. Within a remarkably short time he was making even more money than before, and he had established himself as one of the country's leading barristers in his field.

There was certainly enough to see Tony comfortably through university, and Cambridge was an experience he would enjoy and benefit from for the remainder of his life. He made friendships there that have lasted for over half a century and contacts in the world of journalism and publishing that would be invaluable in his future career as a photographer. This was also the period when Tony realized that his father was not only a doting parent but also his best friend. They saw each other frequently, wrote long interesting letters to each other giving details of what each was doing, and the affection that had always been there grew into a feeling of mutual respect that would never diminish. The day Ronald died in 1965 was one of the blackest in Tony's life. He says about his father: 'He was much more than just a provider. He was a fascinating companion who always found time to spend with his children, and he never lost the knack of being able to say exactly the right thing at the right time when you needed a little comfort. I miss him terribly.'

Tony's first course at Jesus College, Cambridge, was natural sciences, but this held little interest for him and within two weeks he switched to architecture. He loved the subject but he did not study hard enough. He enjoyed the idea of designing new buildings and seeing his ideas in concrete form, but the necessary background work was too detailed and tedious to hold the attention of this energetic and, it was said, frivolous young student. He entered into the social life of the university with great gusto and became a popular and welcome addition at the many parties to which he was invited. His rooms were in Chapel Court and were the scene of many late-night revelries. As he recalls: 'Cambridge was a delight. There was no pressure, and you must remember that it was much easier to get in then than it is today. If you were lucky enough to have been to one of the better-known public schools you were practically guaranteed a place.'

His love life blossomed, even if, in the 1950s, the permissive society was still more than a decade away. Tony was never a great drinker, but he enjoyed himself and joined in all the after-hours activities that make student life so alluring. But university life, like everything else, was changing. As Tony recognized, he was among the last of the privileged class of undergraduate who took it as their right to go up to Oxbridge from public school. He was just eighteen when he went up directly from Eton, but among his fellow students there were many who had served in the Armed Forces and who were three or four years older than the usual intake. They were men compared to the boys who had arrived straight from the sixth form. What's more, they had a different set of values; they were not as frivolous or carefree. They knew they had to work for their degrees if they were going to get decent jobs after university. It was the start of the democratization of Oxbridge. It meant that Tony and his contemporaries met a number of people who had experienced something of the harsh world beyond academia, something that would not have happened in pre-war years. It gave him an opportunity of mixing socially with young men and women from levels of society he had never previously encountered. It was an important learning experience for him. Without this, a man with his background and elitist upbringing might have felt uncomfortable when the cultural revolution of the 1960s rode roughshod over traditional class distinctions. Instead he was able to embrace the changing times and become very much part of them.

He had renewed his love affair with motorbikes, moving up to a Matchless 350, which was an ex-army machine, still painted khaki, and which cost him £60.

> I remember just after failing my architecture exams, a friend of mine called Anthony Barton and I had a date with two girls who shared a flat. Anyway, they stood us up, so we rode back to Cambridge feeling pretty fed up. Anthony was a big chap, about fourteen stone, and he sat on the pillion and promptly fell asleep. We came to a sharp bend in the road and as he was a dead weight – and I was going too fast anyway – we couldn't make the corner and just went straight on and wrapped the bike around a lamppost, ending up in a ditch. He was concussed and I had quite a few bruises, but otherwise we were all right and a kind lorry driver took pity on us and drove us all the way back to Cambridge, which was miles out of his way. I left the bike where it was and collected it a couple of days later.

He decided to invest in his first motor car. 'It was a 1927 open two-seater Singer which I bought for £20. It was a lovely little thing. The only problem was it did thirty miles to the gallon . . . of oil. But I loved it, and I was frightfully pleased with myself, driving it around the countryside. Eventually I sold it to a policeman for £40, one of the best profits I've ever made on a car. I wish I'd kept it though.'

At university Tony had spent much of the time he should have devoted to study on the river, where his passion for the sport propelled him into his college eight and then, in 1950, to the university eight where he was awarded his Blue. The way in which Tony drove himself to become the best cox at Cambridge was a perfect example of his determination never to be defeated at anything. He completely disregarded the infirmity in his leg and forced himself to become fit enough to compete on equal terms with his rivals for the job. Even if guiding a boat does not require the same sort of muscular development as the men who actually row the craft, it still needs a degree of physical fitness above the normal to spend long hours in wet and freezing conditions and being able to maintain your concentration at maximum level. Tony was the most enthusiastic member of the crew. He never missed a practice session, and he invented a series of exercises for himself so that his withered leg would not be a handicap. It was just as well that he did, as the Boat Race in his year was rowed in some of the worst conditions in living memory. Which made their 3½-length victory all the sweeter. It was also the first year that the Boat Race was televised live. So the cox was involved in a part of sporting history.

Recalling the event nearly fifty years later, Tony described the build-up:

The boat was a wooden shell – it was long before glass fibre – and gave you a terrific kick at the base of the spine with each stroke. Every year there were innovations. That particular year I designed and made the rudder from aluminium and laminated mahogany. . . . For a long time I kept the wind-up calibrated clock, a dark-room timer that I had adapted, and which I used to measure the stroke rate. I wired it up with a bell, which could be heard by myself and the bow (Harry Almond, who weighed just 10st 8lb). No one used a megaphone except the Americans; it was extremely *mal vu*. You learnt to throw your voice, like an actor. I can still call a taxi three streets away.

The training was no way near as professional as it has to be today, but it was still fairly rigorous with the day beginning with cold showers. 'They were quite healthy and also quite nice in the summer, but something of a shock on a frosty morning.' Tony was awarded his Blue in his second year at Cambridge, and on Boat Race Day his weight was 8st 8lb. Neither the cox nor the rest of the crew had the problem of overeating, as strict food rationing was still in force in 1950.

After the Boat Race, Tony returned to his architectural studies but it was too late. He had devoted far too much time to his sport and neglected his academic work. He says, 'My tutor asked me to go down for a year (there's a subtle difference between being asked and being sent) . . . I took the hint and never went back.' (In 1998 the aviary he had designed in 1965 for the zoo at London's Regent's Park was awarded a prestigious Grade II* as a listed building, putting it into an exclusive and much sought-after category; Lord Snowdon remarked at the time, 'Not bad for a failed architect!') One other consequence of Tony being 'asked to leave' the university was that if he had remained he would almost certainly have been selected to cox the Cambridge boat the following year as well, so he missed out on that.

It has often been said that the most important thing about having an Oxbridge education is not gaining a first, or even taking a degree at all, but the simple fact of just having been there. It's a worldwide club and once you have been admitted, nobody can ever take it away from you.

Tony Snowdon did not get a degree, but he did leave Cambridge with something even more sought after, a Blue. That elevated him to become a fully paid-up member of an infinitely more exclusive group, those who had represented the university at the highest sporting level. And the fact that in doing so he had helped his team to win made him a special person in the eyes of his contemporaries and opened quite a few doors when he started to look for work. The old-boy network is never more active than between fellow Etonians and former students at Oxford and Cambridge – whether graduates or not.

As Tony set out to make his mark in the outside world, his school and university days behind him, the contacts he had made would stand him in good stead in the years ahead. He relished the challenge that faced him.

FOUR

A Photographer in the Making

After coming down from Cambridge without a degree, Tony Armstrong-Jones did a variety of jobs including being a waiter at the Metropole Hotel in Brighton and selling advertising space in London for a firm which specialized in renting low-cost bedsitters. For this last job he provided his own company transport, his motorcycle, on which he zoomed around collecting the replies to postcards placed in shop windows. He needed to work, even though he had a small allowance of £200 a year from his father and lived rent-free in a room in his father's set in the ultra-exclusive Albany in Piccadilly. Tony had known for years that there was only one job he really wanted to do, and that was to be a photographer, but to please his parents he agreed to try his hand at becoming 'something in the City'. What this meant was joining the family stockbroking firm founded by his grandfather, Colonel Messel, and with this in mind he was invited to lunch with the directors. It wasn't a success. Tony made his excuses and left after the main course, declaring later, 'I just knew the City wasn't for me.'

Tony's parents finally agreed that he could start a career in photography, and he was given an initial boost by his mother, the Countess of Rosse, who had been so implacably opposed when he first suggested the route he wanted to follow. She decided if Tony was to join the ranks of those who took pictures for a living he might as well do it properly and learn from someone who had reached the top. Lady Rosse knew everyone in society – and that was the area she felt would suit Tony best – so she set about arranging for him to work for one of the top men in that field. She thought at first that Cecil Beaton, a near neighbour in London, might do but he was

47

apparently reluctant to take on a beginner, so she settled for the next best thing, the society and Court photographer whose professional name was Baron.

Baron – his real name was Sterling Henry Nahum – was a self-taught photographer who honed his skills as an army photographer during the Second World War, where he saw active service in various European theatres and was wounded in the Italian campaign. In 1946 he opened his first studio in London and quickly earned a reputation as an excellent portrait photographer. He realized that the easiest and fastest way to fame and fortune was to be associated with celebrities, and he managed to find and fill a niche in the market, photographing international statesmen such as Yugoslavia's Marshal Tito and famous literary figures like Dame Edith Sitwell.

It wasn't too long before he came to the attention of the royal family, and in 1952 he photographed the Queen, the Duke of Edinburgh and their two children, Prince Charles and Princess Anne. Baron became a close friend of the Duke of Edinburgh and, like him, also joined the famous (some said notorious) Thursday Club which used to meet for convivial lunches every week. It was inevitable that when the time for the Coronation came in 1953 Baron was appointed official Court photographer.

Baron's pedigree was thus impeccable, and when he agreed to Lady Rosse's request that he should take on her son as an assistant it could not have been more fortuitous for young Tony. But while it was Lady Rosse who helped to secure the opening, it was Tony's father who provided the wherewithal that allowed him to start his apprenticeship. Tony received no wages; in fact Ronald Armstrong-Jones had to pay a premium of £100 for the privilege. He did so willingly in the hope that at last Tony would settle down to make something of himself.

Baron and Tony Armstrong-Jones hit it off immediately and they worked together brilliantly. Both were individualists with their own ideas of how to take the best pictures, and while Tony already knew what he wanted to do and had his own thoughts on the artistic merits of photography (though today he still insists that photography is a craft not an art), Baron was an expert in the technical side. It was he who taught Tony all he knew about the mechanics of cameras. He found Tony a willing and enthusiastic pupil. He had always had this insatiable curiosity about how things worked, he still has, and enjoyed few things more than taking bits of machinery apart to find out how they operated. Nothing was ever sent away to be repaired; Tony would spend hours working out problems and delighted in finding solutions on a trial-and-error basis.

Another aspect of being a professional photographer that Baron took very seriously was the business side. He was no airy-fairy artist with little flair for commerce. He knew to the nearest penny the value of the work he was offering, and he was also a vigorous and energetic salesman. He instilled in Tony the commercial instincts he possessed himself and showed his young assistant how to attract the most lucrative clients. Tony was like a sponge, soaking up all that Baron had to offer.

One other thing they had in common was that both suffered physical pain; Tony from his childhood polio which affected his leg and Baron from the war wound which had been in his shoulder and which also meant that since 1943 he had been unable to bear any weight on that shoulder. He couldn't carry a camera tripod around.

The association between Tony and Baron (who was to die in 1956, at the very young age of 49) didn't last long. It had never been intended to; it was merely a stepping stone or something to enable him to get that first vital rung up the ladder. Tony knew he could not be happy working for someone else, and after six months he left amicably to set up in business on his own. Again it was his father who provided the money. He gave Tony enough for him to secure the lease of a tiny studio in Shaftesbury Avenue, which he shared with a friend, David Sim, and shortly afterwards, on his own, at No. 20 Pimlico Road, a disused ironmonger's shop, where he was to achieve some of his greatest early successes, both in his private and professional life.

It was during this period that rumours started circulating about some of the people he was friends with. He never tried to hide the fact that some of his closest companions were homosexual. Indeed, if anyone had mentioned it to him he would probably have gone out of his way to be deliberately outrageous. He had, and has, that sort of stubbornness that enjoys flouting convention and pricking pomposity.

Equally, though, Tony's studio was a magnet for some of the most attractive girls in London, and he was often seen in their company at fashionable nightclubs and restaurants. Since his university days he had been tremendously successful with women, and there was a seemingly never-ending procession of beauties who beat a path to his door in Pimlico.

It did not take very long for Tony to establish himself as one of the country's up-and-coming young photographers, though in those early months he concentrated mainly on London, using the contacts he had made at university and before that at Eton. He admits that his uncle, the famous stage designer Oliver Messel, opened many doors for him. 'I was lucky,' he says, 'through him I met everybody.' Messel may have enabled him to get a foot in the door, but once there it was up to Tony himself to stay there.

The theatre was his main interest and where he achieved some of his earliest successes, securing commissions from a number of West End theatres to photograph their stars for their front-of-house publicity pictures. Until he came along, the theatres had been satisfied with simple but glamorous portrait photographs placed in solid frames, but these did nothing to draw the attention of the viewer. Tony altered all that. He was responsible for introducing the massive 10ft-tall cardboard cut-out blow-ups that stood in the foyers and demanded to be looked at. It is a formula that has become standard practice on both sides of the Atlantic these days. Tony says the idea was born out of a simple expedient, 'I wanted to get people into the theatres.'

Snowdon openly admits that he loves the company of actors, and it shows in the photographs he has taken in the theatre over five decades. The affection he feels for the stage is clearly shown in the number and variety of pictures he has taken of stars from the 1950s to the present day. His range of work is remarkable and, even without the added cachet of his royal connections, he would still be ranked among the leading theatrical photographers of his generation. Throughout his career Snowdon's photographs have been renowned for their simplicity, and this is a deliberate ploy. He says, 'They are not meant to be clever or to impress other photographers. What I try to do is to make people react. That's another reason why I don't like my subjects to be too relaxed. If they are a little on edge, the result is always better.'

It was in 1954 that he started his lifelong admiration for actors and actresses when he photographed Margaret Leighton and Eric Portman for their roles in Terence Rattigan's play *Separate Tables* at the St James's Theatre. Even then he was experimenting with new techniques, and his double exposure of Miss Leighton (she was playing two roles in the same play) was considered to be innovative and imaginative at the time.

A huge breakthrough for Tony came in 1956 when he had his first photograph published in the *Daily Express*. It was of John Neville and Claire Bloom in *Romeo and Juliet* at Stratford and brought Tony Armstrong-Jones's name to the attention of the public and press for the first time. Although today the picture looks somewhat staged and unnaturally posed, as they were wearing full stage make-up, which he would never allow these days, it does capture the glamour and romantic image that the English theatre projected over forty years ago.

Tony was never satisfied with merely repeating what other photographers had been doing for years. He was always looking for new ways to show the actors in settings beyond the confines of the studio and theatre. When he was commissioned to photograph Dirk Bogarde and Geraldine McEwan for the play *Summertime* in which they were touring Britain, he joined them in Edinburgh and persuaded them to leave the theatre and climb Castle Hill so that he could picture them in a more realistic setting. The action of the play was supposed to take place in northern Italy.

One of the most dramatic photographs of that early period was of Alec Guinness as Monsieur Boniface in *Hotel Paradiso*. Tony took the picture at one of the rehearsals using a small camera with an ordinary lens. Tony said it was his first picture to be published in *Vogue* and added, 'John Barber, the *Daily Express* theatre critic unscrewed the photograph from its display case outside the theatre and published it the next day in the *Express*. This upset the editor of the *Weekly Sketch* as I had already sold exclusive rights to him for £2.'

A long friendship with Laurence Olivier began in 1957 when Tony stood in the wings at the Royal Court during a performance of *The*

Entertainer, with Olivier as Archie Rice. The resulting pictures show Britain's leading actor as a caricature of the seedy second-rate comedian he was playing. It was a brilliant achievement for both men. Tony went on to photograph Olivier many times, and in his book *Snowdon on Stage* he shows a selection of pictures of the great actor in various roles from Othello to Uncle Vanya. There is also one delightfully informal study of Olivier having a quiet supper with his wife, Joan Plowright, in Brighton in 1967. Snowdon said later that most of the biggest stars were the easiest to work with: 'Laurence Olivier and Alec Guinness both went out of their way to make it easy for me.'

When he was asked to photograph the dynamic Hollywood film producer Mike Todd, he went to the Dorchester Hotel where Todd, who was then married to Elizabeth Taylor, was staying in the Oliver Messel Suite. Tony takes up the story:

We went out onto the balcony and I started to look around for something suitable as a background. I thought I'd run off a few pictures and see what happened. What I hadn't realized was that Elizabeth Taylor was sleeping in the next room. Suddenly someone banged a door very loudly, and Todd threw his arms up in the air and made a hell of a face. At that moment I got the photograph I wanted. He had a huge grimace, and it showed his anger and frustration. He then told me, 'That's it, you've got your picture.' So I only had one chance and, thank God, it came off. It was the shortest sitting I have ever known as it lasted only for about fifteen seconds. It showed the importance of always having a camera with you and ready to be used. There often isn't a second chance.

Snowdon has also spent many hours photographing film stars, either in the studios or on location, which he much prefers. When he was working on the film *Death on the Nile*, for John Brabourne and Richard Goodwin, he had to build a small studio just off the main film set so that the stars, Peter Ustinov, Bette Davis and Maggie Smith included, could be taken aside when they could be spared by the director. Snowdon says he rarely had trouble with the actors: 'The bigger the star, the easier they were to work with. It was the directors who were more often the problem. They had such pressure on them that they hated to be interrupted. And let's face it, still photographers are a nuisance on a film set; all they do is get in the way.'

John Brabourne remembers Tony Snowdon differently. 'Tony was always the complete professional; he never got in the way and he got on with the crew remarkably well. The other thing about him is that he obviously loves actors and the film business, and that's important. It shows in his work. My partner [Richard Goodwin] and I were always very pleased with the results of Tony's work, which is why we asked him back so many times. He worked on quite a few of our films, and we never had a single complaint about him, which is fairly unusual in our business.'

Richard Goodwin, whose film credits include box-office blockbusters like *Murder on the Orient Express*, *Evil under the Sun* and the enchanting *Tales of Beatrix Potter*, was also responsible for acting as a conduit between the stars and Tony when he needed them for stills. 'On *Death on the Nile* Tony found that the bleached white cotton sails the locals used in their little boats were ideal as a backdrop, so he fitted up a sort of mobile studio just off the set and the actors would troop off one by one to have their pictures taken. It was a constant battle with the director to get the actors away from the set, and I helped Tony in that respect. Bette Davis said it was like being put in front of a firing squad.'

His reputation as a film photographer brought an offer from Hollywood when Twentieth Century Fox asked him to take the stills for a Doris Day movie, but Tony had to decline because of his other commitments.

Tony has had a lifelong fascination with films, and his introduction to the technical side through his association with John Brabourne and Richard Goodwin fired his imagination and enthusiasm. 'After a while you get the smell of films in your nostrils and it stays with you,' he says. He was friends with Derek Hart, a national television personality from the old *Tonight* programme, for many years and they began a partnership that produced several very successful television films on subjects usually concerned with social issues such as old age, the relationship of people with their pets and a documentary about dwarfs and midgets called *Born to be Small*, though both Snowdon and Hart refused to use the terms, preferring the description 'people of restricted growth'. Eventually Tony went on to make nine television documentaries, of which one, *Don't Count the Candles*, won a total of six international awards including two Emmys. But back in 1965 Snowdon also achieved the distinction of being banned. It happened when a novel by the Irish writer Edna O'Brien, called *August Is a Wicked Month*, was banned in South Africa for being obscene and blasphemous. Snowdon had taken the cover picture that showed the author appearing from behind a bunch of ostrich feathers. There was nothing wrong with the photograph; it wasn't in the least offensive, but as the whole book was banned so was Snowdon's picture.

Then, in 1975, he was arrested while photographing street life in Detroit. The police, who obviously did not know who they had in their custody, hauled him off to a precinct for aiding and abetting a street vendor. He was released when his identity was verified. It was on the same assignment that he was refused an interview with the mayor of the city, who was told only that a British cameraman wanted to see him. A public-relations disaster was averted at the last minute when a keen-eyed assistant realized that the husband of Princess Margaret was the man concerned and an interview was immediately, if hurriedly, arranged. It wasn't Lord Snowdon himself who told them who he was; he was highly amused by the entire incident, including the arrest, but others who could see the headlines looming were quick to try and put things right.

But even back in those early days, Tony didn't deal exclusively with show business. He satisfied his insatiable curiosity about almost every aspect of London life by haunting the old Covent Garden market in the early hours of the morning and photographing the porters as they loaded sacks of fruit and vegetables. He became a well-known figure around the Garden and quickly became accepted by the tough market workers as he snapped away with his hand-held cameras. The

interiors of East End pubs also held a fascination for him and provided subjects far removed from the glamour of the West End. An
early manifestation of the interest in seemingly mundane occupations
and pastimes showed in his dramatic portrayal of such everyday
pursuits as women queuing for food outside a butcher's shop or dust-
bin men collecting refuse in surburban streets.

What he was doing was gaining experience in a wide variety of
locations and with a diversity of subjects. But he knew what it was he
wanted to do ultimately, and he also knew that the most lucrative
side of commercial photography was in fashion and advertising. This
was to be his next target, and he set about achieving it with his usual
single-mindedness and determination. He bombarded the offices of
all the well-known fashion magazines and advertising agencies, at
first without too much success.

Eventually Tony's work started coming to the attention of the right
people, and his pictures began appearing in publications like *Vogue*,
Tatler and *Queen*, which just happened to be owned by a Cambridge
friend, Jocelyn Stevens.

Tony Armstrong-Jones was in exactly the right place at the right
time – and the right profession. The late fifties and early sixties were
a time of great change in Britain. The austerity of the Second World
War was well and truly behind; prosperity had arrived. Unemploy-
ment was at its lowest level for fifty years and people, young people
in particular, had money to spend for the first time.

It was the beginning of the age of true consumerism, with people of
all classes demanding the luxuries they had been denied for years.
Television was sprouting its commercial wings, advertising washing
machines, cars, foreign holidays and a multitude of enticing items that
persuaded potential customers that they could not live without them.

There could not have been a more propitious moment for a young,
ambitious photographer to arrive on the scene. Well-known fashion
models only had to appear at one of London's nightspots in the latest
creations for their pictures to be flashed around the world. It was the
start of what would become known as the Swinging Sixties, and
London was right at its heart. Young designers like Mary Quant with
her miniskirts and Janet Reger with her ultra-expensive lingerie were

the goddesses of female fashion. Stores such as Biba in Kensington were essential meeting places for the younger smart set, while Carnaby Street became the focal point for all the more outlandish outfits. It was an exciting time to be young, talented and ambitious. Glossy magazines sprouted almost weekly, and they all wanted the latest pictures, the more glamorous the better. Pop groups played at society dances and became the darlings of the upper classes. Anyone who was involved in any of the 'arty' professions was thought to be cool, with fashion photographers the coolest of them all. Terry Donovan and David Bailey commanded fees of thousands of pounds for photographic sessions, and they were fêted as celebrities wherever they went. And no one realized his time had come more than Tony Armstrong-Jones. Tony had found his own particular gold mine and he grabbed the opportunity with both hands. For him and his generation it was jackpot time.

In 1956 he staged his first exhibition at Kodak House in Kingsway, and two years later his talent was recognized when examples of his work were featured in a book called *London*. He gained his first introduction to the royal family by the simple expedient of writing to Princess Marina and asking if he might be considered as official photographer for her elder son, the Duke of Kent's, twenty-first birthday pictures. It worked, and the resulting photographs were received so favourably that he quickly came to the attention of other members of the royal family. With royalty no recommendation works better than word-of-mouth compliments from one of the family; the Windsor grapevine spreads quickly and very effectively. Tony became noted for his royal studies, among which were the official portraits of the Queen and the Duke of Edinburgh for their tour of Canada in 1957.

From there Tony went from strength to strength. His old friend, the late David Hicks, summed up Tony's attitude to photography and to life generally when he said, 'He only has one standard, perfection. Mediocrity is not a word in his vocabulary.'

His reputation grew and by the time he became involved with Princess Margaret, the name Antony Armstrong-Jones was already in the forefront of British photographers.

FIVE

Royalty Revealed

When mixing with royalty it is sometimes difficult to understand how delicate is the line that exists between what they regard as acceptable and unacceptable behaviour. You can put a foot wrong without even knowing you have done so, and behaviour which between people of equal class or status is considered to be perfectly normal can often cause considerable disapproval when royalty is involved.

Princess Margaret had a fearsome reputation for insisting, in the most regal style, on the deference she believed was her right by birth. She was the daughter of a king and the sister of a queen. All who met her were made aware of precisely what the 'Highness' in HRH means. She was clearly above the rest of us and demanded to be treated accordingly.

But she didn't get it from the man she was destined to marry. Tony Armstrong-Jones wasn't deliberately offensive or off-hand, but instinctively he realized that if he was to achieve any success at all with her, it was going to be on his terms not hers. Rather surprisingly, it worked.

Surprising because her fate in not being able to marry Peter Townsend, the dashing courtier with whom she had fallen in love, had made her an even more difficult young woman than she had been previously. Quick and witty, clever and bright, lovely to look at and very alluring to men, she was seen by some as selfish and spoilt, but Townsend brought out the best in her, 'a rare softness and sincerity' as he was to recall years later. In her eyes, he was the perfect partner, not only her father's Equerry but very much liked by him as well and treated almost as a son. The King's death in 1952 brought them even closer together in shared grief. The problem was, of course, that the Group Captain had a wife, albeit a flirtatious one, but a wife nonetheless. He could divorce her – and did so – but he could not change the fact that he was a man with a spouse still living, a state of affairs that the Church and the Establishment of the day frowned upon.

The Prime Minister, Winston Churchill, advised the Queen that parliament would be against the marriage. The effect on the monarchy might have been disastrous. At the very least it would have caused major divisions in the country and throughout the Commonwealth. While the Queen may have felt great sympathy for her sister, any threat to the standing and regard for her own position had to be removed. Moreover, as Supreme Governor of the Church of England, if she were to agree to the union, as she would have to under the Royal Marriages Act, she would be seen as condoning divorce. This was unthinkable at the time and the Queen consequently would have had to refuse her consent.

What this meant was that Margaret could have her man if she wished but only at the expense of her royal status. Even then, there was also the danger to the institution of monarchy to consider: barely twenty years after Edward VIII abdicated in pursuit of love, could it stand a second such blow?

It was a painful decision for the Princess, taken in the full glare of press attention and public discussion, with no shortage of eminent churchmen and commentators reminding her where her duty lay. It was a lonely decision, too. There is compelling evidence that her close family were content to duck the issue rather than confront it. The Queen Mother simply sobbed when the subject was raised, and the Queen refused to give any advice whatsoever, except that her sister should be left to make up her own mind. Which she did. The sacrifice was duly made. She would not marry Peter Townsend, the Princess announced in a statement from Clarence House on the night of 31 October 1955 – a decision she was said to regret ever after.

To be fair to her, there wasn't much evidence of gratitude from the people of Britain for the sacrifice she had made, and today hardly anyone even remembers – or cares – about her sense of isolation and despair. She convinced herself that she was a victim of the times. Those with a less charitable view suggested the loss of her royal status might have had more than a little to do with her decision.

From then on she lived a life of luxury and unashamed self-indulgence. At one point her extravagant lifestyle so incensed the press that questions were asked in parliament about whether she was giving value for money regarding her public duties. As a lady who liked to frequent fashionable nightclubs and restaurants, the Princess was never short of escorts, and she only had to be seen in the company of someone the media thought might be suitable for their names to be linked romantically. In that sense she was the Princess Diana of her day.

Her name was associated with just about every eligible European royal including Prince Christian of Hanover, who was not too pleased at the rumours and issued a formal denial of any romance, as did Buckingham Palace. Practically every single aristocrat in England also found himself, at some time, considered as a possible husband for the Queen's only sister. The most serious of these was a young man, barely three years older than the Princess, who did not possess an ancient title. But he did belong to one of the wealthiest families in the land.

Billy Wallace, whose unfortunate appearance made him the personification of the upper-class chinless wonder, became the sole survivor of the Princess Margaret set of the fifties. Most of the others who had formed a tight circle around the Princess had married with her blessing, but Wallace, who had so much money he could indulge himself in his full-time hobby of social climbing, without the tiresome need to earn a living, remained.

Wallace had been educated at Millfield School and Oxford, but after testing the waters in the commercial world of the City, he gave up all ideas of a business career. Instead he concentrated on securing a place in the higher echelons of society, and an almost doglike devotion to Princess Margaret. His social ambitions could not have been higher as he regularly proposed marriage. Just as regularly, Her Royal Highness turned him down.

But his persistence eventually paid off and, on the rebound from Peter Townsend and, perhaps, also seeing the prospect of being an old maid as a frightening but very real possibility, she finally agreed to marry Wallace, but swore him to secrecy for the moment. The Queen's approval was needed, and Margaret wanted more time to consider her future. It is highly unlikely that Wallace was really ever going to become the Princess's husband. In all probability, she accepted his proposal in a light-hearted manner without ever intending it should end in marriage. It was a spur-of-the-moment decision that she regretted and reversed as soon as an opportunity presented itself.

This came about when Billy Wallace confessed to a holiday romance in the Bahamas. It was a stupid thing to do, and he completely misjudged the level of his *unofficial* fiancée's sophistication if he expected her to overlook his little indiscretion. She immediately broke with him, much to his surprise, and did not see him again for several years. He found out with spine-chilling speed the finality of royal disapproval. It was to be nine years before she relented and restored him to royal favour, by which time she was married herself. Wallace eventually married the Hon. Elizabeth Hoyer-Millar, whose younger sister Annabel, became one of Princess Margaret's ladies-in-waiting, and the couple became regular guests at Kensington Palace until 1977 when Billy Wallace died of cancer. He was 50 and the Princess was a mourner at his funeral.

Antony Armstrong-Jones first met his future wife in April 1956, but it certainly wasn't love at first sight. Indeed neither took much notice of the other as one was guest of honour at a fashionable wedding while the other was there purely in his professional capacity, taking the official photographs. One of the guests was said to have later remarked that he was 'just one of the tradesmen'.

It was at Holkham, the stately home in Norfolk of the Earl of Leicester, where his eldest daughter, Lady Anne Coke, was marrying a former escort of Princess Margaret, Colin Tennant. The same Colin Tennant who, four years later, would give the Princess her most treasured wedding present, a parcel of land on the island of Mustique.

Lord Snowdon remembers little of that first meeting, or even if they were formally introduced, and Princess Margaret later had to be reminded that he was the man who took the pictures. For her it was just another social occasion; for him yet another routine job.

Their first real meeting was some time later when both were guests at a small, intimate dinner party given by Lady Elizabeth Cavendish, one of the Princess's ladies-in-waiting, at her home in Cheyne Walk, Chelsea. Elizabeth Cavendish came from a family whose pedigree nearly matched that of Princess Margaret herself. She was the youngest sister of the 11th Duke of Devonshire and the daughter of the Queen's senior lady-in-waiting, her Mistress of the Robes. Known for her unorthodox outlook, she was possessed of a wonderful sense of humour, an ability to get on with people from any walk of life and any rank, and she was also one of the few women not to be terrified of her royal guest. In other words, the perfect hostess.

The dinner was an immediate success. Margaret was still a long way from getting over Peter Townsend, and Tony was the ideal man to take her mind off her troubles. The fact that he came from a different group to her usual set was an added bonus. Perhaps, sub-consciously, she even saw something of Townsend in Tony. They were both outsiders, different from the traditionally aristocratic Palace courtiers who had surrounded her from birth, and each was able to show her something of a life beyond the confines of the Court. In addition, Princess Margaret had always thought of herself as something of a rebel, and she recognized in Tony a man with a similar outlook and attitude.

They shared a mutual interest in the theatre and knew many of the same people, so they gossiped together throughout dinner, prac-tically excluding the other guests, who were all delighted that Princess Margaret appeared to have found a kindred spirit. She was intrigued by the stories he told her of his various assignments and the star names he had photographed; he was equally fascinated by her store of anecdotes about some of the great names in British politics and public life. He was particularly amused by her ability to mimic with uncanny accuracy several of the nation's more pompous figures. It was an entertaining interlude, and their fellow guests were pleased that they had hit it off so well. What they didn't realize then was that Princess Margaret had already decided to take the acquaintance a step further. She found Tony to be a breath of fresh air after the sycophancy of her usual men friends.

It was all too easy for her to arrange to have Tony included in theatre parties and other functions. These were always fairly large gatherings, and nobody took the slightest notice of an extra man in the group. If her closest friends began to sense a different attitude in the Princess's feelings towards their newest recruit, they spoke about it only among themselves. Then, as now, the golden rule for staying within the royal circle is strict silence. Anything less means immediate and final ostracism. When the royal curtain descends, it is with a chilling finality. There is no mercy – and no appeal.

The strongest hint that those in the know had about Princess Margaret's feelings for her new boyfriend came within three weeks of that first dinner party. She invited him to Clarence House to meet her mother, something she would never have done so soon had they been merely casual acquaintances. From that first introduction, Queen Elizabeth was as captivated as her daughter had been and rapidly became the young lovers' champion at Court. Tony's easy-going manner and boyish charm worked on the matriarch of the royal family as completely as it did on all his clients. He knew exactly how to behave; how far he could go and, most importantly, how not to overstep the line between respectful cordiality and familiarity. It was his early success with his future mother-in-law that paved the way for his seamless transition into being a fully fledged member of the most famous family in the world.

When Tony's relationship with Princess Margaret started to become serious, she did not want it made known to the public until it suited her, so she hesitated to make too many visits to his studio at 20 Pimlico Road. Not that there would have been very many comments even if she had been a frequent visitor – nobody at that time would have connected the most regal of princesses with that most unorthodox of 1950s young men. As a working photographer, with no fortune or title to his name, he was hardly considered to be a

candidate for the hand of one of the most desirable, and untouch-
able, women in the world. The men who had been mentioned as
possible suitors previously had generally been from the landed
gentry, and almost all came from families with titles that went back
many centuries. Peter Townsend was, admittedly, not from that
class, but he had the distinction of being a Battle of Britain hero who
had found favour with the royal family. Nevertheless, when his
relationship with the Princess was first revealed, the old guard at the
Palace were horrified. The idea of a member of the royal household
even daring to consider himself as a possible suitor for the
sovereign's daughter was unthinkable and possibly even treasonable.
Just as thirty-five years later, when the Princess Royal's romance
with Tim Laurence, one of the Queen's equerries, was first discovered, the initial reaction was not all favourable. Some members
of the household simply could not believe that one of their
colleagues – and a junior one at that – would dare to think of
himself as a consort to the Princess. Words expressing their
amazement, and, in some cases, fury, were whispered regarding
Laurence and his behaviour; words which had to be quickly
swallowed once the Queen had given her blessing to the union.

So Tony received little attention from the press, and in this context
he was quite content for that state of affairs to last indefinitely. He
was known to most of the photographers and reporters in Fleet
Street, as he had worked with them for years, but they thought of
him as 'one of us' and not for an instant would they have thought of
him as a sweetheart for Princess Margaret. Even if he had admitted
the liaison, no one would have believed him.

But Tony knew that if they were to continue to see each other they
would need a safe house eventually and he found the ideal place.
A journalist friend, William Glenton, owned a small terraced house,
59 Rotherhithe Street in Bermondsey, backing onto the River
Thames, and he had rented a room to Tony. It wasn't very pre-
possessing at first sight so Tony set about making it a little more
inviting. He painted the walls white, built cupboards and raided
local second-hand shops to find articles of furniture and *objets d'art*.
There was no carpeting so he laid rush mats on the floor. It was a

typical bohemian artist's hideaway, and after many weeks' work he invited Princess Margaret to visit. This was in March 1959; eleven months later their engagement was announced.

Princess Margaret found the secret visits to Rotherhithe Street fascinating and highly enjoyable. She had never seen anything like it before. The nearest she had ever been to such an establishment was on official visits to the East End with her parents when everything had been painted, polished and cleaned. She once remarked that she thought the smell of new paint was normal for everything outside royal residences, she had become so used to the odour. The only thing she objected to in Tony's new den was the fact that there was no separate lavatory for her use. The house boasted only one and that had to be shared by everyone.

The difference in their lifestyles added excitement to the relationship on both sides. It wasn't all a case of Princess Margaret enjoying the risks of slumming it. Tony, too, found the affair added an extra dimension as he moved from East End to palace with consummate ease. He quickly became adept at playing the royal game of deception, where anything is permitted so long as discretion is employed. The morality of royalty depended then, as it does now, entirely on the eleventh commandment, 'Thou shalt not be found out'. He became recognized by the royal household and could come and go as he pleased. Generations of royal servants have learned the art of turning a blind eye to anything that involves the family, and it soon became apparent at Buckingham Palace and Clarence House that this young man was no ordinary boyfriend. The most amazing thing of all was that none of the royal servants gave the game away. For years staff at all the royal residences had supplemented their meagre earnings by moonlighting as moles for newspapers and magazines, but on this occasion no one leaked. They missed the opportunity of making a small fortune. Tony was obviously someone special from the way that Queen Elizabeth The Queen Mother greeted him, and they realized that at last Princess Margaret had found someone both she and they needed to take seriously.

By this time Tony had been taking photographs of the royal family for two years, so his visits to royal homes did not attract any great attention or comment. If he was seen leaving Clarence House it was assumed that he had been on yet another assignment. It was marvellous cover and lasted for several months before any news of the relationship got out. They even went shopping along Jermyn Street together without being recognized, and the Princess took great delight in seeing the looks of surprise on the faces of passers-by if they did happen to think they knew who she was.

Of course, this was in the days when junior members of the royal family could safely walk in London's streets without being accompanied by an armed bodyguard and long before the tabloids staked out the homes of royalty. The coming of Diana, Princess of Wales onto the royal scene ended that sort of freedom for ever.

Perhaps the biggest single reason why Tony Armstrong-Jones succeeded with Princess Margaret when so many others had failed is that he didn't try as hard as the others. Or, at least, he gave the impression that he wasn't trying. Maybe this was what attracted her so quickly. She had been so used to men doing her every bidding, and behaving in a strictly conventional way, that to meet someone who not only earned his own living but who introduced her to a way of life that was completely foreign, and slightly disreputable, had considerable appeal.

Much of the excitement of their early relationship derived from the undercover element. The fact that they conducted their affair in secret, out-of-the-way hideaways added a frisson of danger that both found stimulating and sexy. Margaret played at being the little housewife; at least she helped with the washing-up once or twice but stopped short of actually cooking Tony's supper or making the bed.

In those early days they were a good team. His easy-going attitude, spontaneity and flamboyant lifestyle contrasted with her much more structured and conventional upbringing. Each learned from the other. It wasn't all a one-way traffic, with the Princess having the advantages. Tony gained a great deal from knowing her. She would encourage him when he was downhearted, especially if his work wasn't going the way he hoped. When one of his theatrical enterprises failed to live up to its expectations, it was Princess Margaret who pulled him out of his depression. And when she sank into one of her not infrequent moods of self-pity, he could jolly her out of her ill-temper. He was just about the only person who could; all her other friends were terrified of her tantrums and none of them dared laugh, make a joke or even to speak first in her presence when she was in one of her black moods. Tony was the exception. He knew he had nothing to fear, and within weeks of that first meeting they both realized that they wanted a commitment. Tony and Margaret were ready to settle down, and an engagement was in the offing.

Antony Armstrong-Jones had arrived and was ready for the move into the major league.

SIX

An Engagement is Announced

The first time that Tony met the Queen and Prince Philip socially was when he was invited to spend a weekend at Balmoral in 1959. The suggestion had been made, of course, by Princess Margaret, and the Queen had agreed because she and Philip wanted to give Tony the once-over to make sure he was acceptable. The Queen Mother completed the royal line-up waiting to meet their newest prospective member.

Weekends at Balmoral have barely changed since Queen Victoria's day. Guests are expected to rise with the dawn, breakfast by eight and then, dressed sensibly in tweeds and stout boots, to join their hosts in their favourite Highland pastimes of stalking or fishing in the ice-cold waters of the River Dee. Even in her late sixties, Queen Elizabeth The Queen Mother would think nothing of standing up to her thighs in the fast-flowing river for hours on end.

The Princess Royal still maintains that her favourite holiday is a couple of weeks' hard walking at Balmoral. The royal family takes its leisure very seriously, and guests are expected to be fit enough to join in the daily programme. The idea of a lazy holiday, sunbathing and reading, is completely foreign to what they like to do in their off-duty moments. If Tony Armstrong-Jones thought it was going to be a relaxing couple of days, he could not have been more wrong. For him it was a baptism of fire; the sort of initiative test that Mark Phillips, Diana Spencer and Sarah Ferguson would all undergo in future years. Princess Margaret hadn't felt it necessary to warn him, but in fairness, with his social background, he had spent enough country-house weekends of the non-royal type to know a little of what to expect. But there is nothing quite like a royal weekend.

The programme is as rigidly structured as any other royal occasion, with the times for meals, drinks, games and even bathing all strictly adhered to. It is not uncommon, even today, to see male guests running down the corridors trying to fix their bow tie because they do not want to be late, even if they have only just arrived back at the castle after a full day's sport. Prince Philip is a stickler for punctuality; he is never late himself and hates anyone else to be.

Each evening Tony and Margaret would join the Queen, Prince Philip and their other guests for cocktails in the drawing-room, where even the carpets are tartan, before moving into the dining-room for dinner. A seating plan had been circulated earlier. Evening dress was de rigueur, but the less formal black tie and dinner jacket was allowed instead of the white tie and tail coat that King George V had insisted upon. Tony was, however, spared the indignity of having to wear a kilt because of his Welsh background. All the male members of the royal family wore their kilts with the distinctive grey-and-red Balmoral tartan in the daytime and the Royal Stewart dress tartan in the evenings. If they were stalking in the hills they would wear outfits made of Balmoral tweed, which was designed for George VI in 1937 and can be worn by family and household only with the Sovereign's permission.

Tony had little opportunity to observe the niceties of life at Balmoral; for him it was an instant lesson in learning the rules. Nobody told him anything; he was simply expected to know the form.

Prince Philip is not the most patient of men, and the first impression Tony made on him was not the most encouraging. But Tony was clever enough not to try and attempt anything he knew nothing about, so instead of competing with the other men in the party as they shot and hunted their way through the weekend, he watched them, along with Princess Margaret. But contrary to what was reported about those first meetings between Tony and Philip, there wasn't any prolonged or instant antagonism between them. When Tony recalls his treatment by Philip during the Balmoral weekend, he says the Prince could not have been a more considerate host. 'He knew I had problems with my leg, and whenever there was a difficult hill to climb, and there were plenty, he always insisted that a Landrover waited to drive me to the top. He never once made me feel awkward.' Others who were at that weekend remember events slightly differently. One fellow guest said, 'It wasn't that Philip went out of his way to make Tony feel uncomfortable, it was just that he expects everyone to conform to his ways and to jump when he says jump.' The atmosphere was certainly more relaxed when it was just the Queen and the Queen Mother around.

What Prince Philip may not have realized that first weekend was that Tony was nobody's fool. He was willing to learn and, with his quick eye, any mistakes he made initially were soon corrected. He joined in the social life at Balmoral easily, making an instant hit with all the ladies in the party and, with his natural charm, soon had the Queen on his side. They quickly established an easy relationship which has lasted to this day. Her Majesty has always been known to be slightly suspicious of strangers, rarely taking to them immediately. They have to earn her respect and friendship, normally over a considerable period. With Tony there was an immediate rapport, which delighted Princess Margaret and contributed immensely to the success of the weekend. When Tony left Balmoral, the Princess stayed behind and had the satisfaction of hearing from her mother and sister that they fully approved of her choice of husband.

As an introduction to the ways of royalty, however, Tony did not regard it as an unqualified success, mainly because of his uncertainty with Prince Philip. But when the engagement was announced to the family, it was Philip who surprisingly gave the couple the warmest welcome and support. He realized the heartbreak Princess Margaret had gone through over Peter Townsend, and he felt she deserved a little happiness at last. Philip was delighted to be asked to give away the bride at her wedding and performed the task admirably, and with good humour.

The events leading up to the engagement are significant. When Tony came into Margaret's life, she was still romantically involved with Peter Townsend, at least in her own mind. Then in October 1959, almost exactly four years after her heartbreaking decision not to marry him, Townsend wrote to her telling her that he had decided to marry his French girlfriend, Marie-Luce Jamage. The Princess had to face the fact that finally it was all over between them.

She received his letter while she and Tony were staying at Balmoral, and she revealed its contents to Tony while they were out walking. He, of course, knew all about Townsend, but the fact that the former Battle of Britain hero had been Margaret's first love and that she still held a candle for him had not deterred him from pursuing her. He had wanted to marry her from very early on in their relationship, and she knew it. David Hicks said that Tony had told him shortly after that first dinner party that he intended to make the Princess his wife. But he hadn't proposed and, following the disclosure of the letter, she asked him not to.

Tony has never revealed what happened to make her change her mind or the precise wording of his proposal. Princess Margaret later claimed that he asked her to marry him in a roundabout way, adding, 'It was very cleverly worded.' Many years later she was reported to have said that she had not wanted to marry at all after the Townsend affair had ended, but it was surely no coincidence that she accepted Armstrong-Jones just weeks after hearing about Townsend's own plans to remarry.

The couple became unofficially engaged in December 1959, but there was no public announcement until two months later, on 26 February 1960. There were two reasons. The Queen's formal approval had to be obtained, though why this should take months was never explained, and Her Majesty was also pregnant with her third child. The birth was expected in mid-February, and the Buckingham Palace public relations machinery was geared to feature this as the main event of the post-Christmas period, so they did not want another royal announcement upstaging the one they had planned.

Tony bought his fiancée an expensive engagement ring of a large ruby surrounded by diamonds in the shape of a flower (which she kept until the day she died). In January 1960 Tony travelled to Sandringham, where the royal family was in residence, to formally request the Queen's permission to marry. Under the Royal Marriages Act of 1772, any marriage of a lineal descendant of

George II is invalid unless royal consent has first been obtained. The act was passed because the Duke of Cumberland, younger brother of George III, had made an unsuitable marriage in 1771 to Lady Anne Horton, the disreputable widow of a commoner.

No such objection was raised by Elizabeth II in 1960, but Tony's presence at Sandringham was explained by saying he was there to show Her Majesty a model of a pergola which was intended to stand in the grounds. He brought the model with him, even if, privately, he thought the subterfuge unnecessary and slightly childish. There was actually no need for any lies about the purpose of his visit. No one guessed for a moment the real reason, and as a photographer of the royal family for some years, his comings and goings attracted no comment. A month after the Queen had given her permission for the marriage, she gave birth to her third child, Prince Andrew, on 19 February, and a week later, on 26 February 1960, the engagement was officially announced:

> *It is with the greatest pleasure that Queen Elizabeth, the Queen Mother announces the betrothal of her beloved daughter The Princess Margaret to Mr Antony Armstrong-Jones, son of Mr R.O.L. Armstrong-Jones, QC, and the Countess of Rosse, to which union the Queen has gladly given her consent.*

Within days Tony was moved out of his flat in Pimlico Road and into an apartment at Buckingham Palace, where his introduction to the ways of royalty was to be conducted. He was given his own valet, who ran his bath, laid out his clothes and organized his wardrobe. Having been brought up with servants around, it was something to which he was no stranger and he quickly became accustomed once again.

Princess Margaret remained living across the road in Clarence House with her mother, but Tony dined with them every evening, changing into black tie and dinner jacket. Throughout their lives, both the Queen Mother and Princess Margaret retained the custom of dressing for dinner even when they were alone, even though the Queen and Prince Philip no longer do so in private. The newly engaged couple spent their weekends at Royal Lodge in Windsor Great Park, which had been the Queen Mother's country home since 1932.

Following so quickly on the news of the birth of Prince Andrew, the press seized on this latest item of royal tidings with delight and relish. Surprisingly, there was little adverse comment about the engagement. It was almost universally welcomed as a sign of further democratization of the monarchy, and the fact that Tony did not come from the ranks of the expected peerage was seen as positive proof that this was indeed a love match and not a union arranged for reasons of political or monarchical expediency.

The reporters and photographers of Fleet Street vied with each other in their personal accounts of how they, and only they, were his closest friends. The fact that not one of them had the slightest inkling of what was happening gave the immediate lie to those stories. But it was all harmless fun, and even Princess Margaret, who had been on the receiving end, and some said deservedly so, of an appalling press for years, received favourable coverage.

During the months leading up to the wedding, Tony temporarily abandoned his profession as a photographer, which was galling as just about every publication in the world was prepared to offer him a blank cheque to take pictures for them.

There were exceptions to the generally ecstatic reaction to the engagement. Astonishingly – and ominously for their future happiness – these came from people who knew the couple well, not from uninformed outsiders. Jocelyn Stevens, one of Tony's oldest friends, was given the news in a telegram sent to him by Tony. He already knew of their developing relationship and had been in from the start, so his reply was unexpected and not entirely welcome. He despatched a telegram saying, 'Never has there been a more ill-fated assignment.'

An even more surprising reaction came from Tony's father. He was on honeymoon in Bermuda with his third wife, Jennifer Unite, when he was asked for his thoughts. 'I wish in heaven's name this hadn't happened. It will never work out. Tony's a far too inde-pendent sort of fellow to be subjected to discipline. He won't be pre-pared to play second fiddle to anyone. He will have to walk two steps behind his wife, and I fear for his future.' Ronald Armstrong-Jones was a gregarious extrovert who thoroughly enjoyed life, and, while he was not a snob, several of his acquaintances felt he would have welcomed the idea of being related, even through marriage, to the royal family. Tony's feelings at his father's comments have never been recorded, but he must have been dismayed initially at the lack of enthusiasm being shown by a parent he adored.

Within the royal family itself there were certain reservations, not about Tony as a person, but simply about the fact that he was not royal. While the Queen, the Queen Mother and even Prince Philip, who was not known for his friendly attitude to outsiders, generally accepted Tony and made him welcome as a new member of the family, one or two of the more conservative relations were not so amicable. Princess Marina, Duchess of Kent, whose opinion regarding the introduction of commoners to the royal family was well known in Palace circles, was said to be particularly hostile. This, in spite of the fact that it was she who had introduced Tony to royalty in the first place (when he photographed her son, Eddie, the Duke of Kent, for his twenty-first birthday picture and later Princess Alexandra), and that none of her own children married royals. The Princess was careful, though, not to show any hint of her disapproval in front of Princess Margaret, whose displeasure was not to be aroused.

Tony and Margaret were ecstatically happy. Those who were close to them at the time said they were a very tactile couple who could barely keep their hands off each other, and it was believed Margaret had completely recovered from the disappointment over the Townsend affair and that she and Tony were truly in love and could not wait to be married.

SEVEN

A Royal Wedding

Friday 6 May 1960, the wedding day of Princess Margaret and Antony Armstrong-Jones. The ceremony was to take place in Westminster Abbey, performed by the Archbishop of Canterbury and witnessed by the Queen, Prince Philip, Queen Elizabeth The Queen Mother and almost every other member of Britain's royal family. Few, however, came from Europe's other reigning dynasties. Practically all of them had refused their invitations, giving a variety of excuses, though their true reason was generally believed to be because the groom was 'not known to us'. The reasons they gave were ludicrous: King Badouin of the Belgians had tickets for a concert in Antwerp; the entire royal family of the Netherlands refused and issued a statement which said, 'It is the wish of the royal family to say nothing at all. You must draw your own conclusions'; Juan Carlos of Spain, who wasn't even a king then, declined from his exiled home in Portugal. Not that their absence made the slightest difference to Tony, but Margaret was understandably furious at the snub by these Continental royals who she considered were infinitely inferior to the House of Windsor. It took a long time for her to forgive them, if she ever did – and she certainly never forgot.

Margaret also never forgot, and didn't forgive for some time apparently, two of her closest friends, David Hicks and Lady Pamela Mountbatten, who married in a big society wedding a matter of months before her wedding to Tony. She believed they were trying to upstage her, which they clearly were not. The thought would simply never have occurred to them that their wedding might be compared with that of Princess Margaret. In her opinion, they should have done the decent thing and postponed their nuptials until after hers.

75

None of this, of course, was said out loud. That is not how royal disapproval works. Nor would any one else have taken offence. But Hicks felt his friendship with the Princess was never the same afterwards. 'She made it very plain to me that she believed we had done it deliberately, which was absolute nonsense. But she felt slighted and so the ice descended.' But in spite of what Hicks said, Princess Margaret cannot have felt too strongly about his and his wife's presence for not only were they among the guests but the Queen insisted that they walk in the special procession of foreign royalty and members of the royal family, alongside Lady Pamela's father, Earl Mountbatten of Burma. Her Majesty was consulted on every aspect of the wedding arrangements, and her approval was required before any final decision was taken. Even so it is hardly likely that she would have pushed the Hickses into the official line-up if she thought it would spoil her sister's day.

Among the royals who *did* accept invitations, Queen Ingrid of Denmark, Princess Margaret's godmother, was by far the most important so she was given the use of the Belgian Suite at Buckingham Palace during her stay. Lesser royals were allocated suites, or rooms, in other parts of the palace, and there was the occasional amusing incident in the otherwise immaculate arrangements made by the Lord Chamberlain, Lord Scarbrough, and the Master of the Household, who looked after the domestic requirements of the guests. Prince Maximilian of Baden had been expected to fly into Heathrow Airport, and a Royal Mews car and aide were despatched to meet him. Unfortunately there was fog on the morning of his arrival, and his aircraft was diverted to Gatwick. By the time the official had managed to get to Gatwick, His Highness had had enough, so he simply called a taxi and directed the driver to take him to Buckingham Palace – and he paid his own fare. Two of the 'royal' guests were downgraded from being on the 'royal' list to the 'non-royal' list. Prince and Princess Frederick of Prussia were originally invited as 'Royal Guests' until it was discovered that they had become naturalized British citizens. So they were relegated to the status of 'Ordinary Guests'. Attention to such minute detail is the stuff of royal protocol. Eventually only nine royal guests accepted invitations to the wedding, which were sent out by the Lord Chamberlain to the Queen Mother as the surviving parent of the bride. But those to the wedding *breakfast* – about 120 – were issued on behalf of the Queen and Prince Philip. Two people pointedly excluded from the guest list were the Duke and Duchess of Windsor, the bride's uncle and aunt by marriage. Relations between the royal family and the ex-King and his wife were still frosty, nearly a quarter of a century after the Abdication. From their Paris home the Duchess was reported to have said, 'Perhaps there'll be a funeral soon', though what that was supposed to mean was anyone's guess. She later quipped, in a moment of rare wit, 'Now I suppose we'll have to keep up with the Joneses.'

Divorce, the issue which had cost Edward VIII his crown and Mrs Simpson her royal ambitions, still posed difficulties. There had been much speculation prior to the wedding day about the position of Tony's parents, who were divorced. Not only that, but he had a father, mother, stepfather and two stepmothers: his mother's second husband, the Earl of Rosse, his father's second wife, Carol Coombe, who had also remarried after her divorce from Tony's father, and there was also Mr Ronald Armstrong-Jones's third wife. All were invited, and the Lord Chamberlain had the delicate task of arranging where they should all sit. This was, of course, long before the days when royal divorces were commonplace, and divorcees, even the innocent parties, were still, at that time, barred from Court. So for the Lord Chamberlain it was a first, and one he could well have done without because there was no precedent to which he could refer, the usual method when royal protocol is involved. He solved the problem by placing Tony's mother and father in the same row – but not next to each other – as their daughter, Susan, Tony's only sister, who had married the 6th Viscount de Vesci, opposite the royal party in the sacrarium. In the third row, in the main body of the abbey, sat Mr Armstrong-Jones's current wife, just in front of the Earl of Rosse, Tony's mother's second husband, who also had his two sons with him.

It was a happy compromise that suited everyone, and the day passed without any undue complications apart from when they were all due to leave the abbey. Tony's father wanted his current wife to travel back to Buckingham Palace with him, but the Lord Chamberlain wrote to him explaining that she could not '. . . because you are required for official photographs'. Similarly, the Countess of Rosse insisted that her husband and the boys should ride in her car, and the Lord Chamberlain eventually gave in and they all travelled together. Another delicate problem for the Lord Chamberlain was persuading Lady Rosse that she had to walk back down the aisle of the abbey alongside Tony's father. She finally agreed reluctantly, but they did not speak.

The celebrations had begun the night before as 100,000 people flooded into The Mall to make sure of the best vantage points. Buckingham Palace was floodlit for the occasion, and illuminated decorations shone along the wedding route. The crowds had plenty to cheer as the Queen, the Duke of Edinburgh and Queen Ingrid of Denmark drove from the Palace across the road to Clarence House to see Princess Margaret. She had not had a hen-party before the wedding, but Tony did hold a stag night for several of his friends, a couple of days earlier. There is no best man at a royal wedding. They either have supporters or a groomsman, which is what the Court Circular called Dr Roger Gilliatt. He was the second choice, as Jeremy Fry, Tony's best friend and first choice, had been turned down by Buckingham Palace. Roger Gilliatt had an impeccable pedigree as his father was surgeon-gynaecologist to the Queen and as such, a member of the medical household. Roger Gilliatt's wife, Penelope, was a magazine editor who had occasionally employed Tony as a photographer, but neither was in the best friend category. As Dr Gilliatt admitted, 'Armstrong-Jones seems like a nice chap, but I don't know him very well.' Less than a year later, Dr Gilliatt was himself involved in a divorce, as the innocent party, when his own marriage broke up.

On the day before the wedding 20,000 people had been admitted into Westminster Abbey to see the preparations, and when it closed at eight o'clock that evening there were still 3,000 waiting in the queue. The ceremony provided another royal first in that it was the first to be televised live with an estimated worldwide audience of over 300 million being claimed by the BBC. Sound radio commentaries were also broadcast to every Commonwealth country and to France, Italy, West Germany, Greece, Holland, Sweden, Norway, Belgium and throughout the USA. The occasion provided the BBC with its first major international challenge, setting the tone for future royal weddings.

It was a combination of old-style tradition – it was the last wedding at which the royal guests all wore formal full-length dresses, which seemed strangely out-dated even then – and modern democracy, with the inclusion of some of Tony's friends from lower down the social scale. His charwoman from Pimlico and the postman from his family village in North Wales were among the 2,000 guests, together with stars such as Joyce Grenfell, Margaret Leighton, Noel Coward, Dame Margot Fonteyn and the French film star Leslie Caron, plus the Poet Laureate, John Betjeman. A national newspaper listed the names of all the actors, actresses, dancers, hairdressers, interior decorators, song writers, singers and ballet dancers, emphasising that they were all friends of the bridegroom, adding, 'These are the people who will dominate the social landscape.'

One of the most distinguished guests on the bride's side was Sir Winston Churchill in grey morning dress, who, because of his great age, was allowed to enter through the North Door shortly before the royal family and did not have to take his seat hours before the ceremony like most of the other guests. Among the other notable British politicians were Lord Attlee, Sir Anthony Eden, Mr John Profumo, Lord Hailsham and the Earl of Home, who later relinquished his title to become Prime Minister. Princess Margaret's guest list ran to 510 names and included her hairdresser, René Moulard and his wife, 5 members of Norman Hartnell's staff and 2 from her favourite shoemaker, Edward Rayne. The Queen Mother, who paid for the wedding and bridesmaids' dresses, was permitted to invite 100 of her friends, while Tony was allocated the same number.

The pageantry of the occasion was captured by the presence of the Honourable Corps of Gentlemen-at-Arms in their scarlet tunics and plumed helmets, who were on duty in the choir of the abbey, and of the Queen's Bodyguard of the Yeomen of the Guard in their colourful Tudor costumes, standing in the nave. Completing the ceremonial order was a Guard of Honour of the 1st Battalion Welsh Guards with the regimental band and drums and the Queen's Scholars of Westminster School in their distinctive uniforms. Then came the Dean of Westminster in his crimson cope, followed by the High Bailiff and the Chapter Clerk of Westminster, both in their formal dress. One group of notable absentees was the Heralds of the College of Arms. They had written to the Queen asking to be allowed to be present, but Her Majesty decided their presence would make the occasion look too much like a State event when it was simply a family occasion. But in order not to hurt their feelings she instructed the Lord Chamberlain to invite them, and their wives, to the ball she gave at Buckingham Palace on the evening of 4 May, two days before the big day itself.

Shortly before the service was due to begin, scores of police officers searched the abbey following a bomb scare. A telephone call had been made to a man living in London who had the misfortune to share his name with the Home Secretary of the day, R.A. Butler. The non-political Mr Butler had been the subject of many anonymous calls apparently, but felt he could not ignore this one, which said, 'I feel it is my duty to tell you that a bomb has been placed in the abbey.' He called Scotland Yard, and the security precautions were brought into operation. Nothing was found, and the bride and groom were not informed.

The weather was warm and sunny as Queen Alexandra's State Coach, bearing the Queen, Queen Elizabeth The Queen Mother and the Prince of Wales, dressed in a kilt, left Buckingham Palace with a Sovereign's Escort of the Household Cavalry at exactly three minutes past eleven. The bride left Clarence House in the Glass Coach accompanied by her brother-in-law, Prince Philip, wearing a pink carnation in his buttonhole, and escorted by mounted troopers with a Captain's Escort of the Household Cavalry. (The Prince was standing in for her late father, who had died eight years earlier; the Church authorities at Westminster Abbey had discovered that where someone gave away the bride when her father was dead or unable for any other reason to be present, that person should be described as a 'Friend' and that is how Prince Philip was called.) The streets between Clarence House and Westminster Abbey had been lined with white silk banners embossed with the couple's initials 'M & T'. The Minister of Works, Lord Hope, later revealed that each banner had cost £45. The cost of decorating the wedding route was £20,000, with £3,000 being spent on roses alone.

The weather was perfect, and the Crown Equerry's timetable had been worked out with machine-like accuracy. Several rehearsals had been held with stopwatch in hand to make sure everything went like clockwork and the bride did not exercise her traditional right to be late, much to the delight and relief of the Crown Equerry. In 1981, Sir John Miller, the then Crown Equerry, who had followed the same procedure before the wedding day, found, to his dismay, that Lady Diana Spencer wanted to arrive at St Paul's Cathedral several minutes after the appointed time. They compromised with a delay of just thirty seconds, thereby allowing the bride to follow tradition and not throwing the Crown Equerry's meticulous timekeeping too much off balance.

The rehearsals inside the abbey did not interest Tony very much. He gave the appearance of not being too concerned about how the ceremony was conducted as long as they were married at the end of the day. But he perked up when the subject of where to place the television cameras and lights was raised. His natural curiosity and photographic professionalism was aroused, and he agreed when Princess Margaret suggested that television monitors should be installed so that those members of the congregation out of sight of the high altar could see the entire proceedings. This turned out to be one of the better ideas, as guests who had been seated for several hours in parts of the abbey out of sight of the altar were able to see the whole of the ceremony instead of just getting a glimpse of the bride as she passed down the nave. Loudspeakers relayed the service to thousands of people standing outside, many of whom had been there all night, lying on the pavements in sleeping bags. EMI installed television sets in Clarence House so that members of the household who were not attending the service could watch in comfort.

No detail of the service and arrangements escaped Princess Margaret's attention. Her private secretary, Major the Hon. Francis Legh corresponded with his colleagues in the Lord Chamberlain's office, the Master of Household and the Crown Equerry, who was responsible for arranging the transport for every royal guest either by car or horse-drawn carriage. Then there were the abbey authorities and the multitude of civil and military organizations with which the bride was associated. The final total of thousands of documents and letters fills seven boxes, which are now kept in the Royal Archives at Windsor Castle. The Order of Service was just one example of the kind of detail the Princess wanted to be perfect. In a note to the Dean of Westminster, Major Legh informed him that, 'The Princess is quite happy with it now, except for the cover which she wants to be stiffer still (i.e. what the printers call "board"), and the gilt edging to be more prominent; possibly also, the wording on the cover to be in red as opposed to black.' The changes were duly made.

Princess Margaret's wedding dress had been designed by Norman Hartnell, who had also made the Queen's wedding dress, and who was considered to be above reproach when it came to royal outfits. He did not take kindly to criticism or, indeed, suggestions of any kind. So when he was presented, at Clarence House, with Tony's idea of what he thought his bride should wear, Hartnell was not impressed.

Tony felt that Princess Margaret was so beautiful that she did not need anything fussy or too elaborate. In his view the simpler the dress, the more effective it would be. And as he himself would be wearing traditional formal morning clothes, he did not want there to be too great a contrast between them. It was a sensible suggestion, but Hartnell felt that Tony's ideas were a little too severe. Princess Margaret backed Tony, and so Hartnell, who knew when to back down, adapted his original designs to incorporate most of Tony's suggestions. There had been a great deal of speculation about the dress, but when it was finally revealed, it aroused complete admiration. One description said it was 'so simple as to be monastic'. Tony's suggestions had proved to be absolutely spot on. The result was a simple design made of white silk organza with a closely fitted bodice and a high V-neckline. The skirt consisted of three layers of organza over hundreds of yards of tulle, cut into twelve panels that widened from waist to hem. The top layer alone took some thirty yards of material. Princess Margaret's shoes, designed by Edward Rayne, the royal shoemaker, were made of white crêpe with a white satin facing running around the edges; the Princess had insisted on heels 2½in high to bring her up to her husband's height. The entire ensemble was topped off with a magnificent diamond tiara. Known as the Poltimore Tiara, this was not one of the many traditionally handed down through generations of royalty but one which had been bought privately for the Princess at auction for what was then believed to be a record sum of about £5,000.

The eight bridesmaids, led by the 9-year-old Princess Anne, wore dresses which were based, at Princess Margaret's request, on the first evening dress that Norman Hartnell had designed for her when she was just 17. The Princess chose this pattern because the original dress had been a favourite of her late father, and in order to remember him further she wore the rare Order of the Crown of India that he had awarded her in 1947, just before India gained its independence. The bridesmaids' dresses were frilly with puff sleeves, decorated with panels of broderie anglaise with pale blue ribbon slotted through. On their heads they wore coronets made of hyacinth petals and carried bouquets of lilies of the valley, while the bride's bouquet was of orchids. The headdresses had been designed by Tony's friend Carl Toms, who nine years later would cooperate with him on the plans for the Investiture of Prince Charles as Prince of Wales at Caernarvon Castle.

The eight bridesmaids were: Princess Anne; 6-year-old Sarah Lowther, whose mother was formerly a lady-in-waiting to Princess Margaret; 8-year-old Annabel Rhodes, a god-daughter of Prince Philip and whose mother was a cousin of the bride; Lady Rose Nevill, the daughter of the Marquess and Marchioness of Abergavenny, both of whom were very old friends of Princess Margaret and the Queen; Marilyn Wills, daughter of Princess Margaret's cousin, Mrs John Wills (and later a lady-in-waiting to the Princess); the Hon. Catherine Vesey, the bridegroom's niece, whose mother was Tony's sister, Susan; Lady Virginia Fitzroy, whose mother, Lady Euston, was a Lady of the Bedchamber to the Queen; and Angela Nevill, whose father, Lord Rupert Nevill, was to become the long-serving and most trusted private secretary to Prince Philip. When the Queen saw the list of bridesmaids she noted that three of the older children were 'bossy girls, so perhaps they can keep the younger ones in order'.

The high altar in Westminster Abbey was resplendent with historic gold and silver plate as the couple knelt before the Archbishop of Canterbury to speak their vows. The bride was self-assured and confident throughout, displaying no sign of nerves. But, like Diana, twenty-one years later, she did make one tiny mistake in her responses to the Archbishop. In her case, the words 'For better, for worse' were spoken in the wrong place. And she did promise to obey her husband, using the form of words from the older Prayer Book of 1662.

One of the great features of the ceremony was the music, all chosen by the Princess and directed by Sir William McKie, Organist and Master of the Choristers. An anthem by Schubert, 'The Lord Is My Shepherd', was sung before the reading of the Beatitudes and the bridal procession was accompanied by the hymn 'Christ Is Made the Sure Foundation'. Sir Arthur Bliss, Master of the Queen's Music, composed magnificent fanfares which were played by trumpeters of the Royal Military School of Music at Kneller Hall, and during the signing of the marriage registers (there were three: one for the bride and groom, one for the royal archives and one to remain in Westminster Abbey) two anthems, the first by William Byrd and the second by Gustav Holst, were played.

Following the signing of the registers in St Edward's Chapel, the newly married couple paid homage to the Queen as they returned to the body of the church. The Princess gave a full curtsy, while Tony gave the customary neck-bow. The bride's grandfather, King George V, had admonished one of his relatives many years earlier saying, 'Only head waiters should bow from the waist.' Princess Anne also curtsied to her mother, who gave her an encouraging smile for the way she had conducted herself throughout the ceremony.

As they walked out of the abbey, Tony and Margaret were flanked by a guard of honour made up of soldiers from the regiments of which she was Colonel-in-Chief. And, as they drove in the Glass Coach back to the reception at Buckingham Palace, the crowds of well-wishers were standing eight deep along The Mall. Many had camped out all night in order to get a good viewing position. All seemed perfectly happy to do so as The Mall, with its wonderful rose arch, shining coronets and golden domes, was a blaze of colour, proved a fitting background to the pageantry and splendour of this unique occasion.

One of the most remarkable sights of the day was the sea of faces that turned towards the balcony of the Palace, waiting for the appearance of the happy couple. The area around Queen Victoria's memorial was packed solid, with the crowds stretching far back along The Mall. Members of St John Ambulance Brigade treated 1,215 fainting cases. The police tried to control the throng, without success, and later, with good humour, they gave up and joined in themselves as hundreds of thousands of men, women and children broke through the cordons, rushed towards the Palace gates and swarmed up the railings. They were rewarded at 1.20 p.m. precisely as Tony Armstrong-Jones led Princess Margaret out onto the balcony, with the Queen, Prince Philip and the royal children alongside. Cheer after cheer went up as they all waved to the crowds, but there were no public kisses – this being long before the days when Prince Charles and Princess Diana would thrill onlookers and the media with that first balcony kiss in 1981.

The official photographs were taken by Cecil Beaton, still, at that time, the most favoured of royal photographers. Princess Margaret had invited him personally to do the honours in a letter from Clarence House. The setting was the Throne Room at the Palace, which has subsequently been dubbed the 'Jinx Room' by some members of the royal household because of the number of royal marriages that have ended in divorce and whose wedding photographs were taken there: Margaret and Tony, Princess Anne and Mark Phillips, the Prince and Princess of Wales, and the Duke and Duchess of York. The wedding breakfast was attended by 120 guests

(2,000 had been invited to the service in Westminster Abbey, but only family, close friends and royalty were asked to the Palace).

Again the seating plan presented problems for the Master of the Household, who had to make sure the parents and step-parents of the bridegroom were kept apart. As the guests were seated at twelve small round tables of ten it wasn't too difficult to ensure there was plenty of distance between the various Armstrong-Joneses and their former spouses. But the parents of the bridegroom were required to sit near each other on table number one. Ronald Armstrong-Jones sat between the Queen and Queen Elizabeth The Queen Mother, while the Countess of Rosse was two places away between the Duke of Gloucester and Sir David Bowes-Lyon. The Earl of Rosse was on table number three together with the then oldest member of the royal family, Princess Alice, Countess of Athlone, the Duchess of Gloucester and Princess Alexandra. Mrs Ronald Armstrong-Jones was seated at table number seven with, among others, the Princess Royal and the Archbishop of Canterbury, Dr Geoffrey Fisher, who later wrote to the Lord Chamberlain complaining that in the Order of Service his name had been lumped together with a number of other, lesser, bishops when it should have received more prominence as 'I was the person who solemnized the marriage.' Obviously any ill-feelings he may have had were concealed enough for him to accept the Queen's hospitality and attend the wedding breakfast.

It was a comparatively simple three-course meal starting with homard canadien, followed by filet de boeuf Princesse (royal menus often feature dishes named after one of the principals) with haricots verts, pommes croquettes and salade aux tomates. For dessert there was soufflé surprise Montmorency and crêpes dentelles. The wine was the best the royal cellars could provide. Sherry Fino la Ina for the guests as they entered the gold and silver supper ballroom; Château Haut Brion Blanc (Graves) 1955 with Champagne Clicquot 1943 for the toasts, with Fine Old Tawny Port and Hine Cognac 1922 after the dessert.

Prince Philip made a short speech in which he welcomed Tony as the newest member of the royal family, to which Tony replied, and the band of the Grenadier Guards played selections from

Oklahoma! and several other of Princess Margaret's favourite musicals. They cut the official wedding cake – 6ft high and weighing 150lb – presented by J. Lyons & Co. (and made from a recipe the firm used for the wedding cakes they gave to each one of their female employees when they got married 'because we know of no better way of making them'), which was one of twelve that had been delivered to the Palace, with one, at the Princess's request, being sent onto *Britannia* to be eaten during the honeymoon.

Documents released by the Public Records Office in 2003 showed that £1,227 (£18,405 at today's prices) was spent on wines, spirits, liqueurs and cigarettes for the wedding, with an overall cost, including food, of £2,701 (£40,515) for both the reception and wedding breakfast. They also show that £699 (£10,485) had to be paid for the extra staff brought in such as footmen, pages, cellar assistants and glass and silver pantry assistants, with £58 (£870) going to an extra pastry cook and five waitresses from Fortnum and Mason who were hired for the day. The Joe Loss Orchestra, which has played at every royal function for the past fifty years – it still does – was paid £250 (£3,750), while a further £250 was spent on flowers for the occasion and £199 (£2,985) on hiring cars, as the Royal Mews did not have enough vehicles of its own.

EIGHT

Honeymoon Afloat

In preparation for the honeymoon, the Princess changed into an outfit of yellow pure silk shantung, designed by Victor Stiebel, as she joined her husband to drive in an open-topped Rolls-Royce limousine from Buckingham Palace through the City of London to Battle Bridge Pier, where the Royal Yacht *Britannia* was waiting to carry them away on honeymoon.

The short journey to *Britannia* almost proved to be too much for the police to control as the crowds threatened to stop the motorcade altogether in their excitement. As it was, the car was slowed to a walking pace, and they arrived at the pier twenty minutes late, an unheard of delay in royal programming. For Tony Armstrong-Jones it had been a day of formal protocol, and it didn't end there. Before they were allowed to embark in the Royal Yacht there were more formalities as officials from the Port of London Authority waited to see them off. Finally, they boarded the Royal Barge waiting to take them out to *Britannia* in mid-stream. As they moved towards the yacht, all other ships on the Thames saluted them with a cacophony of siren calls. The moment the Princess stepped on board, her personal standard was flown at the main mast, and five minutes later *Britannia* slipped her anchor and set off downstream. Both bride and groom remained on the bridge, acknowledging the cheers and waves from the groups of people at various vantage points along the route. At Gravesend, 4,000 people had waited nearly twenty-four hours to greet the couple as they passed, and there were 10,000 more on the pier at Southend. A flotilla of thirty small craft went out to meet *Britannia* and escort her part of the way to the open sea. Sea rangers on Gravesend Customs jetty sent a goodwill message by semaphore flags, while 250 cadets in HMS *Worcester*, the Thames Nautical Training College ship, gave three cheers. Crowds lined the sea wall on Canvey Island, and everywhere along the Thames Estuary ships were dressed overall as *Britannia* passed by. When the yacht was 3 miles out, an Admiralty barge came alongside to take off the Royal Marines Band which had played to Margaret and Tony on board (one of the tunes it played was 'Oh, What a Beautiful Morning', from one of Princess Margaret's favourite shows, *Oklahoma!*). At last they could settle down to their honeymoon. It had been a fairy-tale day, with Princess Margaret being the focal point of an attention never before seen in Britain. Only the Coronation seven years earlier could compete with the splendour of this occasion, and the bride and groom loved every minute of it.

Princess Margaret and her new husband were the first royal couple to use *Britannia* for a honeymoon. She would later be used by three others: Princess Anne and Mark Phillips, the Prince and Princess of Wales, and the Duke and Duchess of York. As all four marriages ended in divorce, the Royal Yacht's unofficial nickname of 'The Love Boat' was rather unfortunate. But all this was in the future as, on 6 May 1960, Margaret and Tony stepped into the Royal Barge at Tower Pier for the start of a 6,000-mile voyage to the Caribbean.

The Queen had offered the use of the Royal Yacht so that the newly-weds could enjoy some privacy at the start of their married life together. However, even in those days, this most controversial of all items of royal expenditure attracted criticism. The Labour MP Emrys Hughes asked questions in the House of Commons about the cost of the honeymoon, the use of the Royal Yacht for a strictly private occasion and who was paying. He was told that there were 20 officers and 337 yachtsmen on board and that their wage bill amounted to £4,000 a week, whether they were at sea or not, so the honeymoon was not involving *Britannia* in any additional expense. This was the official answer. What it did not reveal was the running costs of bringing *Britannia* from her home port of Portsmouth to London to collect the couple, or how much it would cost for the round trip to the Caribbean. The Civil Lord of the Admiralty dismissed the question of expense by claiming that Princess Margaret deserved the voyage as a reward for the extraordinary amount of work she had undertaken on behalf of the country.

As this was the first royal honeymoon cruise, the commander of the yacht, Vice-Admiral Sir Peter Dawnay, had issued special instructions regarding the privacy of Princess Margaret and her husband. They were to be left completely alone at all times. All work that needed to be carried out anywhere near their apartments was to be completed in total silence, and none was to be started before nine o'clock in the morning.

In 1960 there was still enormous formality at Court, and this was carried through onto *Britannia*. Princess Margaret did not encourage familiarity, or even the slightest show of friendliness, from household or crew, neither did she wish to be included in any informal entertainments held on board. Her idea of a honeymoon cruise was to be left in complete privacy and for the standards she had become used to ashore to be maintained at all times on board.

Twenty years later the crew were surprised and delighted to find the young Princess of Wales wandering about the decks barefoot and even joining some of the junior deck-hands in their mess for a drink and a sing-song. There was no chance of such informality with the Queen's only sister.

Princess Margaret and Tony confined themselves to the royal apartments, and the only glimpse any member of the crew had of them in swimsuits was when they were served cool drinks on the Verandah Deck as they lay sunbathing. Even then they were ordered to avert their eyes. All meals were taken in the State Dining-room. Lunch was served with exactly the same amount of ceremony as that found in Buckingham Palace, and each evening the couple dined formally. Tony wore a dinner jacket, while Princess Margaret was invariably in a full-length evening gown, complete with jewels and tiara, or, as one officer remarked (out of hearing) 'wearing every rock in the book'. They were joined each evening by a lady-in-waiting and the Princess's private secretary, Major the Hon. Francis Legh, also in evening dress, and occasionally they would invite the Admiral and one or two of his officers to dine with them.

These invitations sometimes came at the last moment, so every evening the officers would find out from his valet what Tony's dress was going to be and then they would all dress the same way, just in case they got the call.

For Princess Margaret it was truly the best of both worlds; she was able to enjoy the privacy she demanded without giving up any of the creature comforts she had always been used to. The crew of *Britannia* went to great lengths to provide a romantic atmosphere for the couple, even stocking up on records of the Princess's favourite singers, Nat King Cole and Frank Sinatra, which they liked to listen to while sitting on the Verandah Deck after dinner.

Margaret and Tony had adjoining staterooms with a double bed installed in Princess Margaret's. Press reports at the time falsely said that she had had to bring her own bed because the yacht didn't have any double beds on board. This was untrue as *Britannia* had always had at least one double bed available in a cabin on the Shelter Deck.

Both of them liked to read, and a selection of the latest bestsellers was brought along including Joy Adamson's *Born Free* and the book of the film *The Longest Day*. The Keeper and Steward of the Royal Apartments, a lieutenant-commander, had been informed that neither Tony nor Margaret would read paperbacks, and only hardbacks which were brand new and had never been opened before.

It was revealed that Sylvia Davies, a stylist from René's hairdressing salon in London, had been on board throughout the voyage. But there was nothing unusual in this. Every royal lady (apart from the Princess Royal) takes her personal hairdresser on long overseas trips. But for the first time in his life Tony had a valet to look after his clothes. It made a change from his usual casual attitude to dressing.

All the crew were sworn to secrecy about the royal couple and their habits, likes and dislikes. But inevitably some details leaked and were voraciously gobbled up by the pursuing press pack. The British media had not at that time caught up with their foreign colleagues in terms of intrusive reporting, so they were more circumspect and discreet in their coverage of the honeymoon. But the American, French and Italian cameramen and reporters were nowhere near as restricted and they flashed money around among the crew and workmen in the islands the yacht visited. They all wanted the same thing – that elusive, exclusive picture of Princess Margaret in a swimsuit. When they failed in that target they disclosed (or invented) intimate details of her underwear. Apparently, it consisted of hand-woven crêpe de Chine, while her nightdresses were sheer silk.

Tony wore pyjamas and sported a silk dressing gown, and his favourite nickname for his wife was 'Ducky', something he vehemently denied. Not exactly the stuff to win Pulitzer Prizes, but still it was devoured by the public on both sides of the Atlantic and indicative of the sort of detail that would increasingly be demanded in years to come.

As with most royal occasions, the six-week honeymoon cruise was programmed down to the last detail. Every minute of every day was planned, and the whole thing went like clockwork; the well-oiled machinery of the royal household ensured that nothing was left to chance as they sailed between the islands of Tobago, Antigua and Mustique.

It was Princess Margaret's first glimpse of Mustique, the island that she would become closely identified with in later years. Barely 3 miles long and only 1½ miles wide, in 1960 it was completely unspoilt, with no development of any kind. There were no roads, water supply or electricity. It had recently been bought by Princess Margaret's close friend Colin Tennant, whose intention was to divide the island into building plots for the discerning and wealthy among his acquaintances so that they could enjoy vacations in complete privacy. As it was private property, he was in a position to control who could land on Mustique, which was a valuable selling point to would-be owners.

But by far the most important asset to this enterprising developer was having a member of the royal family associated with the island. Tennant offered the Princess a 10-acre plot in one of the most desir-able positions as a wedding present. She chose it in preference to something in a box from Asprey. It was a good choice as the land, even then, was valued at about £15,000. It was an even better investment for Colin Tennant, as once the news of Princess Margaret's interest in the island became known, members of the international jet set flocked to buy up adjoining plots. The nearer they could get to her, the better, and prices rocketed within weeks of her building a beautiful holiday home overlooking Gelliceaux Bay. Les Jolies Eaux became a haven for the Princess and later also a useful source of income when she rented it out for about £2,000 a week, before giving it to her son, David, who subsequently sold the property.

Tony Armstrong-Jones was not so enthusiastic about the place or, apparently, about Colin Tennant's motives. Whether Tennant was being merely very generous to an old friend or whether there were ulterior commercial considerations behind the gift, the fact is that Tony never once set foot on Mustique again after that first landing on 26 May 1960.

For Princess Margaret there were no surprises during the honeymoon cruise; everything was exactly as she had expected. Anything less would have received the royal glare of disapproval and the Admiral would have been made aware of Her Royal Highness's displeasure in no uncertain terms. The weather was exceptionally mild during the cruise, and neither the Princess nor Tony suffered any bouts of seasickness, unlike Princess Anne and Mark Phillips thirteen years later, when during their honeymoon cruise, they were both sick for the first few days. There were no unpleasant incidents involving the media, and when they arrived back in Portsmouth at the end of their honeymoon, Tony was amazed at the size of the crowd that turned out to greet them. He was also a little disgruntled at the formality of the welcoming ceremonies but managed to conceal his reservations.

For him it meant the end of being a purely private person; from now on he would become public property with his every movement shadowed by the press and his days organized by a private secretary. It was going to take a lot of getting used to.

One of the first tasks the young couple had to tackle when they arrived back in England was to unpack and inspect the wedding gifts they had received. Not all of them could be described as useful, but every one had to be looked at and, for those they wanted to install in their new home, a place had to be found.

The wedding presents numbered well over a thousand and included rare and handsome gifts from all over the world. The President of Burma gave an ornate solid-silver four-piece tea service, while the people of Sierra Leone offered a magnificent uncut diamond weighing eighteen carats in a Georgian silver casket. A bronze statue, standing 15in high, designed by Gregory Maloba, a lecturer at Makere College, and called *Compassion*, was the gift from the government and people of Uganda. Residents of Matlock Bath sent a pair of earrings for the Princess together with a bracelet, and a pair of cuff links for Tony, all made out of rare Derbyshire blue john stone. From South Africa came four gold candlesticks in the Georgian style. Two of the candlesticks bore inscriptions in Afrikaans and two in English. Many of the gifts illustrated part of the culture of the country they came from. Kenya gave a set of crystal glassware engraved with pictures of the country's game, while the government and people of Victoria in Australia gave a handsome rose-bowl complete with kangaroo handle on top. The members of the Diplomatic Corps based in London clubbed together to provide a superb evening bag for Princess Margaret. It was made of interwoven gold-and-silver thread with a crystal clasp with diamonds.

Not all the gifts were in perfect taste, or would be useful in their new home. Some are still stored, in their boxes, in a building in Windsor Great Park, along with unused wedding presents given to Princess Elizabeth and Prince Philip more than fifty years ago.

But for the couple who had everything to start with, there was more of everything to come home to. Few young men and women have had a more auspicious start to their married life.

NINE

Tony & Margaret

Princess Margaret and Tony were always the most interesting couple in the royal family. Their unconventional circle of friends and their obvious love of a social life outside that of the Court, coupled with their willingness to be photographed at film premières, fashionable restaurants and opening nights, made them into newsworthy items from the moment they were discovered to be together.

They were also thought by some to be the black sheep of the royal family, Margaret because by marrying below her station she had let the side down, and Tony because of his apparent preference for a bohemian lifestyle and outrageous dress sense. It didn't bother the couple one little bit; in fact they rather enjoyed their notorious reputation, and it certainly added to their attraction, though, strangely, they were always more popular abroad than they were in Britain. They were acclaimed in the USA, which they visited frequently. In Hollywood they mixed with stars like Paul Newman, Cary Grant and Gregory Peck, Tinseltown's own royalty. In France and Italy, Margaret and Tony were fêted by those countries' aristocracy, and their comings and goings were followed in the press by a public that couldn't get enough of them. All this was twenty years before Diana, Princess of Wales appeared on the scene and eclipsed the rest of the royal family in a matter of months. A glance through the press cuttings of the time reveals that barely a week passed without a picture and story about one or both of them appearing. The leading newspapers and magazines throughout Europe and the USA featured lengthy articles and dozens of pictures, usually in an uncritical manner. In fact, overseas, their glamorous image was welcomed by press and public alike.

Tony tells of one incident that attracted a lot of attention when they were in Sardinia:

We [Princess Margaret and he] were often guests of the Aga Khan, and sometimes we would go out for a day's sailing in his yacht. One day we struck an uncharted rock, which caused a pretty big hole about a metre square, and the boat sank pretty quickly. We weren't in very deep water, but the yacht was completely submerged. Princess Margaret and the other ladies were quickly taken ashore by one of the yacht's small boats and the rest of us swam. I was the only one wearing a rubber wet suit as I had been waterskiing and snorkelling, and as we were having a drink on the beach, one of the other guests said she didn't have any ice, would I swim out to the yacht and get some? It wasn't very far, and I didn't think it was an unusual request, so I swam out and then had to dive down the stairs, which were all under water, find the fridge, open it up, get the ice out, swim back up the staircase and ashore. Then someone else said, 'I've left some quite nice jewellery in my cabin, do you think you could swim back again and get it?' So I swam back, found the cabin and when I opened the drawer all these little Cartier boxes floated out. They were filled with bracelets and necklaces. I put them in a small handkerchief and went back. By this time some of the others had cottoned on, and they were less polite. One said, 'Hang on Tony you've forgotten my cuff-links, which are rather nice. Nip back and get them would you?' So I did. It was an eerie feeling, swimming down into the sunken yacht and I didn't have a proper aqualung, just a face mask, and the strangest thing was that a couple of tourists who were properly equipped swam up to the porthole and looked in and we found ourselves face to face.

The next day the yacht was towed to Corsica for repairs, and I went with the Aga Khan to the naval headquarters where he was saluted by the Admiral. During the trip from Sardinia, I had been looking to see if there were any other valuable items in the cabins. I was wearing just a pair of shorts. I was absolutely filthy, covered in diesel oil, and I had actually swallowed quite a lot, which was very unpleasant. Anyway, after the Admiral had greeted us we had to walk through his house and the floor was of white marble. I didn't have any shoes on and all you could see was a line of oily footprints across his hall. He was kind enough to ignore it, and the press found it all highly amusing.

At home, Tony and Margaret were frequently attacked in the press because of their flamboyant lifestyle. He was the easiest of targets, particularly when he again resumed working as a professional photographer, a profession that somehow did not sit easily with most people's idea of what a member of the royal family – even a semi-detached one who only qualified through marriage – should do for a living. If Tony had been a banker, stockbroker, captain of industry, or ran a large estate, it wouldn't have mattered nearly as much. But being a photographer was regarded as frivolous, not very manly and a not quite worthy enough career for someone married to a woman who was so close to the throne.

One of the early problems Tony had to cope with was Princess Margaret's absolute refusal to alter her behaviour, even when she was visiting her husband's family. Her autocratic manner infuriated some of his relations, and the staff at Plas Dinas couldn't wait to see the back of her. On one occasion when Tony and Princess Margaret were staying there she threw a massive tantrum simply because a housemaid served her with the wrong brand of whisky.

It was claimed they were an ill-matched couple from the start. He, with his easy-going, natural gregariousness, was as likely to stop and chat with the dustman as with a member of the royal family, while she insisted on being treated with due deference and respect by all and sundry. These were aspects of Princess Margaret's character that never changed. For a woman who had everything, beauty, intelligence, a ready wit and unrivalled position, it seemed second nature for her to want to make things go wrong. She was often described as the guest from hell. It was almost as if she needed to deliberately upset the carefully made plans that people made to accommodate her, and nobody quite knew what her mood would be from one day to the next. She could be the most charming and gracious person on

99

earth, and the following day the nastiest. The only people who rarely saw this side of her were her mother and her sister. To say that Margaret was contradictory is an understatement. She could be generous to a fault and enormous fun to be with, and also dismissive and totally selfish. A young officer who had been invited to join a dinner party at which Princess Margaret was a guest around the time when King George VI was ill had the temerity to ask after her father's health. She replied: 'Are you referring to His Majesty?' and proceeded to ignore him for the rest of the evening. Tony was just as complicated but in an entirely different way and with perfect manners. He wouldn't dream of insulting a host at a party, and neither did he enjoy shouting at servants if they did something wrong. But he, too, could be difficult at times as a number of the members of the Princess's household, including ladies-in-waiting, discovered, while several former staff were said to have complained about his awkward attitude on occasions. Both Tony and Margaret had two sides to their characters, but generally he was considered to be the nicer of the two. A former royal butler, Bernard McBride, told the *Sunday Mail* how hard he had to work when he was employed by the Snowdons. 'As well as cleaning the silver, washing, ironing, laying tables and serving meals, I had to lay Lord Snowdon's clothes out each day and attend to the front and back doors for any possible callers.' He added, however, when comparing the attitude of his two employers, 'Lord Snowdon was much more relaxed. He would often give me gifts in the form of aftershave and cigarettes, though I didn't smoke. He treated me as a person rather than the servant Princess Margaret did. You could tell who was the royal.' McBride left after a year with the Snowdons, and he recalled that Lord Snowdon thanked him personally before he went, but the Princess didn't give him a backward glance: 'Then, more than ever before, she made me feel like a second-class citizen.'

However, domestic problems apart, Tony and Margaret also had to cope with the dual role of carrying out a full programme of official public engagements while trying to live a full and rewarding private married life. So it was not too surprising that as far back as 1967 rumours began spreading about a rift in their marriage. And when Tony appeared in Japan, on an assignment for the *Sunday Times*, wearing a beard, reporters immediately jumped to the conclusion that he was in disguise because of the stories that were starting to circulate. He even answered questions about the state of the marriage saying, 'I am very much in love with her [Princess Margaret] . . . what do you want me to be, a playboy? I'm a working man so of course I have to be away from home.' The media wouldn't leave the story alone, and soon Tony and Princess Margaret were being described as 'The Reluctant Couple'.

One of Britain's senior aristocrats, in a patronizing condemnation, explained the reason why the marriage was falling apart a good nine years before the separation, when he said, 'Tony is far too removed from nobility.'

But in the early years of the marriage, although they had frequent rows, some of which, carried out in public, embarrassed others more than they did themselves, there were also moments of intense happiness. For instance, Tony kept his Little White Room at 59 Rotherhithe Street, a 300-year-old house on the edge of the Pool of London, for more than five years after they married. It was their romantic hideaway, and they enjoyed its simplicity after the opulence and luxury of their everyday accommodation at Kensington Palace.

Tony's landlord, the journalist William (Bill) Glenton, received a telephone call from Tony one day in 1965, asking if he might bring his mother-in-law to see the room. It took a little while before the request sank in and Glenton realized that the real identity of the mother-in-law was, in fact, Her Majesty Queen Elizabeth The Queen Mother.

Of course, he raised no objections, and, as with all royal programmes, nothing was left to chance. Tony's secretary formed the advance party, arriving first to tidy up the room. She sprayed it with an air purifier and placed a large bowl of roses on the table. Then she unpacked a hamper containing cold meats, salad, cheese and the Queen Mother's favourite fruit, strawberries. To make sure the party went with a swing there were plenty of bottles of red and white wine plus gin and whisky.

When the royal party arrived in a Clarence House limousine, they parked it some distance from the house to avoid attracting the attention of Glenton's neighbours, and they walked up the street to the house. Queen Elizabeth introduced herself, saying, 'Margaret has often told me about this house, and I've often wanted to see everything for myself.'

Glenton retired upstairs to his own living quarters, and the Queen Mother, the Princess and the Earl sat down around his tiny dining-table and had a picnic meal. Afterwards they gathered around Tony's old upright piano, and Margaret played while the others joined her in a sing-song, an unexpected choice being the French national anthem, 'La Marseillaise', which, apparently, all three sang with gusto in fluent French. They were still there at midnight, with the Queen Mother going out so she could throw crumbs to the swans on the Thames.

Before leaving, Tony and Margaret took her for a drive around the neighbourhood, stopping for a look around one of the oldest church-yards in London. If any late-night revellers had chanced to see the group, they would have been hard-pressed the next morning trying to convince anyone that they had actually seen the Queen Mother and Princess Margaret walking around a Docklands graveyard at midnight. As they left Rotherhithe Street, the Queen Mother was heard to remark, 'I haven't enjoyed myself so much since I was a girl of twenty.'

Tony and Margaret continued to use the room throughout much of the sixties, even after their children were born. If they wanted to get away from the stuffiness and protocol that ruled their lives, they would quietly slip away and spend the evening together, just the two of them, recapturing some of their happiest moments when they first met. Tony always did the cooking, and the menu rarely changed: parma ham, followed by rare steak and salad for the Princess and cold potatoes for him. Princess Margaret, ever figure-conscious, hardly ever touched potatoes. They would usually finish up with Camembert cheese, and the whole meal was washed down with red wine. They both smoked incessantly, even between courses, and then Princess Margaret would wash the dishes in a small tin bowl. She became quite domesticated, even sweeping the rush mats, but once told Tony, 'We should get a vacuum cleaner.' The Princess, who had never shopped for food in her life, once called up the stairs to Bill Glenton's wife asking if she could borrow a cup of sugar. It was the classic working-class cliché situation, but of course she was completely unaware of the irony.

They rarely invited any of their friends to join them in Rotherhithe; it was their secret hideout. An exception was made when Noel Coward turned up for supper and brought a friend along for company, Marlene Dietrich. Tony remembers the occasion well. 'After we had eaten, we sat around my battered upright piano while Noel played all his favourite tunes and Marlene sang all her most famous songs like "Falling in Love Again" and "Boys in the Backroom". It was pure magic.'

During this period of domestic bliss, Noel and Marlene were not the only celebrity friends in Margaret and Tony's life. Chief among the others were the arch Goons Peter Sellers and Harry Secombe. Harry Secombe first met Lord Snowdon at one of the *Goon Show* recordings at the Camden Theatre in London. Shortly before he died, he explained how Tony Snowdon happened to be there. 'Tony was a great friend of Peter Sellers and, as he was also a fan of the Goons, he asked Peter if he could come to one of the shows. I remember his somewhat flamboyant appearance but this was the Swinging Sixties after all. Peter introduced us and straight away he said, "Call me Tony"; he was that sort of fellow, no side at all. When he found out that I had an interest in photography, we had several long chats about the various cameras and lights we used. I discovered that he did not like using too many artificial lights, preferring natural light whenever possible.'

Harry Secombe (later Sir Harry) was one of the easiest men to get along with, and although he lived in opulent surroundings and even greater style than several members of the royal family, he had none of the arrogance some stars seem to need to bolster up their already inflated egos. His mansion was set in acres of rolling Surrey countryside, and he was on first-name terms with most of Britain's aristocracy as well as with Hollywood's royalty. So meeting the newest

103

member of the royal family at that time did not intimidate him in the slightest. 'I never really expected to become close friends with Tony,' he said, 'but it just grew. There was a friendliness about him that was absolutely natural, and what's more Myra [his wife] found him the same way, and she can smell a phony at a hundred yards.' Lady Secombe concurs, 'I love Tony. I think he's lovely. He is so warm, and I'm sure it comes from him being Welsh. You don't get that with many other people. Every time we meet he gives me a kiss and says, "How are you Myra, my love." It's just like meeting one of the family.'

Lord Snowdon invited Harry and Myra, with their elder daughter, Jennifer, to the Investiture Ball in Caernarvon in 1969, and Harry said, 'It was truly a night to remember. Hundreds of Welshmen singing their heads off with Lord Snowdon in the middle making sure there was enough ale to go round.' A short time later they were asked to a function at Windsor Castle. Harry recounted the story: 'When we got to Windsor, Tony came up to us and introduced us to everyone. Then he gave us a personal guided tour around the private apartments, and it was fascinating the way he explained who all the people were in the photographs on the piano. Many of these were foreign royals who had been dead for years, but Tony knew about them all and he made it a wonderfully interesting evening.' It seems that Lord Snowdon took the Secombes under his wing, not that there was any real need, as Harry had known the royal family for years and his friendship with the young Prince Charles stretched back to the Prince's teenage years when he first became a fan of the Goons.

It was at another royal occasion, this time the thirtieth birthday party of the Prince of Wales at Buckingham Palace, that Tony made a beeline for Harry and his wife. 'He smoothed the path for us as he did at a number of royal functions,' said Harry, 'but there was nothing condescending about it. He just wanted us to be comfortable. He was completely natural and totally lacking in pretension. That's the measure of the man. At this birthday party, one of Prince Charles's favourite singing groups, The Three Degrees, were invited, and Tony danced with Myra as they sang some of their current hits.'

While Harry Secombe and Tony Snowdon remained good friends until the day Harry died in 2001, Harry was the first to admit that Peter Sellers was the one who was closest of all to Tony:

They were really great friends. Peter was obsessed with Tony and Princess Margaret, and he would do anything to get himself invited to Kensington Palace. He was so flattered at being befriended by royalty. It became a bit of a joke, he was so obvious, but Peter had these wild passions and when he got an idea in his head you couldn't persuade him to give it up. It had to die a natural death.

On one occasion he gave a dinner party for Princess Margaret and Tony at his home in Elstead, where he lived in some style. Anyway, we were also invited, and while we were sitting down to dinner, which was beautifully served, burglars were in another part of the house stealing all the valuables. None of us knew anything about this until much later, and when Peter found out, he nearly died. To think what could have happened with the Queen's only sister in the house.

One of the most memorable occasions when Harry and Tony got together was at the very last *Goon Show* of all. This took place at the Camden Theatre in London, one of Harry's favourite venues, in 1972. Harry recalled Tony's involvement:

Peter, Spike [Milligan] and I had not seen each other for some time. I was doing my own television shows, Spike was writing and appearing as a solo act, and Peter, of course, had really hit the big time with the Pink Panther films. None of us was quite sure if the chemistry would still work and we were a bit apprehensive for the first few minutes. However, after the first read-through of the script, things started to warm up and we soon got back into the old routine. Tony turned up that afternoon during the rehearsal and took hundreds of pictures. He also showed a remarkable knowledge of Goon history and loved using his own Bluebottle and Eccles voices.

Harry said that Tony had a true Goonish sense of humour and a highly developed sense of the ridiculous 'which puts him on exactly the same wavelength as me'. The programme was to be recorded in the evening, and among the audience were the Duke of Edinburgh, Princess Margaret, Princess Anne and Lord Snowdon. It was slightly intimidating for the cast as Harry Secombe remembered, 'Although the show ran smoothly and it was nice to get back together with Peter and Spike, it was not one of our best. Perhaps the presence of the royal family made us hold back a little. Whatever it was, I didn't think it was a classic. But afterwards, Tony brought all the others backstage to meet us, and we had a marvellous little party with them all joining in.'

The Secombes became very friendly with the Snowdons and frequently joined them at social gatherings, mainly at Peter Sellers's home. At that time Sellers was married to the Swedish actress Britt Eckland, but he had convinced himself that Princess Margaret was in love with him. Harry Secombe said that Tony Snowdon once told him that he had heard that Princess Margaret had had a fling with Sellers. His comment was that of all the people she *might* have had a fling with Sellers was not one of them. The affair was all in Sellers's mind. He really believed that Princess Margaret was crazy about him, without ever having been encouraged by her. Obviously, he misread her naturally flirtatious manner on occasions.

The actor Graham Stark was also witness to Peter Sellers's growing obsession with Princess Margaret:

He persuaded himself, in his own mind, that he was in love with her, and she felt the same way about him. Once he said to me, in a very confidential tone, 'Gra, one day I'll tell you the whole truth about me and Princess Margaret.' But it was all in his imagination. There was never the slightest sign on her part that she thought of him as anything but a friend. He did the same thing with Sophia Loren, who is a dear friend of mine. He wanted everyone to know he was having an affair with her when they co-starred in *The Millionairess*, but it simply never happened. Sophia told me, 'He's just like a little boy.'

106

Apparently, Sellers also tried to steer Lord Snowdon in the direction of his then wife, Britt Ekland, but neither was having that. Britt was a very strong character and only did what she wanted to, but it would have suited Peter very well if Tony and Britt had fancied each other. In his own mind it would have justified his imagined affair with Princess Margaret. Britt Ekland, in her autobiography, *True Britt*, goes into some detail about her introduction to Lord Snowdon and Princess Margaret and described her first dinner party at Kensington Palace. She said that at Sellers's insistence, Lord Snowdon agreed to take some pictures of her. So she was taken to a bedroom where she took off her blouse and bra, and Snowdon gave her one of his white shirts to put on. The photographs were so good that Snowdon had one of them specially framed and then, borrowing a ring from Princess Margaret, he signed the glass with the diamond. Miss Ekland recalled that both Tony and Sellers were camera freaks who exchanged expensive Leicas and Nikons like children's cigarette cards.

Apparently, Tony and Princess Margaret were a very loving couple at this time. Britt Ekland and Peter Sellers, who were frequent guests at Kensington Palace, were intrigued to see that their hosts collected sentimental souvenirs such as theatre tickets from the first show they had seen together, bills from their favourite restaurants and even a blade of grass that held special memories. Princess Margaret used to tease Tony affectionately, and they shared a wonderful sense of fun.

On one occasion, they were all together at the home of Tony's friend Jocelyn Stevens when a couple who lived near by were invited to dinner. The couple had been angling to meet Princess Margaret for months and finally they got their wish. They had been told the dinner was black tie, and accordingly they arrived on the doorstep in evening dress.

When they came into the dining-room they found all the other guests, Princess Margaret and Tony included, wearing casual clothes. The men had even stripped to the waist and, already seated at the table, wearing only bow ties which their host had provided, looked to all the world as if they were naked. Everyone had a great laugh at the expense of the newly arrived guests, which seems rather cruel on the face of it, but eventually they, too, saw the joke and joined in.

Through the good offices of Tony Snowdon, Britt and Peter became part of the royal social whirl, weekending at Windsor with the Queen and Prince Philip, meeting the rest of the family and joining in at shooting parties. Tony was the perfect host, showing them what to do without being patronizing, and Britt says he was always well-meaning, friendly and considerate.

There are stories about Princess Margaret from this period that contradict the general impression that she was aloof. The writer, the late Quentin Crewe, and his then wife, the novelist Angela Huth, entertained Snowdon and the Princess regularly and were entertained in return. The four of them were a close group, and Crewe said the fact that only one of them was royal didn't affect the relationship. He recalled: 'My then wife was pregnant at the same time as Princess Margaret, so that gave them something extra in common. As it happened Angela did not have a very good time and needed to stay in bed for long periods. On more than one occasion Princess Margaret brought lunch to our flat and stayed for several hours chatting to Angela and cheering her up. It was an act of very great consideration and not one that people outside her circle might have associated with her at that time. But she was kindness itself, without ever once seeming patronizing or condescending.'

Quentin and Angela (known as Angie) were renowned for the lavish parties they gave in London in the seventies. Anyone who was anyone, particularly in the arts, was invited, and the Snowdons were regulars. They would be joined by friends such as Peter Sellers and his then wife Britt Eckland, and they would be entertained by musicians like Dudley Moore, another pal, or the outrageous George Melly, with his penchant for turning up in spectacular outfits that were guaranteed to shock.

But while Tony was very friendly and informal, royal protocol could never be completely forgotten when Princess Margaret was around. She was always greeted with a deep curtsy and no one, apart from her husband, ever called her anything other than Ma'am without risking royal wrath. But then again, it was not always possible to judge the moment correctly with the Princess. On one occasion Myra Secombe and Harry were finishing a holiday in Barbados when they received a royal summons. Princess Margaret was staying at Oliver Messel's house on the island. 'We had just finished our packing to go home the next day when, at five o'clock in the afternoon, we were asked to join her for dinner that evening. There was great panic. I didn't know what to wear. Eventually we picked the simplest clothes we could find and arrived to find the Princess and everyone else in swimsuits. When she saw us she simply said, "Oh! You've dressed." We needn't have bothered.'

Tony's friendship with Peter Sellers survived the comedian's various divorces, remarriages and numerous nervous breakdowns. It has been suggested that Sellers used his relationship with both Tony and Princess Margaret to further his own ambitions to obtain a knighthood. If he did, they were not aware of it, and as history records, no honours ever came his way in spite of his closeness to the royal family. Equally, there is no evidence that he was ever worried by the omission.

It was through Peter Sellers that Graham Stark became friends with Lord Snowdon. Stark was Sellers's closest friend throughout most of his adult life, acting as best man at his wedding to Britt Ekland. They had met while both were serving in the RAF during the Second World War and started out together as struggling comedians in the late 1940s and early 1950s. In spite of Sellers's success, their relationship never changed, and until the day of his death, they were closer than many brothers.

Graham Stark is also a very successful photographer, and it was this talent that brought him into contact with Lord Snowdon and Princess Margaret in the first place. He remembers the first meeting vividly:

Peter was a fanatic about gadgets. Whatever came out, he had to have. The trouble was he had no mechanical aptitude at all. He would buy the latest sophisticated movie equipment, open the box and press all the buttons. If it didn't work straight away, back it went to the shop. One day he rang me and said he wanted to show a short film he'd made to a couple of people. Would I come down to his house in Surrey and work the projector and join them for dinner. I agreed, drove down, managed to get the thing working when the door opened and in walked Princess Margaret and Lord Snowdon. Peter hadn't said who his other guests were going to be for the simple reason that it hadn't occurred to him that they were anyone special. Throughout his life, he was never impressed by anyone's rank, which made something of a contradiction of his later infatuation with Princess Margaret. I'm sure the royal bit was a huge part of the attraction, but generally he didn't seem all that impressed with his betters.

Anyway, I nearly fell over when he introduced us. After all, in those days we all thought royalty walked on water. When we started the film Peter and Britt sat with Princess Margaret, and Tony, it was 'Tony and Graham' by now, joined me alongside the projector. The film was one Peter had made at considerable personal expense, spending £6,000 on a professional music track alone, about a quick-change artist, himself, and the climax was when he said he was going to give his impression of Princess Margaret. He disappeared behind a screen and reappeared seven seconds later. But when he reappeared it was actually the Princess herself. It was very funny, and we all fell about. The Princess also did her impression of Queen Victoria, and Tony acted as a one-legged golfer. When it was over Princess Margaret came up to me and said she felt a complete amateur among so many professionals. I said to her, 'Darling, you're very good. In fact you ought to be in the business.' Throughout the remainder of the evening I kept calling her 'Darling', without realizing I could have ended up in the Tower, but the next morning Peter called to say that 'You've made a great hit with HRH. She's just telephoned to say how much she enjoyed meeting you and thought it was hilarious that you called her 'Darling' all night. No one else had ever done that.'

Graham Stark became a frequent companion to the Sellers and Snowdons, meeting in restaurants and at parties, and several times at Peter's palatial home in Elstead. Graham says that Lord Snowdon was the easiest of men to know. They spent much of their time together talking about photography. 'Once he discovered that I shared his passion we were on the same wavelength straight away.' On one occasion Lord Snowdon asked Graham and Peter to accompany him to Olympia where some of his photographs were on show at the Ideal Home Exhibition. 'He was so nervous when we got there,' says Stark, 'and I could feel for him. I've been through it myself.'

Stark and Snowdon also shared the services of a printer employed by Kodak. The company had given Graham an exhibition of his work, and Snowdon went to the opening. 'I found that the printer was a mute and that he had worked for Tony in the past as well. He was brilliant at his job, and Tony insisted that he was used saying that his affliction should not be a bar to him earning a living. He should be judged solely on his ability. There was nothing patronizing in this; it was just Tony's way of making sure that disability should not prevent anyone from following his trade or profession.'

With his photographer's eye for detail, Stark saw something telling about the royal couple in their early days together. 'One thing I noticed about Tony was that his eyes never left Princess Margaret and he never once tried to upstage her. If she was talking he would never interrupt. He had obviously learnt the lesson about how to behave in front of royalty even if you were married to it.'

The lesson may indeed have gone home, but whether the Earl was happy with it – and with his life two steps behind – he had yet to make up his mind.

TEN

Tony & the Royal Household

The first home of Princess Margaret and her husband was a grace-and-favour apartment – No. 10 – in Kensington Palace, given to them by the Queen. The apartment had five principal rooms and various smaller rooms and offices, but for the Princess, who had grown up in Buckingham Palace and since 1952 had lived in the almost equally sumptuous Clarence House, it was the equivalent of being moved into a cottage. She called it 'a doll's house' and was said to have felt insulted by being asked to live there, though, as far as anyone knows, she never complained to her sister about her accommodation. Her cousins, Prince and Princess Michael of Kent, are the present occupants.

The apartment had been empty for three months, since the death of the last tenant, the Marquess of Carisbrooke, a grandson of Queen Victoria. It needed a certain amount of structural building work and complete redecoration, which was done at a cost of £6,000.

A staff of seven was hired: butler, housekeeper, cook, footman, housemaid, chauffeur and the Princess's personal maid, who did nothing apart from looking after her mistress's well-being. Ruby Gordon had worked for the Princess for years, and she was a law unto herself, adamantly refusing to help the other staff in their chores, knowing she had the ear of Princess Margaret if she had any complaints, which she often did. She was also the sister of the legendary 'Bobo' McDonald, the Queen's personal maid and one of the most powerful people in the Palace. Bobo knew everything that went on, above and below stairs, and nobody, not even the Lord Chamberlain himself, head of the entire household, would challenge Bobo. In her latter years when she was bedridden in her rooms above the Queen's private apartments at Buckingham Palace, Bobo was cared for by two nurses provided by Her Majesty, and the Queen visited her every day until she died. Bobo also gave the Queen all the latest gossip from all the other households so she was kept fully up to date with what was happening in Kensington Palace as well. Princess Margaret and Tony also employed several part-time cleaners, plus Princess Margaret's private office staff to look after her official engagements. The weekly wage bill amounted to a princely £130 in total.

It was all a completely new way of life for Tony, and he made a number of initial errors, such as turning up in the kitchen to the dismay of the staff who had never seen a member of the royal family on their side of the green baize door before. Tony thought it perfectly natural to go wherever he pleased in his own house; the butler believed the master and mistress should keep to their own part and leave 'below stairs' to the servants. Within two years, most of the staff, including the butler and Ruby Gordon, had departed, allegedly citing Tony's 'non-royal' behaviour as the reason.

But long before this there were signs of disruption in the Snowdon household.

Shortly after the Snowdons returned from honeymoon, Tony and David Hicks were lunching together and David was invited to see their new home in Kensington Palace. 'I was intrigued as I had never been there, and I wanted to see the style of the place.'

Hicks, a spectacularly successful interior designer and aesthete, knew everyone, kings, queens, princes and princesses from all over the world. He was as welcome in the White House as in Buckingham Palace, not only for his artistic taste and talent but also because he was arguably one of the most entertaining people on earth. As a prolific gossip, his fund of stories was inexhaustible and when he regaled his hosts and fellow guests with outrageous anecdotes, he was not afraid to name names. There wasn't an aristocrat in the country that he was not on first-name terms with, and practically every one of the 100 wealthiest people in the world regarded him either as a friend or had employed him to design a room, a house or a garden. His client list read like pages out of *Who's Who*. It included the Prince of

Wales, Middle Eastern potentates and the *QE2*. Like his good friend, Tony Snowdon, whom he had known for many years, he was very expensive, but again like him, he gave value for money.

'It was a combination of sheer curiosity and professional interest,' he recalls. 'When we got to their apartment, Tony called out, "Darling, I've brought David Hicks back." There was no reply so we went from room to room and everywhere we went we appeared just to have missed HRH. Throughout the entire tour she didn't appear. It was all very strange. I found the apartment very interesting, particularly Princess Margaret's bathroom where the lavatory was placed right in the centre of the room; fascinating. Tony was obviously embarrassed at his wife's absence but covered it up brilliantly.'

Tony's isolation and the beginning of his treatment as an outsider started within months of the wedding. It was not only those distant European relations who refused to recognize him as an equal, but increasingly the royal household let him know he was there on sufferance. It was all done with great subtlety; there was no direct confrontation. The Queen would never have allowed that to happen. But gradually the frustration and irritation grew.

There were several occasions when Lord Snowdon clashed with the royal household, usually over quite minor incidents. With one exception, he invariably came out on top. The one time he lost was during the first two years of his marriage, when he and Princess Margaret had moved into Kensington Palace. There was a continual battle between Snowdon and his butler, Thomas Cronin, over the running of the house. The butler felt the domestic accounts and all purchases of food and wine should be his responsibility. Snowdon thought otherwise. And Cronin was forever trying to get his master to behave in the way that he expected royalty to conduct themselves. The final straw came when Lord Snowdon insisted on taking his coat off at the dining-table and throwing it over the back of his chair (he still does and whenever he sits down in a restaurant he often takes off his jacket).

Cronin walked out of Kensington Palace and sold his story to a newspaper, revealing his former master's lack of acceptable behaviour. It was following this 'betrayal' that the royal family introduced confidentiality clauses in the employment contracts of all their staff so that no one else could sell their family secrets. Forty years later, Cronin's story would pale into insignificance with the revelations of several other royal servants, particularly those of Princess Diana's former butler, Paul Burrell.

The clashes with the household proper at Buckingham Palace usually involved some petty infringement of the royal rules, which no one had written down, but which all were expected to know and obey.

Lord Snowdon's love of speed caused some friction with senior courtiers. Five years after he was married, Tony decided he wanted to ride over the official TT course on the Isle of Man. He had always loved fast motorbikes and had owned one since he was at school. He didn't tell anyone about his plan, knowing they would have tried to prevent him, but on 6 July 1965 he achieved his ambition. The trouble was, as his ride was unofficial, all the roads were open to other traffic. When the Queen's senior aides heard about his daredevil stunt, they let him know that this sort of behaviour was not of the kind that was expected from a senior member of the royal family and asked him to guarantee that he would not do such a foolhardy thing again. He declined to oblige them, and they retreated in disarray. To commemorate his feat Lord Snowdon was presented with a tiny trophy, which stands proudly in his downstairs lavatory at home, complete with an inscription which reads:

6th July 1965
When the Earl of Snowdon lapped the 37¾-mile Grand Prix Course, Isle of Man, with Dennis Craine on a Triumph 650cc Twin. First time round on open roads in 44 minutes. Lap record with roads closed 21 minutes

It is one of his proudest possessions and he admits he can see now how dangerous it was: 'I touched over a hundred on several stretches of the course, and suddenly a bus would come out of a side road. It was pretty hairy.'

Another occasion was again to do with speed – this time on water. Tony, with his friends Tony Richardson, Jocelyn Stevens and Tommy Sopwith, entered the Cross Channel waterski race from England to France in the sixties. Only eleven teams completed the course with Tony's team coming fourth. For him it was harder than the others as he could only use a single ski because of his weakened left leg. Again the household was horrified at the danger and tried to persuade Tony not to compete. His reply was succinct and straight to the point. It consisted of just two words. And to complete the story, Princess Margaret then took up waterskiing, being taught by Tony Richardson, and became very proficient at the sport.

During the sixties and early seventies, Tony Snowdon was frequently photographed wearing what were considered to be outrageous outfits. This was the age of Carnaby Street when anything went, and Tony and friends like Peter Sellers would try to outdo each other in their flamboyant fashions. He wore bell-bottom trousers, velvet jackets in hideous colours, kipper ties and shirts with collars four inches deep. His outlandish clothes ensured that his picture appeared in newspapers and magazines all over the world, often accompanied by captions that today would apply only to the more outrageous pop stars. He didn't mind in the least; in fact he revelled in the publicity his complete disregard for convention brought him. In the summer of 1965, during a visit to Balmoral, Snowdon shocked some of the more staid villagers in Ballater when he appeared dressed in knee-length knickerbockers, dark-brown velvet anorak and a shirt with checks big enough to play hopscotch on. One of the locals said, 'He seems a little more way out every day', and he earned the nickname of 'Trendsetter Tony'. In 1971 Lord Snowdon was hailed as one of the few young royals who set the fashion when he was included in the 'Top Ten Best-dressed Men' of the year. True, he only just scraped in, being placed tenth – two places behind the Duke of Windsor – but the magazine *Tailor and Cutter* said he had a style all his own, adding, 'Like many younger members of the royal family – even though he is only "adopted" – he has done much to make the monarchy more human.'

That, though, was not how it was seen at Buckingham Palace. It wasn't quite the image the royal household wanted to give, and the then Lord Chamberlain, Lord 'Chips' Maclean, was detailed to have a quiet word with Lord Snowdon to see if he would conform a little more. To make the request seem less specific, Lord Maclean also spoke to several other younger members of the royal family (Princess Anne had a penchant for wearing bright-purple trouser suits).

The result with Lord Snowdon (and the others) was another resounding defeat. He remained in the height of fashion until it suited him to change. When I spoke to the Lord Chamberlain about his reasons for making the protest he said, 'Do you think I would have dared to suggest such a thing without the approval of those right at the top?' It was obviously the Queen's or the Duke of Edinburgh's way of getting their message across without becoming personally involved. But it still didn't work.

Princess Margaret, surrounded by the royal family, gives the traditional wave from the balcony of Buckingham Palace after her marriage to Antony Armstrong-Jones, 6 May 1960. Tony's mother, the Countess of Rosse, is seen on the extreme right of the group. *(PA Photos Ltd)*

Princess Margaret and Tony in happier times, July 1964. They knew almost every celebrity in the world and enjoyed meeting the stars and show-business personalities. This was the première of the Beatles' first film, *A Hard Day's Night*, when the famous group was presented to the couple. *(© Bettmann/Corbis)*

Princess Margaret and Lord Snowdon shared a deep love for their son and daughter, David and Sarah. On a sunny afternoon in the garden at Kensington Palace they showed how much they enjoyed their children's company. *(Cecil Beaton/Camera Press)*

Lord Snowdon arrives back in Britain from Australia for the first time after the news of his separation from Princess Margaret became public. The couple officially announced their separation in March 1976, after sixteen years of married life. They divorced two years later. *(PA Photos Ltd)*

Lord Snowdon has loved motorbikes since he was a boy and he was delighted to have the opportunity of riding his Twin Triumph 650cc around the famous TT course in the Isle of Man in July 1965. He completed the course on open roads in 44 minutes. *(Camera Press)*

Lord Snowdon arriving at Caernarvon Castle for the Investiture of the Prince of Wales, July 1969. Lord Snowdon, as Constable of Caernarvon Castle, organized the ceremony. He is seen here wearing his distinctive uniform of dark, hunting green, holding hands with his daughter Lady Sarah Armstrong-Jones, with a rather serious looking Viscount Linley behind. *(popperfoto.com)*

Lord Snowdon leaving the Pant Glas Junior School, Aberfan, in the early hours of 22 October 1966. He was the first member of the royal family to visit this tiny South Wales village following the collapse of a mining tip, which killed 144 people, including 116 children. He is seen here with two of the rescuers, miners from nearby Merthyr Vale Colliery. Lord Snowdon later described the occasion as one of the saddest days of his life.

Lord Snowdon and Lucy Lindsay-Hogg leaving Kensington and Chelsea Register Office following their brief marriage service, 15 December 1978. Neither wanted a fuss or any media attention but press photographers inevitably found out and were waiting for the couple as they emerged after their deliberately low-key civil ceremony. *(Jayne Fincher)*

Even though they were divorced, Lord Snowdon and Princess Margaret often met at social events and always greeted each other with warmth and affection as they did here at the Dunhill Party. *(Ian McIlgrow/Camera Press)*

Tony Snowdon is flanked by his two elder children, David Linley and Sarah Chatto, as they attend the opening of an exhibition of Snowdon's photographs at the National Theatre, January 1997. *(PA News)*

Lord Snowdon's son David, Viscount Linley, with his half-sister, Lady Frances Armstrong-Jones, whose mother is Lucy, the present Countess of Snowdon. *(Rex Features Ltd)*

Lucy, Tony's second wife, with Sarah, his daughter by Princess Margaret. Lucy established a warm relationship with both her step-children. *(Rex Features Ltd)*

Lord Snowdon and his ex-wife Princess Margaret talk together in a friendly fashion as they wait on the steps of St Stephen Walbrook Church in the City of London at the wedding of their daughter Sarah to Daniel Chatto, 14 July 1994. *(Jayne Fincher)*

An affectionate greeting between the Queen and her former brother-in-law in London's Kensington Gardens when Her Majesty officially reopened the Albert Memorial after a four-year restoration programme. Lord Snowdon is wearing his robes as Provost of the Royal College of Art. *(Toby Melville/ PA Photos Ltd)*

Lord Snowdon accompanies Sophie Rhys-Jones (now the Countess of Wessex) as they leave Lambeth Pier for Greenwich. Prince Charles was hosting a lunch there to celebrate the golden wedding anniversary of the Queen and Prince Philip, 1997. *(PA Photos Ltd)*

Melanie Cable-Alexander, who gave birth to Lord Snowdon's son Jasper in 1998. She did not include the father's name on the birth certificate, though Lord Snowdon later acknowledged the boy as his. *(© Brendan Beirne/Corbis Sygma)*

Lord Snowdon attending Princess Margaret's funeral at St George's Chapel in Windsor Castle, 16 February 2002. In spite of the fact that they had been divorced for over twenty years, Lord Snowdon was deeply saddened when his ex-wife died. *(Corbis)*

ELEVEN

The Reluctant Royal

Lord Snowdon held a unique position in relation to the royal family. He was never fully accepted as 'one of us' but neither was he allowed the freedom to behave as someone outside the family. Angus Ogilvy, who followed Tony into the royal family by marrying Princess Alexandra in 1963, had the best of both worlds. He was able to live in St James's Palace, attend State Banquets and Royal Garden Parties if he wished, but was not required to carry out any public duties with his wife, and so he could concentrate on his chosen business career without any adverse comment – or interference – from his new royal relations.

Tony never enjoyed this choice. He was left in no doubt that upon marrying Princess Margaret, he was expected to give up all ideas of a professional career as a photographer and perform as the supporting act to his wife in her role as a leading member of the 'Royal Firm'. At the same time he was given no 'job description' or any indication of precisely where he was supposed to fit in with royal routine. For a man who had always had to make his own decisions – and had managed to do so very successfully – it meant a period of intense frustration before he was able to come to terms with his new status.

It might have been better if Tony had been someone more like Prince Philip, who is also of an independent nature but who realized, once the woman he married had become Queen, that any private ambitions he might once have held had to disappear. Instead, he devoted his life to helping her become a successful monarch and accepted the fact that for the rest of his life he would have to walk two steps behind her.

Of course, in 1960, when Princess Margaret and Antony Armstrong-Jones were married, she was fourth in the Line of Succession to the Throne, behind Prince Charles, Prince Andrew and Princess Anne, all of whom were under-age at the time. So her value to the country was considered to be extremely high, and the number and importance of her royal duties were exceeded only by those of the Queen herself and the Queen Mother.

Newspapers and magazines all commented about Tony's suitability for becoming a member of the royal family. The *New Statesman*, in a patronizing comment that was fairly typical of the time, wrote, when questioning whether he was qualified to join the family, that his credentials had to be judged 'with a leniency which only a few years before would have been unthinkable'.

All of which did not augur well for a young man on the threshold of a new life with the woman he loved, but uncertain of his status in her family. Neither he nor they had any idea of the pitfalls that lay ahead. Princess Margaret had been used to being in the public eye for most of her life; indeed she relished the attention she received from the world's press and asked pointed questions of the Palace press office if one of her engagements did not get the publicity she demanded. Tony, however, was completely unprepared for being thrust into the limelight to quite the extent that marriage brought.

There was no question of Princess Margaret adapting to his way of life. All the changes would have to come from him. They were moving into a home provided by her sister, in a palace where they were surrounded by ancient relatives, most of whom had had little social contact with anyone outside the ranks of European royalty or, at the very least, the British peerage. For Tony it must have been like delving into a history book and suddenly finding all the characters come to life. While other members of the royal family may have had reservations about the union, Prince Philip knew that Margaret had made her decision and he did not see Tony's lack of title or fortune as a drawback or reason why they should not be married. Some of the older-established members of the royal household were amazed; they had expected the severest opposition from Philip. But, as usual, he managed to surprise them with an uncharacteristic display of generosity. This attitude continued once the couple returned from their honeymoon. Prince Philip and Tony, while never the best of friends, were on quite cordial terms with each other, and Philip did his best to show his new brother-in-law how to cope with the subtleties of royal life.

Of course, Prince Philip had been through it all himself in 1947, when courtiers made his early days in the royal family as difficult as possible. The only person he could turn to was his Uncle Dickie, Earl Mountbatten of Burma, who rapidly taught him how to assert himself. 'Remember,' Mountbatten would say, 'no matter how important they think they are, they are only servants. You are royal.' It was a lesson Philip remembered for ever after. Tony never could, or would, think of himself as royal, but his position as husband to the Queen's sister placed him in a very powerful place in the Palace hierarchy, and it didn't take him long to realize it.

He didn't abuse the privilege, but at the same time, no one was left in any doubt that he knew where his strength lay. Princess Margaret would have needed only the smallest hint that Tony was not being given the respect due to him and the full power of her fury would have been felt. Her temper was well known, and even the Queen had been on the receiving end occasionally. She was one lady it didn't do to upset. She was never known to turn the other cheek.

To add to the strain, Tony was not doing any of the things he was used to, or wanted to do. In public he behaved perfectly in those early days, accompanying Princess Margaret on some of her duties, and always keeping well in the background. They went to all the traditional royal functions, Trooping the Colour, the Chelsea Flower Show, Garden Parties at Buckingham Palace and the Palace of Holyroodhouse in Edinburgh. Tony behaved impeccably, and comparisons were inevitably drawn between him and Prince Philip. Observers noted that they dressed alike, spoke alike and Tony even adopted the royal way of walking, with his hands clasped behind his back, just like Philip.

Within a year, his non-aristocratic status changed with the announcement that Princess Margaret was expecting their first child. The Queen was not prepared to allow her first nephew or niece to be a plain master or miss and she elevated her brother-in-law to the ranks of the peerage by creating him the 1st Earl of Snowdon. Princess Margaret had wanted Tony to be ennobled at the time of their marriage, and she never once used the title HRH The Princess Margaret, Mrs Antony Armstrong-Jones as her niece, Princess Anne, did when she married Mark Phillips. Until the time she was created Princess Royal, Anne was known as HRH The Princess Anne, Mrs Mark Phillips. Tony, however, had his own views about a title and wanted to be recognized in his own right and not as a social climber because of the woman he had married. So he rejected the first offer of a title. But the imminent birth of his first child forced him to change his mind. He chose an earldom because that is the lowest form of hereditary title that also confers a courtesy title on the children – a son would automatically be a viscount (Lord Snowdon had decided on Linley as a subsidiary title in honour of his grandfather Linley Sambourne) and a daughter a lady. At the time of his elevation he became the junior of 155 earls in Great Britain, and shortly afterwards when Princess Margaret was visiting North Wales, she was asked if she had seen Snowdon. She replied coldly, and with a certain amount of albeit unintentional wit, 'Do you mean the man or the mountain?'

However, there is no truth in the story that the Queen refused Tony a dukedom simply because she wanted her own husband to have a superior title. Philip had been on the receiving end of such a snub himself when King George VI refused to make him a prince of the United Kingdom on his marriage to Princess Elizabeth. It was his wife who promoted him to the rank ten years later, when she was Queen. And the King had also made his elder daughter a Lady of the Garter one week before Philip joined the order 'so as to protect her seniority'.

With his elevation to the peerage, Tony and Margaret were also moved into a much larger apartment in Kensington Palace, No. 1A in Clock Court. Like their first home, this too had been empty for years, since 1939 in fact, and some £55,000 was spent out of public funds to make it fit to live in. The last occupant had been Princess Louise, Duchess of Argyll, a daughter of Queen Victoria, and since she died nothing had been done to the interior; in fact, Princess Louise had last had the place decorated in 1891.

Forty years after the Snowdons moved in, public records released claimed that the equivalent of £1 million had been spent, including a third on special marble floors. Lord Snowdon was quick to refute the allegations of reckless spending and rushed to defend his late ex-wife, who was blamed for much of it. He pointed out that the apartment was uninhabitable when they first saw it and added:

It's so unfair. It's time things were put right. The whole point about the building was that it had suffered extensive damage during the war from an incendiary bomb. It had a direct hit and after that it remained empty. . . . The government did not want this pointed out. It was much easier for them to blame it on Princess Margaret. . . . What they have tried to make out is that Princess Margaret refurbished it at a huge expense. I remember vividly that she and I made all the doors together. She did the veneering and we did them in the workshop. That didn't cost much. It was the Ministry of Works that wanted marble floors. We didn't want them on grounds of cost. We used stone flags and cut them. I then got slate, and that didn't cost anything because I got it from Wales from a slate quarry which happened to be owned by my godfather, so we got those free.

The government architect who was responsible for the refurbishment supported Lord Snowdon's views, adding that when he first saw the place 'There was even a stream flowing through the basement.' The architect, Harold Yexley, pointed out that he met almost weekly with Princess Margaret and Lord Snowdon to discuss what could and could not be paid out of the public purse, and that one of the rooms, which was lined with gothic panelling, was actually paid for by the Princess.

But even the birth of his first child, David Albert Charles, Viscount Linley, on 3 November 1961, followed on 1 May 1964 by Sarah Frances Elizabeth (now Lady Sarah Chatto and both delivered by Caesarian section), did little to prevent Tony from feeling an outsider. Shortly after David was born, Tony and Margaret were due to leave for a winter holiday in Antigua. He did not want to leave his son, but Margaret, who had grown up surrounded by nannies and governesses, and whose parents had frequently left her and her older sister in their care when their public duties took them abroad, couldn't understand his concerns. So they went on holiday, but Tony could not wait to get back to his son, with whom he was besotted.

With Princess Margaret continuing with her royal duties, Tony had accepted certain positions of his own, none of which was sufficient to satisfy his talents or abundant energy. He had taken on a number of unpaid posts, including being a member of the Design Council, but it was when he decided to earn his own living once more by joining the *Sunday Times* as artistic adviser that his isolation from the rest of the royal family really became apparent. His period of trying to adjust himself to his situation as a member of the royal family was coming to an end.

Tony realized that if he was going to retain his own identity he must get back to full-time work, even though he retained some of his honorary but essentially 'worthy' appointments such as serving on the Council of Industrial Design (and continued to do so for many years).

It wasn't so much the Queen or Princess Margaret who objected to him working, but some of the senior courtiers at the Palace, who feared that if he was seen to accept paid employment, accusations of commercialism might be levelled at the royal family. 'They wanted me to have a safe job,' he recalled many years later. By now, of course, he had become the first Earl of Snowdon, but he was anxious not to be seen to be capitalizing on his title or his royal connections. Yet, instead of using his original name, he decided to adopt his new official name of Snowdon. A decision he has still to explain.

In the early sixties he accepted his first working assignment since the marriage when he agreed to photograph the actors filming the British film *Billy Liar*, starring Tom Courtenay. He had been commissioned by the *Sunday Times*, from whom he had demanded – and been promised – total secrecy. He knew that if the media found out about his plans they would descend in hordes on the location and ruin the day's shooting, not only for himself but also for the film crew. It was the final day of filming in a dance hall in Manchester, and when Tony arrived he found a dozen or so photographers and cameramen waiting for him. There had been a leak. After trying unsuccessfully to complete his assignment, he gave up, packed his cameras and returned to London. Only then did the other photographers leave the crew alone so they could finish their day's work. The *Sunday Times* provided Lord Snowdon with one of his most successful periods when he was given a contract to produce photographs for their colour magazine. His old Cambridge friend Mark Boxer was editing the magazine, and he offered Tony a job. The offer may have originated through the old-boy network, but there was nothing altruistic in Boxer's move. He and his boss, Roy Thomson, the owner of the *Sunday Times*, realized the publicity value of having Snowdon working for them. It was the first time a member of the royal family had accepted paid employment, and it guaranteed unprecedented prestige to whoever managed to secure his services. Boxer also knew that Snowdon was a first-class photographer, so they weren't just paying for his name.

Before he accepted the job, Tony had to get the approval of the Queen. If she had said no that would have been the end of the matter. But Her Majesty realized that he needed to work and that, in spite of the criticism the news of his appointment would invoke, the fact that he was in gainful employment would ultimately be favourable to the family.

She was right about the criticism. A veritable storm broke once the news was released with most of the *Sunday Times*' rivals furious that they hadn't landed this singularly big fish. The *Observer* was particularly vitriolic, saying, 'It will inevitably seem unfair to rival newspapers and magazines that the Queen's close relative is used for the enlargement and enrichment of the Thomson empire.' They also brought Princess Margaret's name into the affair: 'Had the Palace not considered that the commercial benefits to the Thomson Organization of Lord Snowdon's link with the *Sunday Times* would be almost as great as if the paper had hired Princess Margaret?' They also suggested that the *Sunday Times* believed that Snowdon's appointment would help them to add 200,000 to their circulation; in terms of hard cash, a bonus of a couple of hundred thousand pounds in increased advertising revenue. Roy Thomson retaliated, saying, 'It is not right to suggest we are employing Lord Snowdon for his name. Anyone knows he has great accomplishments in this line of work. If his name helps, well that's all right, but he will have a job to do, don't make any mistake about that.' The row went on and on, with everyone speculating on how much Snowdon was being paid, and exactly what his terms of reference were. He had been appointed as artistic adviser, not just photographer. This meant he was to attend editorial conferences, suggest stories and, of course, take any pictures the paper wanted.

His salary was kept a close secret, but it was believed that he received a little over £100 a week; in 1962, a considerable sum for a part-time job when the Queen's senior aide, her private secretary, worked all week for less than half that figure. David Astor, the editor of the *Observer*, appeared on television to claim: 'I should have thought this would harm the monarchy. To use the fame of the monarchy to put money into the pockets of a private firm is a doubtful procedure.' Had any of the other newspapers thought of the idea first, it's unlikely they would have shared the same sentiments. There is nothing so self-righteous as a newspaper which has lost out on a scoop.

Gunn Brinson worked with Snowdon for more than ten years, first as deputy and later as Picture Editor of the *Sunday Times Magazine*. She was responsible for commissioning him for many stories in the 1980s, and their association was equally beneficial. Gunn recalls their initial meeting: 'His first words to me were, "Call me Tony", which apparently he did with just about everyone he worked with. It set the tone for our future relationship, which was always friendly and he was invariably courteous and very professional. But he knew what he wanted and wouldn't give an inch if he thought he was right – which was usually the case.' One thing that singled him out from most of the other photographers was his attitude. 'He did more homework than anyone else and was never satisfied until he knew all he needed to know about the subject. It wasn't enough just to give him the assignment and tell him who or what he was supposed to photograph. He wanted to know all about the person or subject, or whatever it was. He needed to know the entire context of the story.'

Snowdon himself explains why he does so: 'Before I go to photograph someone I usually do my research properly first. Even if I never use it, it's only good manners. It's nice when others do the same.' This last remark refers to those journalists and photographers who turn up at his house and invariably ask him to pose with a camera around his neck, without having checked to find out that he never uses that sort of camera but always uses a tripod. It's this sort of slipshod approach to work that is guaranteed to infuriate him. He takes his work seriously and cannot understand why others think they can get away with anything less.

From the moment he stepped across the threshold of the *Sunday Times* it was obvious that Snowdon was a 'special case', and everyone knew this. These were the days when car phones were the exception rather than the rule. But Tony demanded one, and he got it straight away. He was perfectly entitled to it; it was all part of his contract and no one was more on the ball when it came to reading the small print. He made sure the paper paid for the maintenance of his car – that too was in his contract. He was expensive, but the *Sunday Times* got good value for its money. He got some exceptional pictures and, of course, his publicity value to the paper did no harm either.

Snowdon knew then, as he does today, the undoubted value of his name, but in those days he insisted that his title should not be used when assignments were being arranged. It was a bit unrealistic because as soon as people met him they recognized him. It was inevitable. He had one of the most well-known faces in the world. And there was no doubt that being who he was, married to a member of the royal family and having a title, opened many doors for him, and for the paper.

Snowdon was already very well known as a photographer under his original name of Tony Armstrong-Jones, but he became even more famous as simply Snowdon. He has never explained why he abandoned his first professional name, but he did insist on his credits being simply 'Snowdon' without the title 'Lord'. One of the idiosyncrasies that Snowdon employed at the *Sunday Times* was his refusal to have anybody present (apart from his assistant) on a sitting. It was an inflexible rule that he worked alone or with his personal assistant. He hated anyone to see him at work. No one knew why and he never offered an explanation, but it was his decision and they had to abide by it.

Gunn Brinson says his work was brilliant: 'His portraits in particular were outstanding. He was imaginative, witty and innovative. When I sent him to Bayreuth to photograph Peter Hall, the director of the 'English Ring' together with Georg Solti, William Dudley and Wolfgang Wagner, the result was magnificent. When I asked him how he had managed to get such an effect, he replied, "I designed the whole backdrop myself. I knew how I wanted the group to appear so I had the canvas specially painted and took it with me." That was the sort of thing he could get away with that few others would have dared to even try.'

That attention to detail became standard practice for Snowdon and elevated him to a position where he could make his subjects do things that were out of character because they knew he was going to produce the best results. He was as much a director as a photographer. Gunn Brinson remembers that when he was asked to photograph Dame Edna Everage's alter ego, Barry Humphries, he made him look out through an upturned lavatory seat. It was perfect.'

Snowdon had the ideal contract with the *Sunday Times*. He could pick and choose his assignments, of which he usually did about eight a year. His expenses were generous, but not higher than some other photographers who insisted on being accompanied by a large entourage, and he enjoyed the best that money could buy when he travelled overseas for the paper. But nothing interfered with the job in hand. Everything took second place to his photography. Time meant little to him when he was working, and often he would work throughout the night to try and get things exactly the way he wanted them. He didn't spare himself – or others – when he was on a job. Perfection was his only standard. He built a massive reputation as a photojournalist, believing that every picture should tell a story. There was one occasion, however, when things did not go quite as he would have wished. Tony had been sent to photograph William Golding, the author of *Lord of the Flies*. He opened the session by telling Golding how much he had enjoyed *Lord of the Rings*. The author was understandably not terribly pleased, and apparently the session turned out to be one of the shortest Snowdon had ever had. But the results were superb, so whether Tony had deliberately attributed the wrong title to the author or it was a genuine mistake, only he knows. As he has often said, he doesn't always like his subjects to be too relaxed, so the former might well be the case.

Gunn Brinson says his relationships with other photographers were amicable but never close: 'He never became buddies socially with any of the other photographers we used.' She also says he was discretion itself when it came to the royal family. 'He never once discussed them to my knowledge. Even casually with those he worked with. He was open and friendly with all his colleagues, but when the subject of royalty came up he veered away from it. He didn't do it in a nasty or arrogant way. That wasn't his style at all. He simply deflected the questions and turned the conversation in another direction. He was quite brilliant at seeming to be totally open, and then you discovered he had told you nothing.'

Eventually Snowdon's contract with the *Sunday Times* came to an end, suddenly and without notice – and not without a certain amount of acrimony. The reason was purely financial. He was offered a deal by the rival *Sunday Telegraph* at almost four times his *Sunday Times* salary and he went. It was as sudden as that. He was serious about his photography, and even more serious about the money he could make. He knew it was the right time to make what he believed would be an advantageous career move. It was simply time to move on. The same could also be said of his private life.

By 1964 cracks had started to appear in the marriage. They began when Tony first started to become disillusioned with his role in the royal family. The reflected glamour, the kowtowing and prestige that came with belonging to the most famous family in the world, gradually wore off. He could see there was going to be no end to the boredom. For the rest of the royal family, including his wife, the means were an end in themselves. There was no alternative, and even if there were, they would not have been interested. Royal protocol and routine were all they had ever known, and they were quite content for the status quo to be maintained indefinitely. It would not be until the late 1990s that the family would realize that if they didn't modernize they would not last – and it came as a bucket of cold water to the more traditional members. Back in the sixties and seventies, the very idea that the monarchy needed any changes was unthinkable. Lord Snowdon knew they were in dire need of some fresh blood, both in the family and the household, but he also knew they would not welcome any such suggestions from an outsider like him. So he decided to make his own life beyond the confines of the Court. When he and the Princess started to take separate holidays, word leaked out that they had problems in their marriage. Princess Margaret had reverted to her original lifestyle and circle of friends; her brief flirtation with Tony's unconventional previous life was over.

His photographic work took him all over the world, and the further he became distanced from royalty, the happier he seemed to be. One of his often quoted remarks at the time summed up his attitude: 'I am not royal. I just happen to be married to a member of the royal family.' It may have appeared to him to be a modest declaimer, but it was not very realistic. In most people's eyes he was royal, whether he liked to admit it or not. Inevitably both husband and wife developed relationships away from each other. A former courtier claimed that in all probability it was Princess Margaret. Which of them started to 'play away from home' first is hard to say. Tony met many attractive young women in his travels, and not many of them were unavailable. He had always liked the company of beautiful girls, and in his then frame of mind he found it easy to console himself with the thought that they were not serious affairs, just casual relationships that could easily be forgotten once he came home. Princess Margaret, too, began indulging in liaisons, some of which were undoubtedly serious, the first of any note being in 1966 with her husband's close friend from his Cambridge days, Anthony Barton.

The short-lived Barton relationship would have remained a family secret had not Princess Margaret, in an extraordinary display of conscience, telephoned her lover's wife, Eva, to confess all, and ask for her forgiveness. What is even more remarkable is that Barton and Snowdon remained reasonably friendly, such is the degree of sophistication in their level of society.

Over the next ten years, as Princess Margaret and Tony moved further apart, their lives polarized to such an extent that they rarely saw each other, although nominally still living under the same roof. He was away most of the time, and when they did meet they could hardly bear to speak to each other. They lived entirely separate lives with each one knowing about the other's affairs, but so long as they were discreet, neither objected. The main difference between them was that Princess Margaret fell in love with her men and became highly emotional, while Tony simply played the field. His only serious affair of the heart, with Lucy Lindsay-Hogg, who was to become his second wife and the next Countess of Snowdon, did not begin until after he was separated from Princess Margaret.

TWELVE

The Royal Impresario

'I, Charles, do become your liegeman of life and limb and earthly worship, and faith and truth I will bear unto you to live and die against all manner of folks.' The words were spoken by Prince Charles to his mother the Queen on 1 July 1969, at his Investiture as the 21st Prince of Wales. As he pledged his loyalty, kneeling before Her Majesty, he was watched by 2,500 specially invited guests inside the 700-year-old Caernarvon Castle and a worldwide television audience estimated at over 500 million. The ceremony had been dubbed the mini-coronation, and certainly all the Queen's horses and all the Queen's men were there, bringing with them the pomp and pageantry that had characterized royal ritual for centuries.

The formal ceremony itself lasted for barely two hours, yet the preparations had taken over three years. The man with overall charge of the arrangements was the Earl Marshal, the Duke of Norfolk, the premier earl of Great Britain, a man whose vast experience of such affairs included his management of the State funeral of King George VI in 1952, followed by the Coronation in 1953 and the marriage of Princess Margaret and Antony Armstrong-Jones in 1960.

But, in reality, the stage-management of this unique royal occasion was the responsibility of Tony Armstrong-Jones, now, of course, the Earl of Snowdon.

The Duke had a formidable reputation as a man who would suffer no interference from any source when it came to handling formal royal occasions. At the time of the Coronation, Earl Mountbatten of Burma, Prince Philip's uncle, suggested that the Royal Navy might supply the Guard of Honour, instead of the traditional Household Brigade. The Duke of Norfolk was heard to reply contemptuously,

'Bloody kingmaker.' So Lord Snowdon knew he had to handle His Grace with care. At the same time he was just as determined that this particular royal show was going to be run the way he wanted it – and as the brother-in-law of the Queen, he had an ace up his sleeve that even the premier earl of England could not match.

Snowdon's recall of events is generous, as ever. 'I knew the reputation that the Earl Marshal had as an impatient tyrant who liked everything his own way, but I have to say he could not have been easier to work with. He just said to me, "Tony, I don't know anything about design I'll leave it all to you. Just get on with it." And that's what I did. He was wonderful and a tremendous support.'

Lord Snowdon's involvement came about because of his appointment, six years earlier, as Constable of Caernarvon Castle. This ancient office had existed for centuries, with its holder being the Sovereign's representative at the castle, and without whose permission no function could be held or work carried out. He had received his invitation to become Constable in a personal handwritten letter from the then Prime Minister, Harold Macmillan, in March 1963. In it, Mr Macmillan had said that the duties were mainly ceremonial and would require his presence only on those occasions when the Queen, or any other member of the royal family, visited Caernarvon. The Prime Minister was not in a position to offer the post himself, but, as with all such honours, he asked for Lord Snowdon's agreement to his name being submitted to Her Majesty for her approval. In this way, had Lord Snowdon declined the post, he would not have been seen to have refused a direct request from the Sovereign.

Of course, the Queen had been consulted before the Prime Minister wrote to Lord Snowdon, and so, too, had Princess Margaret. If there was any possibility of an embarrassment to the royal family, the offer would have been withheld. But protocol having been satisfied, Lord Snowdon accepted the office of Constable, his first and only royal appointment, and immediately travelled to Caernarvon to look over his new domain.

He took, and still takes, the role very seriously, and nothing goes on in the castle without his knowledge and approval. When the souvenir shop inside the castle walls wanted to sell soft drinks, he refused to allow it 'because of the litter problem and also because there are plenty of shops just outside the castle selling drinks and ice creams, so why should we try to take their living away from them'. He has also been involved in trying to make access to the castle easier for disabled people. 'Just because someone is in a wheelchair, there is no reason why they shouldn't enjoy the facilities that able-bodied people do. It's simply a case of using your common sense. Every problem has a solution if only you know where to look.'

The first Prince of Wales had been presented to his Principality, without ceremony, at Caernarvon Castle more than 600 years ago. Then, in 1911, at the instigation of David Lloyd George, who wanted a massive Welsh ceremony to boost his own ego, about 11,000 of the fortunate elite were crammed into the castle to see Prince Edward (the future King Edward VIII and later Duke of Windsor) invested as Prince of Wales. Snowdon was determined that the 1969 occasion was going to be nothing like either of those that had gone before. 'I saw it as an entirely different exercise. Prince Charles's Investiture was to be seen, as it took place, by probably 500 million people on television. It would have been wrong, therefore, to design the ceremony for the few lucky people who were there; it had to be designed as a theatrical experience for television. That was the number one priority; to be able to show the huge audience worldwide what was happening.'

With this aim in mind, Lord Snowdon knew he needed professional help, and he also knew who he wanted.

What was in my mind was to make the simplest and best kind of visual televisual production both in black and white and colour. Remember, colour was not as universally used then as it is now. I didn't want to clutter up the castle with irrelevant bits and pieces but to show its grand simplicity, and to match the essential minimum of contemporary decoration to the medieval architecture. There were two men, both experienced designers and with whom I had worked before, who I knew would be ideal for the job. So I asked the Ministry of Public Building and Works (who were the official contractors) to commission Carl Toms, the theatre designer, to join me, together with John Pound from the ministry.

Carl Toms, a romantic, and John Pound, a modernist, sounded to me like the perfect combination. Between the three of us we tried, and I think succeeded, in arranging a simple elegance for everyone, television viewers and those inside the castle, to participate in and enjoy the ceremony.

One of the early problems was the lack of money, as Lord Snowdon explained: 'We were on a tiny budget; altogether we only had something like £50,000, which included the cost of scaffolding, so we couldn't go mad. But what I wanted was to have as simple a ceremony as possible, with the minimum decoration and to let the castle speak for itself.'

To make sure he had the cooperation of the media, Lord Snowdon made himself available practically twenty-four hours a day in the weeks leading up to the ceremony. He gave interviews to television and radio reporters, celebrity writers and famous columnists from newspapers and magazines. 'I was just one of a tide of radio reporters, cameramen and star television commentators, including Richard Burton and Emlyn Williams, both native Welsh speakers, who had achieved fame in Hollywood as actors and who thoroughly enjoyed their celebrity status, and who, in Williams's case liked to shock people with his outspoken views. They all flocked into the quaint North Wales town to witness this historic event.'

Lord Snowdon was the perfect choice for the role of royal impresario; he loved the rich pageantry, the sense of history and obviously relished the opportunity to display his own unique talents as an organizer of such a magnificent royal spectacle. With a lifelong interest in the theatre, he brought to the ancient ceremonial a feeling of pure drama that captured admirably the sense of occasion the event demanded.

The most important part of the design inside the castle was the dais on which the thrones for the Queen, Prince Philip and Prince Charles stood and the canopy which covered the dais. Lord Snowdon and Carl Toms knew what they wanted:

One needed the romanticism of Carl Toms's ideas for things like the dais and canopy. The dais and thrones were made entirely of Welsh slate – from a quarry owned by my godfather, so cost nothing – and the canopy was of transparent perspex. It could easily have come from the thirteenth century, if perspex had been invented then. Several people on the Investiture committee felt we should have a green-and-white striped canopy as they did in 1911. But this would not have worked in '69 because of the TV cameras. I was being practical but some of the others on the committee thought I was the rebellious whiz kid who just wanted everything my own way. I'm sure that what I was doing would have been approved by Henry V if he'd been around. We had great problems getting the canopy into the castle. We thought at first of having it lowered by helicopter, or even using hot-air balloons to float it in, but then decided it was worth trying to get it through the main gate. We measured it and the opening a hundred times and finally we got it in with two inches to spare on either side. The perspex canopy measured twenty-five feet square and thirteen feet high, on top of which was the emblem of the Prince of Wales, three feathers, nine feet high and carved in polystyrene. There was also, right inside the castle in a very prominent position, the Prince's coat of arms, which looked very impressive. It was fourteen feet wide and eight feet high, but as it was made entirely of plastic, you could practically lift it with one hand.

When it came to the thrones, the Queen's was in the centre of the dais, made of two slabs of Welsh slate with one on either side for Prince Charles and the Duke of Edinburgh. These were more like stools as I didn't want there to be any backs on them. It would have altered the perspective too much, and I needed to be able to place a television camera to shoot over Prince Philip's shoulder. So I asked him if he would mind if his throne did not have a back to it. His reply was typical: 'Of course not. I never lean back anyway.' So that was one problem solved. I think when we had completed the thrones they were just what we wanted, simple and modern but at the same time dateless. The chairs for all the guests, including the royal party of Queen Elizabeth The Queen Mother, Princess Margaret and Princess Anne, were the same for everyone. Made of wood, painted red with the Prince of Wales feathers on the backrest, with cushions of Welsh tweed on which was embroidered the emblem of Wales, the Welsh dragon. To make sure all the royal family would be comfortable, as they are not all the same height, we experimented with old telephone directories. By adding and subtracting we found the right dimensions eventually, and they all seemed perfectly happy. The chairs all came flat-packed in very attractive boxes, which we also designed, and later they were sold off as souvenirs at £12 each, a realistic price at the time, but these days they change hands for hundreds of pounds.

During the run-up to the ceremony, Lord Snowdon worked at the castle for up to eighteen hours a day, but as he recalls it wasn't all work.

I had my speedboat moored in the straits, and most mornings we would go waterskiing for an hour or so. It was great relaxation, and we thoroughly enjoyed it as the weather was perfect. On one occasion though we nearly had a tragedy. Our route took us past Lord Newborough's home, and on this particular morning as we roared past he fired a cannon which just missed us. I saw him later that day and asked him what he was playing at. He said, 'I didn't know it was you. I thought it was just a couple of local lads.' Obviously it wouldn't have mattered to him if it had been. And one of the town's inshore rescue team told me that he wished it had been me that had been hit because 'Then we could have come to rescue you and it would have been a great honour.'

If Lord Snowdon's relations with the Duke of Norfolk could not have been better, the same could not be said of his working relationship with another important figure in the ceremonial, Garter King of Arms, Sir Anthony Wagner, Head of the College of Arms. Garter was impossible; a most difficult man to deal with:

All he wanted was to make money for the college, and to do that he needed banners all over the place because the College of Arms supplied them all. We disagreed on just about every point. I wasn't having all those banners flying from every nook and cranny. It would have completely destroyed the look we were trying for. He also wanted to put red carpets along every inch the Queen was going to walk. When I asked his reasons he said, 'Because you cannot expect Her Majesty to walk on grass.' It was the most ridiculous reason I'd ever heard and I told him so. I said had he never been to a Garden Party or seen the Queen walking at Sandringham. She was perfectly happy to walk on grass and as long as we let her know well in advance she would know what sort of shoes to wear. It was as a simple as that. Garter was not a happy man, but he didn't get his own way. After one of his more ridiculous suggestions I said to him, 'Garter, darling, couldn't you be a little more elastic.'

Television was the dominant factor in practically all the decisions made surrounding the Investiture.

I was determined that we would have no lights of any kind inside the castle. That would have ruined the atmosphere. That was the main reason why I refused to allow a tent to cover the guests, as they had in 1911. If we had erected a marquee then obviously we would have needed to light it and ruined the effect I was looking for. The idea of the tent was to protect those inside if it rained, and when the Earl Marshal was asked at a press conference what would happen if it did rain, his reply was succinct and beautifully phrased. 'We all get bloody wet,' he said. As it happened the weather was kind, and only one person in the entire gathering wore a raincoat and that was Jeremy Thorpe [former leader of the Liberal Party]. In fact the only people for whom we provided cover were the members of the orchestra, and obviously that was because of their instruments. I also did not want to spoil the natural skyline or see hordes of photographers up on the ramparts, so I persuaded the BBC to use cranes that could be lowered when they were not being used. In this way you just saw the battlements in plain silhouette. I also insisted that all the reporters and cameramen should wear dark clothes so that they wouldn't stand out against the grey of the castle walls. All this was done – and at their own expense.

Lord Snowdon didn't get everything he wanted however. One lovely idea proved impracticable. 'I thought it would be nice to have the Royal Yacht *Britannia* moored out in the [Menai] straits. It would have been a marvellously romantic background. The Admiral went and checked it out and found that at low tide there would have been just 2in of water to spare underneath her. So that was out. It would have been beautiful, but not possible.'

In order to ensure that everything went smoothly on the day, Lord Snowdon asked Prince Charles to visit Caernarvon some weeks before the ceremony to familiarize himself with the geography of the place:

I wanted Prince Charles to be able to see what the thing looked like without any other people around, so on the day he came there were just four of us: Prince Charles, his protection officer, Carl Toms and myself. It was well worth the effort as otherwise he would have gone into the ceremony completely blank, without any knowledge of where everything was. We also had a rehearsal at Buckingham Palace in the garden, which was hilarious. All the important areas were marked out with pieces of string, and Garter was there wearing a bowler hat and holding an umbrella instead of his stave which he would carry on the day. When he came to a certain bit of string he had to pretend it was a set of steps and you saw him pretending to go up and down. He was hilarious and it was very funny, at the time.

At the beginning of the ceremony, Lord Snowdon, as Constable of Caernarvon Castle, had to offer the keys to the Queen. This posed certain problems:

When we first found the key – which wasn't very old in fact; there was nothing ancient about it, it was just something Lloyd George had dreamed up in 1911 – we discovered it weighed a ton, or it felt like it. Anyway, we experimented with various ways of me carrying it. One idea was for me to have a sort of tray around my neck with the key laying on it. I soon threw that out. All I needed was a couple of ice creams and I would have looked just like an usherette at the local Odeon. Eventually, I wore it around my neck with a sturdy ribbon, and when Her Majesty arrived I pretended to open the castle door with a huge amount of rattling of the lock and so on, taking a long time over it. It was all sound effects but it was great fun. Then I offered the key to the Queen through Patrick Plunkett [the late Lord Plunkett was a senior member of the royal household], and Her Majesty placed her hand on the key and asked me to keep it in safe custody.

Lord Snowdon became a familiar figure in the weeks leading up to the Investiture, either riding around the town on his Triumph motorbike or driving his open-topped blue Aston Martin DB5 sports car. He enjoyed the attention he received, and even though there were threats from the self-styled Free Wales Army, who opposed the Investiture, he never felt threatened himself. 'I was Welsh, in my own country, so I was never afraid that I might be a target.' Nevertheless, an incompetent would-be assassin killed himself when the bomb he was making blew up a few miles away from Caernarvon, and police activity was very evident in the days before the ceremony.

Lord Snowdon involved himself in every aspect of the ceremony, even the music.

We had a problem with the trumpeters, who apparently needed a conductor. I didn't realize until then that trumpeters needed someone to tell them when to play the fanfare [specially composed by Sir Arthur Bliss, Master of the Queen's Music], so that the television cameras could pan down onto the principal figures in the ceremony. Anyway, we could not find a suitable place to put the conductor as the trumpeters occupied the whole of the space on the ramparts allocated to them. Finally, after driving around the outside of the castle, I hit upon the idea of placing the conductor on the roof of the post office opposite, and that is what we did. It worked perfectly.

If there is one thing that most people remember about the Investiture of the Prince of Wales more than thirty years ago it is the outfit worn by Lord Snowdon as Constable of the castle. He designed it himself and wore it with pride.

The problem was that I had never been in the services. If I had, then a dress uniform would have been the obvious choice. But I did not pass the medical examination when my time for National Service came – I was the lowest possible classification – they would only call me if they were really desperate. I was sorry about that because I wanted to serve in the army. I think I would have enjoyed it. Anyway, I needed some sort of uniform for my duties at the Investiture so I designed this outfit in dark-green material with zips up the front. It consisted of a short tunic, tail coat over tight trousers, and the belt buckle came from one of the local regiments, the Cader Idris Volunteers, the only regiment in the British Army never to go to war. It seemed appropriate to me in view of my own lack of military service.

The uniform attracted a lot of attention from the world's media, and Lord Snowdon still has it in his wardrobe. 'I can still get into it but the neck is a little tight now.'

The general consensus of opinion about the Investiture was that it was a magnificent success, both as a spectacle and as a piece of royal and Welsh history. The benefits to North Wales in general and the town of Caernarvon in particular are being felt to this day. Thousands of visitors pay to look around the castle and spend much needed money in the surrounding shops and hotels. The castle is in splendid condition, with a military museum dedicated to the Royal Welsh Fusiliers, a Mecca for hundreds of former servicemen and women who come from many parts of the United Kingdom and abroad.

Several of those involved in the staging of the Investiture were rewarded with honours. Carl Toms received the OBE, John Pound the MBE, while Lord Snowdon was made a Knight Grand Cross of the Royal Victorian Order, the personal gift of the Sovereign. He is able to look back on the events of 1969 with pleasure and a certain amount of satisfaction. As the first royal occasion for which he had total responsibility, without having any previous experience of such matters, it could so easily have been a disaster. That it wasn't is a tribute to his own dedication and determination and also his skill in picking the right people to support him. He always insists that this was a team effort and that much of the credit must go to Carl Toms, John Pound and the others who worked with him. But in every team there has to be a captain, and in this one, no one was ever in any doubt who that captain was. His debut as a royal impresario succeeded beyond his wildest dreams. The Prince of Wales sent his personal thanks and congratulations, while the Mayor of Caernarvon, on behalf of the people of the town, who reaped the benefits of the massive influx of visitors, thought it would be a good idea to have an Investiture every year, saying, 'It's a pity it was for one performance only.'

THIRTEEN

A Parting of the Ways

Princess Margaret was said to have claimed that Tony caused their marriage to break up when he went against her wishes and renovated a property on his grandfather's estate for their joint use. If that was a ridiculously simplistic claim, it was, nevertheless, a symptom of a marriage that was falling apart.

Old House was situated in 250 acres of woodland in deepest Sussex and was part of Nymans, Grandpapa Messel's estate, where Tony and his sister Susan had spent many happy days when they were children. The main house and extensive grounds had been taken over by the National Trust, but Old House, which consisted of two former estate workers' cottages knocked into a single dwelling, was available and Tony jumped at the chance of making a country retreat for his family away from royal eyes. Princess Margaret loathed the idea, although she, too, wanted a weekend home apart from Royal Lodge at Windsor where they always stayed with her mother. What she would have preferred was to build a completely new house on land at Sunningdale that had been offered to them by the Queen. Tony agreed to make plans for the new house, but secretly he had no intention of giving up his original idea.

Margaret told Tony she didn't like the place, but he went ahead anyway, spending his own money and seeing his own designs come to fruition. For him it was a dual challenge. He desperately wanted to provide a home that wasn't a grace-and-favour gift from the Queen, and he genuinely believed that Old House could be the saving of his marriage.

When the local people heard that Princess Margaret might be taking over the cottage they were incredulous. There was no mains water or electricity, and water for the bathroom had to be hand carried from a pump in the garden. It needed a great deal of imagination and hard work to put the house into anything like a weekend retreat fit for a princess, but Tony relished the challenge. It also came at the right time. Their old hideaway, his room in Rotherhithe, where he and Princess Margaret had enjoyed so many romantic evenings, was due to be demolished by the local authority. They needed somewhere new.

The house was a mixture of styles and ages. A fine Tudor chimney towered above the wing of a part of the house built in late Georgian times. Tony removed an ugly Victorian chimney and converted the fireplaces beneath it into extra cupboard space. The cottages retained the original leaded windows, while the oldest walls were hung with ancient red tiles and the roof was of Horsham tiles. A massive beam above the fireplace in the kitchen bore the date 1652.

Tony designed a brand new kitchen and installed bow windows in the sitting-room. But even though he changed almost every room and imprinted his own personality on the house, he retained practically every original feature in some shape or form. When the renovations were complete, Tony, with his love of the dramatic, organized an opening ceremony attended by the Queen Mother, who performed the ribbon-cutting duties. Princess Margaret was a reluctant witness, but she made no attempt to like the place and after a few short visits she refused to go there again. She wasn't the only one who disliked the house, as Tony recalls: 'The very grand old-fashioned nanny hated it, too, and she used to put her shoes outside her door for me to clean.'

The marriage already had huge cracks in it and, for Margaret, Old House was the final blow. She later said that once she realized Tony was going ahead with the place in spite of her objections, she knew there was no future for them together. She had already had a brief fling – the one with Anthony Barton – and shortly afterwards a much more serious affair began with another old friend of Tony's. This time it was Robin Douglas-Home, nephew of former Prime Minister Alec Douglas-Home, who spent his time playing the piano at fashionable London nightspots, including the Berkeley.

This happened in 1966, some twelve years before the divorce became final and was just one of several affairs the Princess would embark upon.

Robin Douglas-Home was hardly the most suitable lover for a member of the royal family. He was regarded as unstable because of his drinking and gambling, and he was also a serial womanizer who loved to talk about his conquests. Discretion was definitely not part of his make-up, neither was loyalty. He later sold letters written to him by the Princess that clearly revealed their romantic liaison even though it had lasted barely a month. Some years later he killed himself, but not because of any unrequited love of Princess Margaret.

Tony had professed indifference to Margaret's flings, but in reality he was extremely jealous of any other men in her life, and she knew that when he heard about Douglas-Home, he would be furious. She wasn't wrong. In the society in which they moved it was inevitable that someone would talk; malicious gossip was part and parcel of their everyday life, and soon word reached Tony that he was being cuckolded by another of his friends.

In spite of his private fury, he retained a calm public exterior, and when, in February 1967, rumours of a marriage breakdown became rife, he issued a statement from New York where he was on assignment for the *Sunday Times*. It said: 'Talk of a rift is totally unfounded. It's news to me and I would be the first to know. I am amazed.' The statement followed a story in the *Daily Express* which was headlined 'TONY DENIES RIFT WITH MARGARET'. He held a press conference denying the story, adding, 'Nothing has happened to our marriage. When I am away – and I'm away quite a lot on assignments for my paper – I write home and I telephone like other husbands in love with their wives. I telephoned today.' It was the first of many items of misinformation that were issued on instructions from the Palace officials during the remaining eleven years of their marriage. At the time it was made, both Tony and Princess Margaret knew their marriage was virtually over and they were living separate lives. But with royalty, image is all, and both husband and wife were united in trying to protect the Queen from any involvement and possible embarrassment. Neither thought, at that time, that divorce would be the eventual outcome either. The Princess flew to New York to meet Tony and together they travelled on to the Bahamas for a holiday during which they appeared to be quite happy in each other's company. But it was all a front, erected to give the impression that there was nothing wrong when they both knew the marriage was all but over.

They continued to attend official functions together and even undertook a three-week tour of the Far East. Fellow guests at several parties they attended remarked on the obvious animosity between them, and at one point they were barely speaking to each other. Tony was his usual diplomatic self in public, but Princess Margaret didn't even attempt to keep up the façade on some occasions. At one embassy reception, when they had quite obviously had a major row, Margaret ignored everybody, refusing to acknowledge other guests, while Tony tried to act normally as if nothing had happened. If she felt any embarrassment, she didn't show it, but the rest of the guests felt very uncomfortable.

As the glitzy decade of the 1960s came to an end, Tony's name became linked with Lady Jackie Rufus-Isaacs, the only daughter of the Marquess of Reading, near neighbours of Tony in Sussex. The Readings and the Snowdons were friends, and as Tony was seventeen years older than Jackie there was no reason why anyone should be suspicious of their relationship. They managed to keep it quiet for over a year in spite of the fact that at a show-business party following the première of Peter Sellers's film *The Magic Christian*, it was noticed that Princess Margaret sat at one table, with Sellers, while Tony was at another, with Lady Jackie.

It was reported in the media that the relationship began sometime late in 1969 and became public knowledge in January 1971, when the *New York Daily News* broke the story. Later that same day the London newspapers picked up the story and it was mentioned on radio and television news broadcasts throughout the United Kingdom. Tony and Margaret were furious at the revelation, and the Palace also let them know of their displeasure. Jackie's father, the Marquess, was understandably outraged at what he regarded as the ultimate betrayal by someone he had befriended, and it was alleged that he, in a return to old-world attitudes, said he would horsewhip Tony if he ever saw him again.

Tony declined to comment on the allegations, and there was never any proof that a physical relationship actually took place. Lady Jackie, when confronted with the newspaper stories said, 'The report is absolute rubbish. Our families are old friends and Lord Snowdon has a house on his late grandmother's estate, which is less than a mile from our Sussex home. Naturally he drops in to see my parents from time to time as he drives past our house.' Whatever happened, it was quickly over, but the damage was done and the media forecast that it was only a matter of time before the marriage finally folded.

Friends of the couple who had known them both for years claimed the marriage would have been doomed even if they had not both been 'playing away from home'. Tony was far too independent a character to be prepared to tag along behind the Princess during her stultifyingly boring round of public engagements. At first being part of the royal family had a certain novelty value but that soon wore off, and when he began to realize the restrictions that were being placed on him, he was desperate to get out. Unlike his wife, who had never known anything outside the royal circle, and who could not see any reason why she should change or, more importantly, why her husband could not adapt to it.

Tony needed to return to his chosen profession. He knew he was good at his job, and when he finally started again, with, it has to be admitted, his wife's approval, a few of the couple's best friends knew it was the beginning of the end. Their paths were bound to diverge. Tony has a low threshold of boredom. He has to be active all the time. The idea of a future consisting of nothing but the endless round of visiting factories and the eighty or so organizations with which Princess Margaret was associated was anathema to him.

Some close friends had been pessimistic about Tony's involvement with royalty right from the start. The late David Hicks, husband of Lady Pamela Mountbatten, one of the Queen's oldest and closest friends (Lady Pamela was with the then Princess Elizabeth in Kenya on the day she heard that her father, George VI, had died and she had become Queen), was a man who told Tony the truth, even when he did not want to hear it. Hicks had known Snowdon since they were young men. 'We went to the same parties, and dated some of the same girls,' he explained.

David Hicks believed that Snowdon's relationship with his brother-in-law, Prince Philip, was never going to be easy. 'They were completely different in just about every imaginable way.' A senior courtier later confirmed this, saying, 'Tony was never going to sit back and take some of the insults thrown at him. His natural instinct was to fight back, and that is something you just do not do with the royal family.' David Hicks lived an unconventional existence all his life. He was never overly concerned with other people's opinion of him, and in this he shared a common bond with Tony Snowdon. Both were rebellious, independent spirits, and while both achieved fame, and a certain amount of notoriety, through marriage, their vitality and energy was such that they would undoubtedly have succeeded in spite of, rather than because of, having wives who were rich and famous. Hicks believed the marriage was doomed to fail: 'Tony was far too independent a character to simply enjoy living in the shadow of his wife. He needed to work and never really enjoyed the royal role anyway. It wasn't his style. A life of luxurious indolence, while having certain initial attractions, wasn't his scene.'

By this time they were virtually living separate lives, with Princess Margaret still being pursued by Peter Sellers. But it was in 1973 that the Princess met the man who would be responsible for the final break in her marriage. Roddy Llewellyn, younger son of Olympic showjumper Sir Harry Llewellyn, and brother of Dai – described in the gossip columns as the 'Seducer of the Valleys' – was brought in as an extra man to partner Princess Margaret at a Scottish house party.

And if it is true that women always go for the same type, then Roddy could not have been a better choice for her. Slim, fair-haired, with boyish good looks and an unconventional lifestyle, he might have been the Tony of the seventies. At any rate, the Princess found him just as entertaining as she had her husband at their first meeting. They hit it off immediately, and within a few months she had invited him to join her on holiday on Mustique. It was the start of an affair that was to become world news and which would eventually be the catalyst that forced the Snowdons to separate for good.

At almost the same time, Tony was seeing the woman who he would make his second wife and the new Countess of Snowdon.

Lucy Lindsay-Hogg, born Lucy Davies in 1941, grew up in Ireland, where she enjoyed the comforts of the family home set in 300 acres of parkland near Enniskerry. She and Lord Snowdon had a mutual friend in the late Derek Hart, a star television presenter of the sixties and seventies. Tony eventually made three highly acclaimed television documentaries with Hart: *Born to be Small*, *Don't Count the Candles* and *Love of a Kind*. Lucy had married, in 1966, the film director Michael Lindsay-Hogg, but they divorced five years later. They had no children. She was given a job as Lord Snowdon's assistant, and it was after she was divorced that their relationship developed. However, they were not seen as a couple until after the Snowdons' separation. Even then, friends who visited Lord Snowdon's house in Kensington often found Lucy there, occasionally acting as hostess for a dinner party, but equally often as just another guest. She made no attempt to impose any part of her personality on the house at that time; everything in it belonged to Tony and reflected his tastes alone. And throughout the two years of their relationship before Tony's separation, not one word appeared in the press about them.

For Princess Margaret, the exact opposite occurred, with stories and pictures of her with Roddy being featured prominently on almost a daily basis. Tony once described Roddy as being 'light-weight', and when the affair with Princess Margaret became known throughout the world it placed public opinion firmly behind Tony. No one blamed him, everyone seemed to believe that Margaret was the guilty party.

For years before Princess Margaret and her husband officially separated, there had been rows and reconciliations, private tears and renewed efforts to maintain a public front. It was all to no avail and the unremitting attention of the press meant that every aspect of their life, together and apart, was remorselessly pursued. In view of their total incompatibility, which finally turned to mutual hostility, the marriage would have been difficult to sustain even if they had been a private couple. As two of the most famous and photographed people in the world, who lived their lives in a goldfish bowl, it was impossible for them even to try to solve their problems with any degree of privacy. And neither did all that much to silence the rumours. While they may have been discreet in what they said about each other, neither was particularly careful about where they were seen, or with whom.

The public airings of their marital problems on both sides of the Atlantic ensured that they could not remain under the same roof, and after several months of discussions, which included the Queen, Prince Philip and the Queen Mother, they decided that the best solution was a legal separation.

When the marriage of Lord Snowdon and Princess Margaret was finally seen to be in ruins and a separation was inevitable, the Palace public-relations machine was brought into action. Princess Margaret had her own press secretary, a delightful and well-intentioned former army officer, Major John Griffin, who, Tony remembers, 'even came on our honeymoon'. He was based at Clarence House, where his responsibilities included handling all media enquiries regarding Queen Elizabeth The Queen Mother and Princess Margaret, even though the Princess had her own office at Kensington Palace. But on the day it was decided to announce that Princess Margaret and Lord Snowdon were to separate, a more senior figure was brought in to supervise the media arrangements.

Ronald Allison was the Queen's press secretary. A distinguished former BBC Court correspondent with years of journalistic training behind him, Allison was one of the most successful and popular occupants of the Palace press office. Among the many important royal functions he had organized for the media was the engagement and first wedding of Princess Anne in 1973, so he knew what was needed during this crisis. The late Sir Martin Gilliat, Queen Elizabeth's long-serving private secretary, asked Allison across to Clarence House, explained the situation and invited him to 'take over for us please'.

Like most of those in senior Palace circles, Allison had known for some time that the marriage was in difficulties and, being a thorough professional at his job, he had made some private arrangements in anticipation of being asked to handle the matter. He explained what happened next: 'I had a meeting with Princess Margaret and spoke to Lord Snowdon. What I needed to know from them was the timing of the announcement and what they wanted me to say. The timing is always of the utmost importance so that the people involved are not caught in a vulnerable position. I then drafted a short announcement which I intended to release to the Press Association at the agreed time. I sent it across for the Princess and Lord Snowdon to see, and make any changes they felt were necessary. As it happened they were happy with what was written, and, of course, the Queen also needed to approve the statement.'

Lord Snowdon was flying to Australia on a photographic assignment when the statement was issued. It read:

Her Royal Highness, the Princess Margaret, Countess of Snowdon, and the Earl of Snowdon have mutually agreed to live apart. The Princess will carry out her public duties and functions unaccompanied by Lord Snowdon. There are no plans for divorce proceedings.

This last sentence was unnecessary and also untrue. The separation was agreed in the full knowledge that the marriage had finally and irretrievably broken down, and both parties knew that divorce was the next step. This same sentence has also been added whenever subsequent royal separations have been announced; it happened with Princess Anne and Mark Phillips, and again with the Prince and Princess of Wales and also the Duke and Duchess of York – with the same predictable results.

Lord Snowdon arrived in Australia to find the nation's media waiting to ambush him. He called a press conference at the airport and in a halting voice read out his own statement:

I am naturally desperately sad in every way that this had to happen. And I would just like to say three things. First to pray for the understanding of our two children. Secondly, to wish

Princess Margaret every happiness for her future. Thirdly, to express, with the utmost humility, the love, admiration and respect I will always have for her sister, her mother and indeed her entire family.

One week later the Queen celebrated her fiftieth birthday with a large party at Windsor Castle. Among the guests was Ronald Allison: 'I was delighted to see Lord Snowdon there and spoke to him for a long time during the evening. He seemed in great form, and what was particularly pleasing was that, in spite of the break-up of the marriage, the Queen still kept him on her guest list. It showed how much she still thought of him.' Princess Margaret was also at the party and spent over an hour chatting animatedly with her estranged husband. Other guests said they had not seen them so friendly for years. As with many couples who separate after years of acrimony, Tony and Margaret settled into a period of wary friendship once the shouting was over and the decision to end the marriage was finally taken.

Once the separation had been officially announced, Tony moved out of Kensington Palace and his role as a member of the royal family was virtually over. Away from the constraints of being married to a senior member of the royal family, he was able to move openly back into the circle of friends he had enjoyed before his marriage, and to carry on with his career as a professional photographer without worrying about the effect that anything he did or said might have on his in-laws. More importantly, he was also able to show his love and affection for the woman he intended to marry. He was impatient for his divorce to be finalized so that they could marry and settle down together.

When Princess Margaret's affair with Roddy Llewellyn became public knowledge, she had played right into his hands. He knew he could get his divorce, even though, when it happened, he allowed her to start the proceedings. He didn't care who was awarded the divorce as long as he could get out of a marriage that had been a sham for over ten years. It was on 24 May 1978 that the divorce was granted, just one of twenty-eight that same day at the London Divorce Court, and six weeks later, on 11 July 1978, Princess Margaret was granted a decree absolute. As it happened, on the day the divorce was finalized, Tony was at Kensington Palace, but at Clock Court not his old apartment. He was photographing Princess Alice, Countess of Athlone, the last surviving grandchild of Queen Victoria. Hearing that he was in the Palace, Princess Margaret went over to see him and casually remarked that they were no longer married. They gave each other a hug and according to the Princess 'Danced a little jig' in the courtyard. Both were relieved that it was all over at last and that the constant rowing and shouting matches were ended. The marriage had officially lasted 18 years, 2 months and 5 days, and the old adage 'Marry in May and rue the day' had come true.

Having to cope with a divorce so close to home took the royal family onto new and uncertain ground. The Queen had been firmly opposed to divorce, as had her father, grandfather and great-grandfather before her. She had been brought up to believe in the indissolubility of marriage and also that, as the leading family in the land, the Windsors should set an example to the rest of the people. King George V had resolutely refused to acknowledge divorced couples, and even in the early years of Elizabeth II's reign, no divorced man or woman was permitted to be presented. There were exceptions, as there always are. Government ministers who were divorced, for example, could not be excluded from Court in the course of their duties, but they were invited only as officials and not personally.

When her cousin Lord Harewood was divorced by his first wife in 1967, on the grounds of his adultery with the woman he had lived with for three years and who had borne him a son (he later married her), Her Majesty refused to allow him at Court for many years. Not only that but he was ostracized by the rest of the royal family until divorce became so commonplace throughout the country that it would have been both unrealistic and hypercritical to have continued the boycott. Nevertheless, there was still a huge stigma attached to divorce in royal eyes in 1978, and Princess Margaret's divorce was considered to be the first by an immediate member of the royal family. Lord Harewood was the son of the Princess Royal, King George V's daughter, but he had played no part in public duties and while he was well known for his career in music, his royal profile had been low-key, so his divorce did not attract the same sort of attention that inevitably was focused on Princess Margaret.

The position of the Queen as Supreme Governor of the Church of England was also a matter of some delicacy, as she could not be seen to be condoning an act that was officially disapproved of by the Church. Later, of course, the divorces of three of her own children and the remarriage of one, her daughter, Anne, the Princess Royal, would bring the Queen into a situation she shared with many of her subjects. And if in 1960 the royal families of Europe were aghast at the thought of Princess Margaret, the daughter of a king and the last Emperor of India, marrying a mere photographer, what did they make of Princess Anne marrying Tim Laurence, who was not only untitled and from a modest background but had been his future mother-in-law's servant for three years. At the time of the marriage of Princess Margaret and Lord Snowdon, the royal household resolutely refused to allow divorced men and women to be employed, or to remain if they divorced while on the staff, at Buckingham Palace, even if they were what was called in those days the 'innocent party'. By the time of the Snowdons' marriage break-up, the household found among its numbers a large number of divorcees, even in the most senior positions such as private secretaries. And if divorced men and women were barred from the royal household today, the royal family would suddenly find huge gaps in the ranks of their servants, and if divorcees were still excluded from Court, Buckingham Palace and Windsor Castle would find themselves strangely empty places at Garden Party and State Banquet time, not to mention at family get-togethers!

The importance of Tony is that his was the first toe in the water, taking the temperature of the royal family's approval or disapproval after their intimate introduction to what, rightly or wrongly, was rapidly becoming one of the facts of life in the real world. And, in truth, there was no way that they could freeze him out entirely. As the father of the Queen's only niece and nephew, he would continue to occupy a special place, in the same way as the late Diana, Princess of Wales and the Duchess of York did because of their children.

He remains close to the Queen, who includes him on several royal guest lists. And throughout her life the Queen Mother would not hear a word said against her former son-in-law. They talked frequently on the telephone after the divorce, and he was kept informed of her condition when she was in hospital in February 1998 and during her final days. Similarly, his relationship with Princess Margaret settled into a friendly understanding, after a very acrimonious divorce. He was among the first people to be informed when she suffered a stroke while on holiday in the Caribbean, and she telephoned him several times from her hospital bed.

But his relationship with the royal family remains ambivalent because Prince Philip is not a man who forgives easily. While his behaviour is correct, it is never cordial. He saw the Snowdon divorce as the beginning of the breakdown of the royal family that subsequently saw the divorces of three of his own children. Just as the marriage of Antony Armstrong-Jones and Princess Margaret was seen as the first steps in democratizing the monarchy, so their divorce was regarded as revealing the first cracks in the fabric of the institution.

Today Lord Snowdon feels no bitterness towards the royal family. In fact he retains a great affection for most of them, regarding Prince Michael of Kent with special favour. But his experience has left him with a sceptical if not cynical attitude to royalty and a wariness of the so-called glamour and prestige their very presence is supposed to engender.

Neither Lord Snowdon nor Princess Margaret commented publicly about their marriage break-up or tried to lay the blame at the other's door. And he remained on the friendliest terms with his former in-laws, particularly his sister-in-law, the Queen, who sympathized with his position as an outsider coming into the royal family, having to cope with the many difficulties and problems that this entailed. It is a situation few people, men or women, have faced successfully.

The separation and divorce, as with the marriage before, meant that Tony Snowdon would continue to live his life, both professional and private, in the full glare of international publicity. Never again would he be allowed to do anything without the attention of the media. Surprisingly, his popularity never waned and throughout he managed to maintain an air of calm dignity and good humour. And he became even more sought after than when he was a member of the most famous family in the world.

The divorce was a dramatic indication of changing times in Britain. Tony Snowdon may have failed to democratize Britain's royal family from the inside, but at least he had shown they were human. With their family problems, they were little different from the rest of us and, perhaps more significantly, no better than us either. In the years that followed a gradual but fundamental change in our perception of the monarchy began to emerge.

Reaction to the break-up of the marriage indicated that many people tended to favour Tony and there was little initial sympathy for Princess Margaret. Letters to the press illustrated clearly the divisions in the country over where to lay the blame. The middle-aged middle class were practically unanimous in their condemnation of the Princess, describing her as 'that spoiled woman' and 'the fairy-tale princess who turned into the wicked witch'.

The veteran anti-royalist MP Willie Hamilton took full advantage of the break-up to raise the matter in parliament. He suggested to Denis Healey, the Chancellor of the Exchequer, that Princess Margaret should be sacked, adding, 'Even when she is here, a lot of her so-called engagements are audiences which last perhaps a couple of minutes. There are charity balls and premières which are really entertainment, yet which are called official engagements. The figures show that very few of those engagements are outside London.' There was never any chance that his suggestion was going to be acted upon, but it gave Hamilton, who never lost an opportunity to attack the royal family, the sort of publicity he craved.

There was more criticism over the Princess's allowance from the Civil List. Indeed, some indicated that she should repay the money now that her marriage had ended. It was as if Margaret had personally let down the nation by divorcing her husband, and in doing so she had also, apparently, forfeited her right to continue to be subsidized by the people of Britain. It is an attitude that never really changed. Princess Margaret never again captured the affection of a country which once thought of her as 'our little Margaret Rose'.

The affair with Roddy Llewellyn was never going to go away. Every time she was in the news, his name was mentioned, even though he later married and raised a family, and they were all on friendly terms with the Princess. In the same way that Teddy Kennedy will forever have the spectre of Chappaquidick to haunt him, Princess Margaret, who might have lived a blameless life for the last twenty years or so of her life, would never live down the fact that she had a highly publicized affair with a man very nearly twenty years younger than herself, most of which was carried on while she was still married.

If Tony had had a hundred affairs with younger women, few would have blamed him. Many (men at least) would have cheered him on. In Margaret's case, her public image took a blow from which she never recovered. Such is the hypocrisy of a public that demands that its heroes and heroines live up to an image they have created for them, and not as they really are.

In sheer physical terms, Tony was also the winner. In 1978, once more a free man, he looked at his best. Gone were the haggard looks of someone trying to rid himself of the golden shackles of royalty. He was as fit as he had ever been, since his childhood polio. There was plenty of work available, at very lucrative rates, and the woman he loved was by his side. He no longer had to endure the petty insults and restrictions of the royal household, yet he was still in favour with the chatelaines of Buckingham Palace and Clarence House.

Princess Margaret was not so fortunate. The stress of years of marital unhappiness had taken their toll. She had been a heavy smoker since her teenage years, and during the time she and Tony were going through the worst of their many rows, she grew to depend on nicotine even more. She was rarely seen, even at breakfast, without a cigarette, which she smoked through a long holder, and her well-known inclination for a drink increased at the same rate. All this, plus her tendency to overeat, caused her to have a weight problem; at barely 5ft tall, she was beginning to resemble Queen Victoria. And her looks also suffered. Princess Margaret had been an outstanding beauty whose vivacity and intelligence had made her arguably the most attractive woman in the world in her twenties and thirties. The separation and divorce, coupled with several bouts of ill-health, showed her at 48, to be an overweight, depressed and obviously middle-aged woman, very much past her best. The contrast could not have been greater, and she acknowledged, privately, how much the deterioration in her looks bothered her.

Following the divorce she remained a controversial figure, determined to live her own life yet equally intent on being treated with the deference she always demanded. Nobody was allowed to get away with the slightest hint of familiarity in her presence, and her attitude never softened if she thought someone had transgressed.

In her youth Princess Margaret was everyone's idea of a fairy-tale princess, blessed with outstanding beauty, brains, wit and an impeccable pedigree. What she did not possess was tolerance, modesty or the slightest degree of humility. On these matters she never changed. While intelligent, curious about many aspects of life, artistic and fun-loving, she was also described as ungraciousness personified by some hosts, who found her imperious presence too much to handle. She still enjoyed parties with her small circle of close friends – not one of whom was ever permitted to address her as anything other than Your Royal Highness or Ma'am – and she insisted on everyone remaining at her beck and call until she decided it was time to leave. No one was allowed to retire until Princess Margaret decided she had had enough, and that was frequently not until well after midnight. This is not an idiosyncrasy peculiar to her alone in the royal family; they all use their royal status in the same way. Even at Sandringham, when it is usually just the family present, nobody goes to bed before the Queen retires; even the Queen Mother, in her old age, obeyed this unwritten rule of protocol.

This was just one of the facts of life surrounding the royal family that irritated Tony Snowdon. While he was perfectly behaved in the presence of his in-laws and rarely, if ever, did or said anything to upset them, his talent, his individuality and the experiences of his previous lifestyle placed him at odds with the royal family's traditional emphasis on conventionality and conformity. They simply do not care for anything out of the ordinary.

When Princess Michael of Kent was first introduced to the royal family, with her statuesque figure, flair and sense of style, Her

Majesty was heard to say, 'She's far too grand for us.' At the other end of the scale, she paid what was for her the ultimate royal compliment when she first met Prince Edward's girlfriend, Sophie Rhys-Jones, saying, 'You wouldn't pick her out in a crowd.' That is the royal family's ideal, someone who doesn't stand out, and Tony Armstrong-Jones was never in that category. A colourful character who has never lost his zest for life or his insatiable curiosity, he could have been a breath of fresh air to a family that regarded stodginess as an admirable quality. Instead he remained an outsider – and the first of the royal rebels. There were to be others, notably the young woman who would have been his niece by marriage if his marriage (and hers) had not failed – Diana. They were all of twenty-one years apart, a whole generation, in joining the House of Windsor, but Tony and Diana had a remarkable amount in common.

FOURTEEN

Tony & Diana

When Antony Armstrong-Jones first joined the royal family, he was not a great enthusiast for field sports and was never a serious horseman, though he had ridden since he was a child when he enjoyed his first outings on horseback. 'We lived in Eaton Terrace, and my sister Susan and I would be taken most mornings to Rotten Row in Hyde Park where we loved riding our ponies.' And even though he had been educated at Eton and Cambridge so most of his friends were from the moneyed classes, he did not number dukes and duchesses among his everyday acquaintances.

In other words he did not conform to what the aristocracy expected in a royal bridegroom. He may have spoken with a natural upper-class accent, but in most other respects he was totally class-less. His friends and professional colleagues came from all walks of life and many levels of society, and he had little patience with the petty jealousies that plagued life in and around Buckingham Palace.

In those early days he was accepted into the royal family but always recognized as being different from them, and was treated with genial condescension by some of his wife's relations. He is a curious mixture of the grandiose and self-deprecating, with the ability to pre-empt criticism of his title and royal connections by faintly ridiculing them himself before anyone else can. It's a ploy that works very effectively for a man who has always considered himself to be an outsider looking in.

'Tony is one of the warmest people I know, but, like me, he knows what he wants out of life and is determined to get it. He's nobody's fool and his gentle exterior hides a toughness that he has had to learn – again just like me. People think because we never lose our temper in public that they can do anything they want and we'll let them get away with it. Well, I won't, and neither will Tony.' The words are those of the late Diana, Princess of Wales, talking about Lord Snowdon and spoken to the author shortly before she died in August 1997.

After her divorce from Prince Charles, Diana had seen quite a lot of Lord Snowdon and his wife, Lucy, and was full of praise for them. 'They are both super people, who welcome me every time I see them. I couldn't wish for better friends, and I know if ever I needed real help, Tony would be there for me. He's a lovely man.'

Above all, she drew parallels between her position in the royal family and his. 'We were both outsiders,' she said. 'Neither of us really had a chance.' However, she added, poignantly, given the sudden, awful death that lay only weeks ahead of her, they were both survivors. She admired the way he had behaved since his divorce from Princess Margaret and said she sometimes wished she had followed his example and been more discreet. 'He's managed to find happiness, and it couldn't have happened to a nicer guy.'

When we spoke about some of the photographs Lord Snowdon had taken of her, she could not praise him highly enough. As perhaps the most photographed woman in history, she said of him: 'He has the knack of being able to make you relax totally. We all tense up a bit when we are being photographed, but with him he just talks about anything and everything and somehow you forget the cameras and lights and everything. Of course it helps when you know someone as well as we know each other. Tony always seems to know what he's looking for. There's no messing about, and I've always been very pleased with the result – I only hope he was too.'

Diana also mentioned something that was perhaps a little more revealing than she intended about both their characters: 'Because he's got such perfect manners, some of his natural courtesy seems to rub off on those he meets. I hope it did with me.'

Diana obviously saw herself and Lord Snowdon as two of a kind, people who had experienced the same problems; a man and woman who had been plucked from relative obscurity and thrust into the spotlight of royal publicity without any warning of the consequences. When Antony Armstrong-Jones walked down the aisle at Westminster Abbey on 6 May 1960 and became, at a stroke, a member of the royal family, he was unwittingly paving the way for another, younger and more naive 'commoner' (albeit in her case, from an aristocratic family) to follow in his footsteps some twenty-one years later.

It was Armstrong-Jones who effected the entrée to royalty that ultimately enabled Lady Diana Spencer to become the most famous woman in the world. He was the trailblazer who prepared the way for Mark Phillips, Diana Spencer, Sarah Ferguson and, more recently, Tim Laurence. For it was when he was accepted as a suitable husband for Princess Margaret that the doors opened for other non-royal spouses. Until then, it was the sons and daughters of a fast dwindling European royalty who had generally been considered acceptable. If new blood was needed, then it was to the royal houses of Denmark, Norway, Belgium and Sweden that the British royal family looked for a transfusion. Tried and tested princes and princesses who knew the form were regarded as the natural partners. The offspring of the crowned heads of Europe were selected practically from birth as future consorts.

Even then there were reservations about certain monarchies. There was a definite league table among the royal families, with some relegated to the ranks of the second division. When Prince Philip married the then Princess Elizabeth, heir to the throne, in 1947, there were many, including most of the royal household, who were horrified. 'Phil the Greek' was the disparaging nickname he was given in the early days (even though he does not have a drop of Greek blood in his veins), and it was many years before he was fully accepted by the Establishment in the United Kingdom. Even today there are members of Britain's so-called gentry who refer to him as 'that penniless foreigner', though always safely behind his back of course.

In the early part of the century, Princess Mary, the Princess Royal, only daughter of King George V and Queen Mary, was never quite forgiven – or understood – for 'marrying a subject', even though her chosen husband was Viscount Lascelles, who later became the 6th Earl of Harewood and was definitely out of society's top drawer.

The rule generally was: royals marry royals. 'It's safer and we know what we are getting – and so do they.' The exception – Elizabeth Bowes-Lyon, who splendidly turned the shy Prince Albert into a man who could be king – was seen as just that: the exception that proved the rule.

Tony broke the mould and was followed by the Hon. (now Sir) Angus Ogilvy, who married Princess Alexandra, the Queen's cousin, in 1963. Ogilvy was the second son of the Earl and Countess of Airlie. His father had been a lord-in-waiting to King George V, his grandmother was a Lady of the Bedchamber to Queen Mary, while his older brother David, went on to become Lord Chamberlain to Elizabeth II and Head of the Queen's Household. So he wasn't exactly a run-of-the-mill outsider, and anyway, he was marrying someone who was pretty far down the Line of Succession to the Throne. Theirs is a marriage that has stood the test of time, in spite of several rocky patches, and public family rows with their daughter, Marina. Thirteen years after Tony married Princess Margaret, Mark Phillips, who also had family connections at Court, as his maternal grandfather became a valued friend and trusted aide to King George VI, married Princess Anne in 1973 – and was then divorced from her in 1991. Lady Diana Spencer's marital path followed the same route in 1981 and 1992, and Sarah Ferguson, who was married to Prince Andrew in 1986 – and divorced from him ten years later – completed the disastrous misalliances of four of the Queen's closest relatives, three of them her children and the other, her sister.

It is easy to say now that neither Tony nor Diana should have married into the royal family. Neither was the type to settle for having to live in the shadow of a wife or husband – Tony because of his unwillingness to sacrifice his independence and lose his own identity, and Diana because she would quickly emerge as the star of the royal family who outshone her husband, apparently without effort. Both were independent spirits who would eventually attempt to break free, in Diana's case with tragic results. But both would blossom after divorcing their royal partners and achieve happiness elsewhere, again for Diana, for an all too brief period.

It was in the final years of her life that Princess Diana became a close friend of Tony Snowdon, though she had known him since her marriage in 1981. He was one of her favourite photographers and visited Highgrove to take pictures of the Prince and Princess of Wales and their children when they were still a united family. He also photographed her alone in the final months of her life.

On the surface it would appear to have been an odd relationship; he, nearing 70, she, a mere 31-year-old who had had more than her fill of the old fogies at Buckingham Palace. And he had more or less severed his formal relationship with the royal family some three years before she even arrived on the scene. But she felt they had a great deal in common, not least 'the way we were both treated'. He has never claimed that this forged a particular bond between them, and neither has he spoken about her comments about him, but the parallels in their lives are, on examination, quite extraordinary and uncannily similar.

They were both the children of broken homes whose mothers had been regarded as outstanding beauties in their day. Tony's mother, Anne, was frequently described as the most beautiful woman in London, while Diana's mother, Frances Shand-Kydd, was rightly regarded for her outstanding looks. Tony and Diana were both sent away to boarding school at an early age – and on their own admission, neither was an academic. Tony managed to stumble through Eton, preferring woodwork to mathematics but was asked to leave Cambridge without taking a degree because of his poor scholastic record. Not that it bothered him in the slightest, then or later. As she freely admitted, Diana was no intellectual, and at school she failed at everything. She was fond of claiming she was as 'thick as two short planks', and the only prizes she ever won were for trying hard and one special award for service. But once she appeared on the world stage, her lack of formal qualifications did not hinder her progress or prevent her from becoming the most sought-after woman in the world, or speaking out with confidence for the causes she espoused. Her quick wit enabled her to adapt to her new role, and her natural affinity with people of all ages and from all walks of life soon showed the rest of the royal family where they were going wrong.

When they joined the 'Royal Firm', neither Tony nor Diana was given a job description or any training for the role they were required to adopt, and when each of them refused to conform to accepted, if outdated, royal behaviour, they were subjected to extreme pressure and (private, if not public) vilification from some members of the family and even more so from the royal household.

When Tony Armstrong-Jones first arrived at Buckingham Palace as a fully fledged member of the family, he was warmly welcomed by the Queen and, surprisingly to some, also by Prince Philip. Philip's reaction came as a shock because close friends of the couple knew how impatient and even downright rude he could be with outsiders. His own early treatment by the Court still rankled, and few expected him to be considerate towards his new brother-in-law, particularly as they appeared to have little in common. Philip liked to ride, hunt and shoot anything that moved, while Tony's preference was for the arts, the theatre and a somewhat more bohemian lifestyle than that found at Windsor, Sandringham and Balmoral. While Philip liked to portray himself as the sixties equivalent of macho man, Tony cared little about such outward appearances, though, in reality, his sporting achievements as cox of a winning Cambridge boat far outweighed those of his brother-in-law. But in many ways, Philip took Tony under his wing, showing him the way things were done at Balmoral, which Tony didn't really need but he appreciated the gesture.

Diana, too, experienced the kinder side of Prince Philip's character in those early days. In fact, the honeymoon period with her father-in-law lasted far longer than the official one with her husband. Diana could do no wrong in Prince Philip's eyes. He had always loved blue-eyed blondes, and he believed she was the woman who could help Charles prepare for the throne he would eventually inherit – and also make him into the stronger man his father knew he needed to be if he was to become a successful sovereign.

When the marriages of Tony and Margaret and Diana and Charles broke up, Philip was among those who showed their extreme disappointment, laying most of the blame on the two non-royals, regardless of whether they were the guilty or innocent parties. He had tried desperately to get both couples to stay together, if only for the sake of the monarchy. But when the divorces became inevitable, he immediately took the side of the two royals – the 'Firm' had to appear solid, even if, privately, his sympathies were with Tony and Diana.

If Diana had bothered to look back at the events of 1978, when Tony and Margaret separated, she would have seen the way in which Tony became isolated from the rest of the royal family, in spite of both the Queen and the Queen Mother retaining an affection for him. Where Philip was concerned, there was no such warmth or understanding. Not because of any personal antagonism, but simply because Tony had, in his view, let the side down, and done so publicly by virtually forcing Princess Margaret to divorce him. And when Diana separated from her husband she encountered the same reaction. It was history repeating itself. They were both outsiders who had deserted the 'Firm' and, as such, deserved little consideration – or redundancy pay-off – if he, Philip, had anything to do with it.

The true facts of Tony's divorce settlement are an indication of how much of an outsider he became. Reports at the time suggested that Princess Margaret had given him £100,000 to buy a house. What actually happened is that the Queen paid £70,000 for the house in Launceston Place, where he now lives, and which is currently valued at just over £3 million, given the celebrity status of its present occupant and, of course, the royal connections. But the house was never registered in Lord Snowdon's name. Instead, Her Majesty placed it in trust for his children by Princess Margaret, Viscount Linley and Lady Sarah Chatto, with the proviso that Lord Snowdon could live there rent-free for the rest of his life. But he does pay for the considerable upkeep of the house.

That is almost precisely what happened when Her Majesty bought Gatcombe Park for Princess Anne and Mark Phillips and Sunningdale House for the Duke and Duchess of York. Neither Mark nor Sarah had any ownership title to their homes. There was no way that, should their marriages end – as they did – the outsiders were going to get their hands on any royal property.

Prince Philip has always believed that the image of royalty has to be preserved at all costs. Personal happiness comes a poor second to public duty every time. If an action by a member of the royal family is seen to reflect badly on the Queen personally or the monarchy generally, then that person has committed an unpardonable offence. There is no mitigation, and the question of guilt or innocence does not arise. In this, Prince Philip is not alone by any means. There has long been a feeling within the royal household that people should put up with anything rather than expose the family to ridicule or criticism. There is only one question that is asked whenever a member of the royal family has a controversial or difficult decision to make: is it good for the Queen? If the answer is no, or even if there is the slightest doubt, then the advice is, don't do it.

Like Philip, Margaret jealously protected the family image. This was what had persuaded her to abandon her love for Peter Townsend. The Princess always regarded loyalty to her family – by which she meant her mother and her sister – as the most important element in her life. Although her own behaviour had been erratic from time to time, the only occasion when she brought the royal family into serious disrepute was during her affair with Roddy Llewellyn. Apart from that, the minor disturbances she was involved in were seen as mere peccadilloes which did not reflect badly on the Queen or the Queen Mother.

Understandably, therefore, she was outraged when younger royals took the opposite course of action. In the early days of the marriage of the Prince and Princess of Wales, Margaret became very close to Diana, offering advice and comfort to the newest royal recruit. But once the marriage was in trouble and separation and divorce looked likely, the curtain descended. And when Diana cooperated with the author Andrew Morton in the writing of his book about her problems, Princess Margaret felt it was the ultimate act of betrayal. In her eyes, Diana no longer existed.

For a time Diana and Tony unashamedly enjoyed the reflected glory of belonging to the most famous family in the world, but they both suffered an identity crisis in those early days of marriage. Although Tony was much more sophisticated than Diana when he entered the royal family, he too had little idea of what he had let himself in for. As Diana would find out twenty years later, he gradually came to realize that he may have married someone he was in love with, but the contract included being inextricably attached to an institution. Neither Diana nor Tony fully realized then that from the moment they married into the royal family, their own wishes would be secondary to those of the person they had married. They would never be considered to be of equal rank, and even if Diana was to go on to become much more of a star than Prince Charles, and Tony would achieve great prominence in a variety of activities, within royal circles they would always be regarded as second-division lucky outsiders whose good fortune it had been to marry royalty. It was this common factor that partly drew them together after Diana and Charles were divorced.

Initially they also found it difficult to accept the responsibilities that went with their new-found positions. In their early days in Kensington Palace – though separated by twenty years – their uncertainty manifested itself as arrogance, and one of the ways they showed it was by firing staff at regular intervals. It was common knowledge in the early sixties that Tony could not hang on to a butler because, it was said, quite wrongly, that 'he simply did not know how to deal with servants'. Similarly, when Diana moved into her palatial apartments at Kensington Palace, there was a rapid turn-over of domestics who either would not put up with her demands or who she felt did not live up to her high standards. Although Diana had grown up surrounded by servants, she had never had to deal with them directly and she found it difficult to cope.

Both Tony and Diana tried to adapt to being royal – and both failed, not through any faults of their own, but just because, being natural outsiders, they were not prepared from birth for the stulti-fying routine that comes as second nature to those born with blue blood in their veins. The seasonal treks to Sandringham, Balmoral, Windsor and back to London, which were as natural as breathing to Princess Margaret and Prince Charles – because they had never known anything else – quickly lost their charm for the newcomers. Another of the similarities between Tony and Diana is the way in which each reacted when they discovered their spouse had been unfaithful and their marriages were a sham. Both demanded a showdown. They were confrontational, which is anathema to the royal family. They loathe the idea of facing up to personal problems, preferring to push them under the carpet in the hope they will go away. No member of the royal family has ever been known to fire a servant themselves; they always delegate such unpleasant tasks to other servants. Even the Queen Mother was known for her insistence on ignoring unpalatable facts in the belief that if she did so they would disappear. The Queen too has a reputation for refusing to confront private, family problems. When told that her daughter, the Princess Royal, wanted to leave her first husband, Mark Phillips, Her Majesty is understood to have replied, 'I think it's time to walk the corgis.'

When Diana found out the truth about Camilla Parker Bowles, Prince Charles's mistress, her immediate reaction was to get out of that unfortunate marriage. Similarly, when Tony was faced publicly with Princess Margaret's affair with Roddy Llewellyn, even though he had known about it privately for months, he knew there was no alternative to divorce. Roddy was Margaret's Camilla and continuing public humiliation was something that neither Tony nor Diana was willing to accept. This is where they differed from other generations of royals. Wives had always accepted that their husbands were unfaithful and had mistresses. As long as discretion was employed, they were prepared to turn a blind eye. And royal husbands were equally obliging when their consorts took lovers. Tony and Diana did not obey the rules – even if they knew they existed.

Both Princess Diana and Lord Snowdon will be remembered in various ways by different people, but the most important legacy of each of them will be their children. They may have made mistakes in their own private lives, but no one could ever accuse either of them of neglecting their parental duties. One thing that Princess Margaret and Tony were agreed on – as were Prince Charles and Princess Diana in 1992 – was the welfare of their children. That was regarded as being of paramount importance. Diana often said that her children were her first priority and that her natural role in life was motherhood. She was determined to bring them up in as normal a way as was possible for two children whose grandmother was Queen and whose father would one day be King. She was a thoroughly modern parent who ran in the mother's race at their school sports days; she took them to the cinema and allowed them to sample the delights of McDonald's burgers. When the time came for William to go to public school she expressed a clear preference for Eton because of its nearness to her London home, in spite of Prince Charles's association with Gordonstoun and also Prince Philip's natural loyalty to his old school.

Diana impressed on William and Harry the future responsibilities they would one day have to shoulder by taking them with her to visit a centre for the homeless and on a number of engagements to deprived areas. At the same time she wanted them to grow up enjoying their childhood and adolescence and experiencing as much of ordinary life as was possible for boys in their position.

Similarly, Lord Snowdon tried – and succeeded with Princess Margaret – in raising their two children to be normal youngsters with an appreciation of life beyond the confines of palace and castle.

David and Sarah and William and Harry are four well-adjusted and uncomplicated young people who are a credit to their parents, while Frances, Lord Snowdon's younger daughter by his second wife Lucy, is one of the most delightful young women one could hope to meet. He may not be in a position to leave them quite as many millions as Diana did for her sons, but their inheritance will be just as precious in other ways. What Tony Snowdon has instilled in his three grown-up children is an appreciation of life's true values and he is able to give them more than mere money; he gives them his undivided attention and unqualified love in unlimited quantities.

And if Diana will go down in history as the inspirational 'People's Princess' who wanted to be known as a 'Queen of Hearts' then perhaps Lord Snowdon's epitaph might also include the word 'humanitarian'.

While she involved herself in childcare, famine relief, AIDS awareness and, in the final months, that spectacular campaign to rid the world of anti-personnel mines which brought her international acclaim, he, too, has been working quietly at a variety of worthy causes, though with not quite the same amount of publicity.

Lord Snowdon's efforts on behalf of disabled people for over twenty years have brought immense benefits to thousands of men and women. Tony and his friend Quentin Crewe served together on the Council for the Crippled Child, now Action Research, and many of the advantages taken for granted by wheelchair users today came about through their efforts.

Snowdon traces his first feelings of compassion for disabled people (he hates the term 'the disabled') to his childhood illness. And also the idea that he might be able at some time to do something positive to help. He designed a wheelchair which was a vast improvement on the standard issue, and that came about because Quentin Crewe was confined to a wheelchair; the last time he had walked was when he led his second wife, Angela Huth, down the aisle at their wedding, and Tony believed he could build something a lot better. 'I saw this dreadful thing they had provided him with; it was so basic, I knew I could improve on that, so I built one myself.' In fact, Lord Snowdon says it wasn't just his own experience of polio that first made him aware of what it was like to be disabled: 'I may have felt something at the time, but really it was the business with Quentin that started me off.'

Crewe concurred:

It was inevitable I suppose, given my obvious condition and Tony's childhood experience with polio. But it was quite extraordinary how he managed to turn his ever practical eye to some of the problems. On one occasion he asked me to go to an exhibition at Olympia. I can't remember what it was, but he had some photographs on show and wanted me to see them. Anyway, we got to the entrance and the man on the door refused to let me in because of my wheelchair. This was in the early seventies; it certainly wouldn't happen today. Tony couldn't believe what was happening, and he determined that it would not be repeated. So he set about designing a new wheelchair for me that would be more convenient for everyone.

The way he did it was typical of Tony. He always liked using his hands and making use of whatever material is lying around. On this occasion he found a small motor attached to one of his son's toy cars. He stripped it from the toy and modified it to be used on a wheelchair, and it worked. The wheelchair was also more compact than the one I had been using previously; it was really nothing more than an ordinary chair set on a platform, but it made life a little more comfortable, and I used it for many years.

Later, Tony published an interview with the then chairman of British Rail, Sir Robert Reid, in which he virtually made him promise to look at some of the problems experienced by people who had difficulty in getting on and off trains, problems the chairman admitted he had not considered, simply because they had not been brought to his attention before. During the interview it was clear that Tony Snowdon was becoming increasingly angry and frustrated at the way wheelchair-using passengers were treated – and at the attitude of the head of British Rail, who kept giving political answers to Tony's searching questions.

In 1981, the International Year of Disabled Persons, he began the Snowdon Award Scheme. He saw that many physically disabled young people were being denied the opportunity to pursue further education or training because of a lack of funds that were not forthcoming from the State at that time. Using an initial £14,000 – money he had received as fees for photographs he had taken of the royal family during the period when he was married to Princess Margaret, and which had been placed in a trust fund – he worked out a scheme that would encourage young men and women to take their place on a more equal footing with their more able-bodied contemporaries. Since it began, the Snowdon Award Scheme has made awards to well over 1,000 students and raised over £1 million from various sources including other trusts, companies, commercial organizations and generous individuals.

Simon Weston, the Welsh guardsman, who was horrifically burned in the Falklands Campaign in 1982, says, 'Without Tony Snowdon's personal involvement, there are many young people who would not be able to use computers or enter higher education or get the right training for the jobs they want. He puts his money where his mouth is.'

So perhaps Princess Diana was not all that far off the mark when she said she and Tony Snowdon were alike. There may have been a generation gap between them, but it never seemed to affect their friendship. Tony had already left the royal family long before Diana came on the scene, yet both she and Prince Charles welcomed him to their homes, and of course the fact that Tony's daughter Sarah was invited by Diana to become godmother to Prince Harry strengthened the ties between the two families. Perhaps Diana recognized in Tony a kindred spirit, even in those early days; someone who, like her, rebelled against the rigid strictures of Court life. Diana used to visit Tony in his Kensington home, and she was particularly fond of Lucy. Another aspect of her character that endeared her to Tony was that she was completely non-judgemental as far as he was concerned. If there was any gossip about either of them – and they were rarely out of the news – they would both enjoy a good laugh about it.

Where Princess Margaret and Tony Snowdon were among the iconic glamour couples of the sixties, Charles and Diana held that position twenty years later. But where Princess Margaret and Prince Charles had been born royal and never knew anything different, Tony and Diana were required to adapt to the incredibly changed circumstances marriage into the royal family forced on them. The similarities between them, their early hopes, their failed marriages and acrimonious divorces, their pride in their children and their achievements after leaving the royal family, all show how history has repeated itself.

But it was a wasted opportunity. They had so much to offer to change and improve the House of Windsor. But they remained outsiders. The stories of Lord Snowdon and Diana, Princess of Wales have this in common too: they both show how royalty rarely changes – and never learns.

FIFTEEN

Life after Margaret

Tony enjoyed his new-found freedom, dining at the most fashionable restaurants in London, travelling to New York and Los Angeles on photographic assignments and being seen at first nights and the latest shows in the company of celebrity friends like David Frost, Peter Sellers and Rudolf Nureyev. He tells of one amusing incident in New York: 'David Frost and I tried to go into a very posh restaurant wearing evening dress, but we were turned away. The trouble was we were both wearing what was then the latest white silk polo-neck evening shirts that you wear without a tie. The Americans hadn't seen these before, and as we didn't conform to their dress code they refused us admission.' He was getting back to his 1972 image when he had been voted one of the 'Ten Sexiest Men in America', being narrowly beaten to the top only by Clint Eastwood.

By mutual agreement Princess Margaret had been granted custody of their two children, with Tony having unlimited access. They both realized that it would be much more practical for David and Sarah to live at Kensington Palace, and they wanted as little disruption as possible to their lives. Throughout the entire period of acrimony and frustration between Margaret and Tony, they had never rowed in front of their children and they had never disagreed about their welfare and upbringing.

Once the marriage had been dissolved, Tony was free to court publicly the woman he intended to marry. Their friends had known about their plans for some months, but discretion being an integral element in Tony's character, he had managed to keep secret the identity of his new love and very little had appeared about her in the newspapers. If there is one thing that Lord Snowdon is better at than almost anything else, it is keeping a secret. He confides in no one and is able to keep his own counsel about practically every aspect of his private life. It is not something that has happened because of, or since, his marriage to Princess Margaret, and the caution that being a member of the royal family demanded. He has always been secretive – about his private life, about his ambitions and about his finances.

This is why, when he first began dating Princess Margaret, nobody guessed at his intentions or even got an inkling that he was seeing the most eligible – and seemingly unattainable – woman in Britain. None of his closest friends, or his press colleagues, received the slightest hint that he was courting the Queen's only sister, and when the engagement was finally announced it came as a complete surprise. Similarly, when the marriage broke up, although there had been rumours of a rift for years before, no one really expected a royal divorce or believed that such an occurrence would take place. If Tony had confided in anyone, there would inevitably have been a leak. But he knew, and still knows, that the only way to make sure his private life remained private, was to say absolutely nothing to anybody. It is a rule he has adhered to religiously for forty-five years, and he believes it has stood him in good stead. It is a part of his character that the royal family has much to be grateful for. A generation later, all sorts of secrets came tumbling out that have not served the monarchy well. But there was never any question of him cashing in. The opportunities were certainly there, and if he had decided to tell his story, it would have been open-cheque time from any newspaper in the country.

When Tony decided to marry for the second time, to Lucy Lindsay-Hogg, it was no surprise that the first the media heard about it was when he announced his plans to the Press Association, the day before the wedding. Tony knew that if he had not done so, the press would have found out about it anyway from their contacts at the various register offices in London, so he pre-empted the anticipated media intrusion and showed once again his mastery in handling the press. By making the announcement as and when he chose he was able to prepare himself for the reporters and cameramen and not be taken unawares. He also displayed a nice line in flattering the press by saying, 'I would also like to take this opportunity to express my gratitude for the understanding and very many kindnesses shown to me over the past two years [the period since his separation from Princess Margaret].' The hidden message was obvious: 'Please give us a break this time around.'

The ceremony was held at Kensington and Chelsea Register Office on 15 December 1978, some five months after his divorce from Princess Margaret was finalized. The Princess had known that he intended to marry Lucy, but she apparently had not been informed of the actual date, claiming later that she heard about it only when she read it in the newspapers. Tony's children, David and Sarah, were in on the secret but did not attend the ceremony because their father felt they would attract too much attention, and he had always done everything in his power to protect them from media intrusion. He still does.

In sharp contrast to his first marriage in 1960, with royalty present and the Archbishop of Canterbury in charge of the proceedings, the second occasion was deliberately kept a low-key affair with only a few close friends of the bride and groom present. Tony's friends, Adrian Garnett, who had been at Eton with him, and John Humphries, his solicitor, who had represented him in the divorce proceedings, were witnesses, plus the writer Caroline Moorehead with her husband, Jeremy Swift, old friends of Lucy. Humphries had to produce £18.25 in cash to pay the remainder of the registration fee; Lucy had previously paid the £3 deposit a few days earlier.

Tony had arranged the timing of the brief ceremony like a military operation so that there would be no embarrassing moments with either of the principal characters having to hang around. He arrived promptly at ten o'clock and immediately ordered the main lights in the register office to be turned off so that any photographers outside could not sneak a picture through the windows. Lucy turned up on time ten minutes later, hatless and not even carrying a wedding bouquet.

After a ten-minute civil ceremony, supervised by the Superintendent Registrar, the couple emerged to find a battery of photographers and reporters waiting to greet them. They didn't make any statement or answer any questions, but smiled and thanked the people on the pavement who wished them good luck. As both Tony and Lucy had been married before, they agreed that a quiet ceremony was what they wanted, and as they drove away to a private celebration at a West End restaurant, they were both relieved that it had all gone as planned. There was no honeymoon after the wedding; they waited until after Christmas and then took David and Sarah on a skiing holiday in Switzerland.

Princess Margaret spent the morning Christmas shopping in the nearby Fulham Road with a friend, and that evening she attended the Royal Ballet performance of *Sleeping Beauty* at Covent Garden.

Tony's new wife could not have been more different from his first. Where one was precocious, spoilt and demanding, the other was practical, serious and wanted nothing more than to be kept out of the limelight. Lucy hated publicity and would have been perfectly happy never to have seen her picture in the tabloids. Next to the Duchess of Kent, she is arguably the most private person ever to be linked to the royal family – even by marriage to a former member – and yet she is no shrinking violet. She has very definite opinions of her own, and while she was and remains a tremendous admirer of Tony's talent and energy, she never acted as a rubber stamp to all his views. If she disagreed with something he said or did, she told him so.

As an established film researcher long before she met her future husband, Lucy had her own career in a profession that required self-assurance and confidence, and she was never lacking in either. Tony and Lucy liked to entertain at home, and their close circle of friends were as loyal as those surrounding the royal family. None ever broke the unwritten rule about not revealing what goes on at Launceston Place. Tony regards discretion as the most important and indispensable element in his friendships. Old friends like Jeremy Fry and the late Quentin Crewe could always be relied upon, but newer pals proved to be equally staunch in guarding the couple's privacy.

Lord Snowdon has rarely been out of the news since he first became public property on his engagement to Princess Margaret, and he is not exactly averse to publicity when it comes to one of his pet projects, or furthering his own commercial interests. But he draws a distinct line between what he regards as legitimate media interest and his private and personal life. He is obsessively protective of Lucy and their daughter, Frances, and neither has ever given an interview or posed for pictures.

It is an attitude that has to be respected and admired, even by frustrated would-be interviewers, as Tony knows from personal experience the problems an intrusive press can bring. He realizes that he is fair game for reporters and magazine writers, and he accepts the situation with resigned tolerance. But he has become a past master at fielding awkward questions and deflecting potentially embarrassing enquiries. He knows that the less he says, the less chance there is that his own words will come back to haunt him. High on his list of no-go areas are the royal family and his children, and many an experienced journalist has come away from an interview with him wondering how he managed to say so much without telling them anything they didn't already know.

The media treated Tony and Lucy kindly following their wedding. There was no sniping or snide comments about the difference in style of his two wedding ceremonies. Since his separation from Princess Margaret, nearly three years earlier, Tony had had full exposure to media attention and he had suffered it with good humour, quiet patience, restraint and dignity. His conduct had been exemplary and held as an example of how to behave in such circumstances; now it had paid off. He had managed to continue his career and handle his private life without upsetting his own children or the royal family. And perhaps just as importantly, for someone in the public eye, he had also maintained a good working relationship with the press, whose goodwill he needed if he was to avoid any of the harassment that subsequent royal divorcees claimed they were subject to.

Before Tony married Lucy he introduced her to his former mother-in-law, Queen Elizabeth – whom he always called Ma'am. It was by all accounts a friendly introduction, and Lucy was welcomed by the Queen Mother, who never laid the blame for the break-up of the first marriage at Tony's door. The Queen continued to favour Tony as a royal photographer, and in the year of the divorce and his remarriage, he was invited to take the official pictures for Her Majesty's fifty-second birthday. It was a public seal of approval that did his business no harm whatsoever, and within weeks he was inundated with commissions.

One thing that Lucy did that Princess Margaret had never done was to encourage Tony to work. She knew he needed to keep busy, as she did herself. And she enjoyed the hustle and bustle of his various activities. On the day they were married, Tony said, 'We both look forward to a life of quiet happiness like any other family and intend to carry on our respective careers.' The couple had been professional colleagues for six years before they married, working together in Australia for six weeks in 1975 on a BBC television series called *The Explorers*. This was four years after Lucy's divorce in 1971 from Michael Lindsay-Hogg, the successful film producer by whom she had had no children. The divorce was as friendly as these things can be in the circumstances, and both Tony and Lucy remained on friendly terms with Michael. As they began their married life together, Tony had never been happier. The tension of the past few years fell away and, at the age of forty-eight, eleven years older than his wife, he felt that life was beginning again for him.

The only constant reminder of his previous existence as a member of the royal family was his earldom; but he had grown so used to it that it would only have caused more publicity if he had decided to renounce his title and revert to being plain Antony Armstrong-Jones. In any case, his peerage had been a gift from the Queen, and there was no way that Tony would have insulted her by throwing her generosity back in her face. However, there were now two Countesses of Snowdon as Princess Margaret continued to be styled HRH The Princess Margaret, Countess of Snowdon, while Lucy, as the wife of the Earl, was now *the* Countess of Snowdon.

Princess Margaret never explained why she chose to retain the subsidiary title after her divorce. But as she rarely felt the need to explain any of her actions, perhaps that is not too surprising. Many people expected her to cut off all connections to her former husband, as the divorce had been particularly acrimonious. But for the rest of her life, Her Royal Highness insisted on using the title; unlike Princess Anne, who was styled HRH The Princess Anne,

Mrs Mark Phillips, until she was created the Princess Royal, when she abandoned her husband's name even before their marriage ended. One possible explanation for Princess Margaret's decision was that as their son, David, will one day inherit his father's title, she felt it incumbent on her to keep it so that, in the event that she survived her former husband, she would then become the Dowager Countess of Snowdon. But then, of course, so too could Lucy have been known by that title.

Away from the confines of royalty, Lord Snowdon appeared more relaxed and infinitely happier than he had in years. Lucy was obviously the best thing that had happened to him in his life, and when in the spring of 1979 she discovered that she was pregnant nothing could have pleased him more. Their daughter, Frances, was born in the Westminster Hospital on Tuesday 17 July 1979, prematurely, seven months and two days after her parents had married. Tony described her to reporters as very small, but beautiful, as he left the hospital later that morning to fly to Switzerland on a photographic assignment.

If Princess Margaret felt any bitterness or envy of her ex-husband's fortunate second family, few could blame her, but if this was the case, she gave no sign to those around her. Her relationship with Tony, Lucy and Frances was reasonably friendly and comfortable without any intimacy. She was, of course, fully aware of her children's closeness with their stepmother and half-sister, but again, there was no disapproval on her part.

Tony was never going to lose the tag of being the ex-husband of Princess Margaret. Even now, more than twenty-five years after they split up and despite the fact that he was married to Lucy longer than he was to Margaret, he is still, in the public eye, connected to her, and he will be until the day he dies. When she suffered a stroke in 1998, he was one of the first people to be told, and reporters all wanted a comment from him. He was besieged by callers telephoning from all over the world, offering their sympathy or wanting his reaction. It is the classic situation regarding outsiders who marry into the royal family. Angus Ogilvy, Mark Phillips and Sarah, Duchess of York have all been woken in the early hours by reporters wanting their comments on a variety of topics relating to the royal family, even if, in reality, they know as little as the rest of us. Angus Ogilvy and Mark Phillips have been very successful in deflecting intrusive questions, and therefore their reputations have survived more or less intact; the Duchess of York less so.

Anyone meeting Lord Snowdon today would soon realize that he came out of his first marriage with far fewer wounds than Princess Margaret. The transition from minor royalty to major celebrity was apparently seamless, and for many years his second marriage appeared to be one of those made in heaven. He certainly gave the appearance of being a happy man.

And if most men who are divorced as they approach their fiftieth birthday would find their lives in ruins, he could truly be said to have landed on his feet. That is until the revelation that another woman had been involved in his life for some years.

The woman in question was Ann Hills, an unpredictable and capricious 55-year-old divorced mother of two, who had had a series of lovers besides and throughout her alleged affair with Lord Snowdon. Their long-standing relationship only came to light when she committed suicide in January 1997, taking an overdose of pills, washed down with champagne, while she was on the roof garden of her £400,000 penthouse apartment just north of London's Oxford Street. A message from Snowdon, together with two other messages from friends, was recorded on her telephone answering machine. He used the code letter 'T' they had agreed on twenty years earlier, and the message ended with the words 'chin up'. They were the last words from him she would hear.

The relationship began back in 1977, when his marriage to Princess Margaret was already in its closing stages, and before he began seriously courting Lucy Lindsay-Hogg. Mrs Hills, a freelance journalist, is said to have met Tony by the simple expedient of arriving on his doorstep and announcing, 'I want to interview you and then go to bed with you.' He said it just wasn't true. It was a great line, but former colleagues of Mrs Hills said they had actually met at a press conference. Not quite as dramatic but obviously as effective.

Their clandestine affair continued off and on for the next twenty years, but Mrs Hills knew from the beginning that there was no hope of her becoming the new Countess of Snowdon. She had given up all hope of marrying him and had started another serious relationship with a businessman who she hoped would marry her. It was when he refused to spend the Christmas and New Year's holiday with her that she took her own life.

Tony had become a steadying influence in her troubled life and throughout the entire period they knew each other they would meet from time to time and she would pour out her woes – usually about the current man in her life – and he would listen sympathetically and offer a shoulder for her to cry on. The amazing thing about this extraordinary incident is that few people, apart from a select group of their closest friends, had any idea of the relationship.

Perhaps it was because they moved in vastly different social circles. Tony kept Ann separate from his everyday life; she was placed in an isolated compartment and she never attempted to encroach on any part of his life, as long as he came to see her. Neither of them ever intruded upon the other's circle. In turn, he remained loyal, though on his side, in the later years, his feelings were more platonic than passionate. Had she not died when she did, and in such tragic circumstances, it is highly unlikely that their names would ever have been linked. Certainly there had never been the slightest hint of any extramarital behaviour on his part in any newspaper. It was only when Mrs Hills died, with the surrounding publicity, that evidence of their closeness became public knowledge. Ann Hills was a journalist who liked to drink and loved to gossip with colleagues. The one subject she apparently never talked about was Lord Snowdon, though she was rarely reticent about other lovers and frequently boasted of her sexual conquests. There was a degree of loyalty on both sides even if that loyalty was confused with the caution necessary to keep anyone from finding out their secret.

On Snowdon's side it would not have been too difficult to abandon her if she had proved to be a nuisance. There is no evidence that she ever made any demands on him. That he did not do so says something about his character. Perhaps it demonstrates that even in the rarified royal society that he enjoyed there is still a code to be observed, and good manners dictate that even when a one-time lover threatens to become an embarrassment they should still be treated in a civilized and courteous manner.

The affair was romantic, sad and, in the end, tragic, giving yet another all too brief glimpse of the private man behind the public face. Sticking to his inflexible rule of never discussing his private life, Tony confined himself to saying that Ann Hills' death was a very, very sad incident to have happened, adding, 'She was terribly nice and great fun.'

More than a year after the affair became public knowledge Lucy left the Snowdon home in Kensington for what she described as a trial separation. Talking to newspaper reporters on the day after it was revealed she said that all marriages suffer hiccups and this was one of them. She gave no hint as to the reason why she had left, and several newspapers commented that if the revelation about Ann Hills was responsible it had certainly taken a long time – eighteen months – for it to take effect.

No one, apart from those involved, knows whether Lucy was aware of what was going on and was prepared to keep quiet as long as it was kept within the family, or if the newspaper accounts of her husband's relationship with Ann Hills came as a complete shock and she had no alternative but to leave.

Eighteen months later there was further humiliation for Lady Snowdon when it was revealed that Tony had fathered an illegitimate son by a woman thirty-four years younger than him. Melanie Cable-Alexander met Snowdon when she was Features Editor of *Country Life* and he was invited to be a guest editor of the magazine. When the child was born the father's name was left out of the birth certificate, but in September 2000 Lucy Snowdon filed for divorce on the grounds of her husband's adultery. Lord Snowdon later acknowledged his son Jasper, and in 2001 all three were photographed together on a trip to Wales. Miss Cable-Alexander writes articles about being a single parent and even wrote in the *Sunday Times* giving advice to the actress Liz Hurley about bringing up a child on her own. There is no indication that she and Jasper occupy a regular part in Tony's life today, and anyway he was not about to enter the marriage stakes for the third time. He was, and remains, still legally married to Lucy as she has not to date applied for a decree absolute. She lives just around the corner from him, and they see each other constantly. Ask him what the situation is and he replies: 'Of course we are still married.'

SIXTEEN

The Snowdon Children

It says much for Princess Margaret and Lord Snowdon, two of the most volatile people on earth, that their children were brought up in an atmosphere of peace and tranquillity, sharing the love of both parents.

David, Viscount Linley, who is now twelfth in the Line of Succession to the Throne, was born on 3 November 1961 at Clarence House, and christened on 19 December in the Music Room at Buckingham Palace, where he was given the names David Albert Charles. His godparents were: Lady Elizabeth Cavendish, Lord Plunket, Lord Rupert Nevill (Prince Philip's private secretary) and the Revd Simon Phipps. David's sister, Lady Sarah Frances Elizabeth, who is fifteenth in the Line of Succession, was born on 1 May 1964, at Kensington Palace and christened in the Private Chapel at Buckingham Palace, with Lady Penn, Mrs Jane Stevens, Miss Marigold Bridgeman, the Earl of Westmorland and Tony's old friend Anthony Barton acting as godparents.

While it would never be possible for David and Sarah to forget that their aunt was Queen and their grandfather – whom they never knew – was King and Emperor, Tony instilled in them a belief that they would never be able to trade on their royal lineage, and that if they wanted respect from their peers, they would have to earn it. Nothing was going to come to them because of an accident of birth.

The facial resemblance between David Linley and his father is uncanny. They are so alike that, age apart, they could almost be twin brothers. Sarah has her father's smile, but there is no doubt that Princess Margaret was her mother.

Both children were educated at Bedales School in Hampshire before Sarah won a place at Camberwell Art School. Sarah married Daniel Chatto in July 1994, and they provided Lord Snowdon with two grandsons, Sam (born in 1996) and Arthur (born in 1999).

David Linley set up his own business making furniture and is now regarded as one of the leading designers and manufacturers of exclusive furniture in the world. He is married to the Hon. Serena Stanhope, whose father is Viscount Petersham, and they live in south-west London. They also have the tenancy of a charming cottage on the Cotswold estate of Sir Anthony Bamford, the multimillionaire industrialist who inherited a fortune from his father, the founder of the famous JCB earth-moving equipment company, and this is where they spend most weekends. The Linleys have a son and daughter: the Hon. Charles Patrick Inigo Armstrong-Jones, born in 1999, and Margarita Elizabeth Alleyne Armstrong-Jones, born in 2002.

Serena's father is the eldest son and heir of the Earl of Harrington, a well-known and highly respected bloodstock agent and breeder who adopted Irish citizenship in 1965 after selling the family's Elvaston Castle and Derbyshire estate of 4,500 acres. Lord Petersham, who was divorced from his wife, Virginia Freeman-Jackson, in 1983, lives in a magnificent Georgian manor-house in Wiltshire, after moving back to England from his tax haven home in Monaco. Both Serena and her elder brother, William, an estate agent, are believed to have been made financially independent when their father sold part of his property holdings for around £20 million.

Serena's family have been prominent in Anglo-Irish society for generations. The first Earl Stanhope was Lord Lieutenant of Ireland from 1746 to 1751. Her mother was a successful horsewoman, being the youngest member of the Irish team competing at Badminton in 1959, and then crowning her riding career as a member of the team which won the World Cup at Burghley in 1966. Her maternal grandfather, Captain Freeman Jackson, led the Irish Equestrian Team at four consecutive Olympic Games, beginning in Helsinki in 1952, until his final appearance in Rome in 1964. Serena's father also achieved success in the saddle as an amateur, winning the Grand Annual Chase at Cheltenham in 1971. So Serena's pedigree was perfect for a young woman about to be assimilated into the royal family. She enjoys the country pursuits so favoured by the Queen and her family, while at the same time sharing the sophisticated tastes of David, who really prefers life in town.

Another character trait that endears her to her new family is her discretion. In spite of the prominence of her parents in Irish life, the Stanhopes have always insisted on keeping a fairly low profile; ostentation does not figure largely in their make-up. Serena also gets on very well with David's sister, Sarah, and also with his half-sister, Frances, said to be the most retiring of the Snowdon family.

Both David and Sarah are still very close to their father, and when I spoke to David Linley about his relationship with his father, he began by telling me how often they speak. 'If a day goes by without us talking to each other at least two or three times, then something's wrong. We've always been close. There's never been a time when we weren't, and since I've started the business he has been a tremendous help. The backbone really. We enjoy the same things. We both love old cars and motorbikes and share an enthusiasm for architecture and design.' David went on to explain how his father helps him:

He has this incredible eye for detail. When I was starting up he would come down to the workshop and straight away put his finger on what needed doing. He could also look ahead. For example, he told us we needed another kitchen and a separate loo for the ladies. At that time we didn't actually employ any ladies so I didn't see the point, but in time we did and of course we did need the lavatory for them. We try to be fastidious in our quality control and that has all come from him. Nothing is ever too small or insignificant for his attention, and that's something I've learned from him. He was born with a brilliant eye for proportion, and he can make something out of wood without using a set square or any other instrument and somehow it will look right.

David Linley added how both parents had been totally supportive to him and to his sister, Sarah, from the days when they were very young:

As children we were given every opportunity to discuss whatever we felt like with our parents. There were no taboo subjects. They were extremely open with everything; they treated us just like grown-ups ever since we were born. When it came to deciding on where we would go to school it was natural that they said, 'Where do you want to go?' I was more taken with Bedales than with Eton. It was in the countryside, which I preferred, and I knew they concentrated more on the practical aspect of making things than the academic side. My parents told me to give them three good reasons why I should go to Bedales rather than Eton, and I managed to convince them that it would be the best place for me by saying what I've just told you. There was no pressure from either of them and I know that my father had been consistently compared at Eton with his own father and grandfather, so he understood my reasons. We've always had that very good relationship where we could talk about things, anything really.

Sarah joined David at Bedales and enjoyed it as much as he did as she could concentrate on her painting which she loved. As David said: 'When my father came down to the school he was much more interested in seeing what we had made rather than looking at our marks in class.' The choice of Bedales was obviously a good one as David Butcher, the man who taught David woodwork, has remained a friend since he left the school in 1980. 'He treated me like an adult and never patronized me. Whenever we launch a new product these days, he always comes along, and he and my father get on brilliantly.'

Even when David and Sarah were very small children, their father made sure they would appreciate the world around them.

We used to do a lot of driving, and whenever we went out he would always make a lesson out of a game. We played the old observation game, I Spy, but with him if it was a tree he would make us learn what sort of tree it was and tell us about the seasons and that sort of thing. He is still the most observant person I know. And he never gave us any pocket money either. If we wanted a toy he would make it for us. I remember once I wanted a submarine I'd seen in a shop window. He wouldn't buy it but managed to make a model out of bits of wood, a coat hanger and a hook, and it worked perfectly. There's nothing he can't turn his hand to. He used to make wonderful models out of the silver wrapping paper you'd get in a bag of sweets. And he rarely used any machinery; it was all done with his hands.

David Linley has inherited much from his parents. Artistic talent from both sides, a love of classical music from his mother and his looks, dexterity with his hands and obsession with all things mechanical from his father ('We both love gadgets'). He even started out to emulate Lord Snowdon as a photographer, winning the prestigious Vogue-Sothebys Cecil Beaton Award for portrait photography in 1983. But as he says now, comparisons were always being made. 'It was certainly the case when I started doing photography. I was constantly being compared with him. Every time I took a picture that was published the press would inevitably mention me as his son and compare my efforts, usually unfavourably, with his work. As a result my career as a photographer didn't last very long, and I'm now able to do it as a hobby. My first love had always been woodwork anyway; I'm more comfortable with it; it's my world.'
But just because father and son are so close, it doesn't follow that they agree on everything.

Quite often I'll send him a little present I've made, and if he doesn't like it he'll return it with suggestions about how it can be improved. It's a bit of a pain giving him things – he's so hypercritical he'll give them back. And if he comes here and sees an article we've made that doesn't meet with his approval, he always lets me know, but then his criticism is invariably constructive. He cannot let anything pass if he believes it could be better. He also has a way of questioning me that is quite hard-hitting, and I have to accept that. He may be my father – and my closest friend – but when it comes to the business, he's very professional. He's generous to a fault, but as he's done it all before when he started as a photographer, he knows the pitfalls and he doesn't hesitate to tell me if I'm going about something the wrong way.

But Lord Snowdon is justifiably proud of his children and in particular of David's international reputation as a bespoke furniture maker and his undoubted talent with wood. On his desk in his studio is a three-tiered box which David made for him and which he never fails to show visitors.

I asked David Linley how he would describe his father. He did it in two words: 'creative genius'.

One other trait that David has inherited from his father is his sense of style. When Snowdon first appeared on the royal scene forty-five years ago, no one was ever going to miss him; the clothes he dressed in made sure of that. His son has also established a style of his own, with a wardrobe of colourful clothes that might best be described as adventurous. He certainly has an eye for the flamboyant and eye-catching, which is shared by his fashion-conscious wife. Some of the outfits he wears could only be worn by someone who is completely self-confident and uncaring about public opinion. Some people say he has the courage to wear what the rest of us would like to if only we dared. In his personal life, David Linley is secretive, obsessive of his privacy and guarded about revealing anything about his lifestyle or his family. Where his fashion is concerned though, he certainly does not hide his light under a bushel. And he can get away with clothes which on almost anyone else would look ridiculous. What other businessman would walk around London in blue knickerbockers, brocade waistcoats and yellow suede shoes?

And a businessman is what he is above all else. He is constantly on the move; London one day, Los Angeles the next, Tokyo the following week. Wherever there is a chance of selling his very expensive but beautifully crafted furniture, he is there. Not an opportunity is missed; no possible opening is allowed to pass. He once, somewhat ingenuously, remarked, 'I've never sold a piece of furniture because of who I am or because of a press article.' While it is true that he does not deliberately trade upon his famous parents' name and reputation, he would be hard put to deny that being the son of the Queen's only sister has opened many doors for him. But like the children of other equally famous parents he has found that once the door has been opened, you are on your own. And often it can mean that you have to be even better than the average because the expectations of you are that much greater. His ambition is there for all to see, and he has never denied that success is his goal. It's the most important thing, he says. His talent is in his hands but he also has an inherent business sense that has taken him to a position where he is now among the world's leading suppliers of bespoke furniture.

He dislikes talking about money and how much he spends on clothes but the names of the designers he patronizes gives some idea of the cost of his outfits. The younger generation's favourite, Richard James, whose jackets can cost up to £800, has found a welcome in the Linley wardrobe, and his collection of richly embroidered brocade waistcoats is worth several thousand pounds. In another age he might well have been a Regency dandy – the term 'male peacock' could have been coined for him.

While David prefers the casual look during the day, wearing dark, muted colours, soft loafers and rarely a tie, he can, when the occasion demands, appear as conventional and conservative as his cousin the Prince of Wales.

His tailor, Doug Hayward, whose prices start at around £1,000, makes his suits, and he buys the shirts to go with the suits from the royal shirtmakers, Turnbull & Asser, in Jermyn Street. On occasions such as the late Queen Mother's birthday, when he used to join the rest of the royal family at Clarence House, he always dressed formally, out of respect for his grandmother, and looked every inch as royal as the rest of them.

Serena Linley matches her husband's distinctive style, and her wardrobe includes outfits by designers such as Herve Leger, which cost up to £5,000 each. The couple are frequently seen at top society events, often in attention-seeking clothes, yet Serena is no way near the rich man's spoilt child her pedigree and lifestyle might suggest. Those who know her say she is down-to-earth and completely lacking in pretension, with an easy charm that is hard to resist.

She has inherited her father's relaxed easy-going nature and a little of her mother's natural reserve.

David Linley's unique style is reflected not only in the clothes he wears but also in just about every aspect of his lifestyle. Every item of furniture in the home he shares with his wife, Serena, has been chosen to blend in with its surroundings. He will sometimes wait months, leaving an empty space in a room, until he finds the right piece. He instinctively knows what goes where, and he is genuinely offended if an article appears to be out of place. He is also fortunate enough to have enough money to indulge himself and to add to his collection of classic cars and motorcycles. His father gave him the Aston Martin that once belonged to Peter Sellers (it has since been sold), and he has restored an old Morris Minor convertible to its original condition – at the same time converting the engine to take unleaded fuel – and now puts its value at over £13,000. He also collects old road fund discs, and on one of his forays he discovered one that had belonged to a Triumph 500 motorcycle, once owned by his father. He traced the current owner, who had stored the bike in a garage for many years, persuaded him to part with it and after cleaning it up and replacing a few parts, decided to make it the centrepiece for his extended showroom – another example of his artistic talent blending with his commercial instincts, with a touch of showbusiness thrown in for good measure.

David Linley does not undertake any public engagements on behalf of the royal family, which some people think is a pity as he would undoubtedly add an extra dimension to the dreary round of formal openings and obligatory attendances. His quiet, self-deprecating sense of humour disguises a ready wit and, surprisingly, an innate shyness. Before he was married, his image was of a frivolous, upper-class twit who dumped girlfriends with the abandon of a modern-day Casanova and loved nothing more than all-night parties in the company of acquaintances of a similar disposition and class. Today nothing could be further from the truth, if it ever was. He once successfully sued a newspaper for saying he had been banned from a pub for loutish behaviour, and for much of his adult life he has had to fight off the inaccurate descriptions of him as a Hooray Henry.

He is serious, without being dull, intent on creating a successful international business, and is a devoted husband. He is naturally suspicious of newcomers, as are all members of the royal family. And their distance from their more newsworthy cousins has not deflected any interest in them in the slightest.

The media has always been fascinated by David Linley. Since he was a child he has lived in the glare of press attention and provided dozens of entertaining pictures and columns with his galaxy of society girlfriends before he settled down. David is clearly a thoughtful and creative man who cannot stand still. He finds it difficult to explain what motivates him; what it is that forces him to work so hard. Perhaps it is the fact that it was suggested that because of his background he would never have to push; everything would come easy. But he was always going to have to work. Unlike his royal cousins, Charles, Andrew and Edward, there was never going to be a predestined career of public duties.

His wife might be the heiress to millions eventually, but David does not have quite the same expectations, even though he is believed to have benefited from his mother's will and has a worth estimated to be well into seven figures. And while he plainly enjoys many of the advantages of the rich and famous because of his royal pedigree, he obviously feels the need to achieve success on his own. He also wants to be able to pay for the good things in life himself. He has expensive tastes, but with a couple of profitable property deals under his belt already – he has recently completed the purchase of a flat in Chelsea for over £1 million – his bank manager is surely happy to see him these days.

His father is justifiably proud of what David has done so far and believes he will go even further. Still only in his forties, he relishes the opportunities and challenges ahead. At the time of writing, he is planning to open a branch of his business in New York. He may not be entirely a self-made man, but he is certainly the nearest thing there is to it in the most famous family in the land.

For someone of royal birth, blending into the background and not being noticed in a crowd is a rare occurrence. Almost every member of the royal family, even those on the fringe, are used to being subjected to the scrutiny of public and press from early childhood. They become hardened to being the focus of attention, accepting it as part of the job, even if they never learn to like it. Some, like the Prince of Wales, come to accept it and even expect it. He would find it very disconcerting if he wasn't followed by a host of photographers and reporters on any public engagement, and he employs a dedicated press office to make sure of it.

Lord Snowdon's elder daughter, Lady Sarah Chatto, is arguably the most unspoilt of her generation of royals, and also one of the strongest. When her parents split up, she remained close to her father but never lost her love for her mother and provided staunch support in the immediate aftermath of the divorce when Princess Margaret was being severely criticized for her lavish lifestyle and unfortunate relationships.

When Princess Margaret made her famous – and probably well-meant – remark about her children not being royal, 'They just happen to have an aunt who is the Queen', she was laughed at by those who believed she was being ridiculously naive in trying to distance her children from the inner circle of royalty. What she was trying to do was explain that they would never be part of the inner circle of royals who do not have to seek outside careers because of their public duties. She was also anxious to provide Sarah and David with a life that was completely different from her own and her sister's; in other words, something that could be considered to be as normal as is possible under the unique circumstances of their birth. Neither Sarah nor David believes that they could ever fully escape the attention their rank and famous parents attract; neither do they try to shirk the responsibilities involved with being so closely related to the Queen. They are aware that their behaviour is likely to reflect on the royal family, so each has been careful not to allow themselves to be compromised. On occasions such as the Queen Mother's birthday, they always made sure they were present at Clarence House for the duty photo call, and if the Queen requires their presence at a Buckingham Palace function, as occasionally happens, her niece and nephew never fail to attend.

But Sarah and David have proved it is possible to live a normal life, and at the same time enjoy some of the advantages of being minor royals. They both enjoy a level of independence that in their mother's day would have been unthinkable and which their cousins, Prince William and Prince Harry, will never be able to have. Sarah was only 14 when her parents divorced. It was a traumatic experience for one at such a formative period in her young life, but one which friends claim laid the foundation for the sensible and unflappable character she displays today. When she left school and started her career as an artist, she went first to art school and then to the Royal Academy, proving herself to be an accomplished and talented painter.

Her capacity for getting down to hard work is attested to by film producer John Brabourne, husband of Countess Mountbatten of Burma, who once gave her a temporary job as a wardrobe assistant on the set of *A Passage to India*. Her father had made the introduction, but after that she was on her own. Brabourne said:

There was no favouritism because of who she was, and she didn't expect any. She is such a natural person she can mix with all types. The crew found her to be delightful, and what's more she earned her money. The conditions weren't ideal, with a very hot, humid climate and so on, but they didn't seem to bother her too much. She certainly was not a passenger. The film business is so competitive these days that there is no room for carrying anyone who doesn't earn their keep.

Leaving Kensington Palace, Sarah chose to live on her own in a London flat before she married, and quickly established her own identity. While she remained close to relations of her own age, like the Duke of Kent's daughter, Lady Helen Windsor (now Lady Helen Taylor), she also branched out and made many friends from all levels of society, whom she met at college. She could be seen riding her bike around London, doing her own shopping and generally acting like any other young woman – who was not in the direct line of succession to the throne.

It was because she was so unaffected and natural that she became close to the late Diana, Princess of Wales, who asked her to be godmother to Harry. Diana, who as previously stated, felt a close affinity with Lord Snowdon, liked Sarah enormously and often asked her to lunch where they would talk about the latest fashions and who was going out with whom. Sarah had a number of casual boyfriends, but none was regarded as being the one until she met Daniel Chatto, the man she was to marry.

Daniel, educated at Westminster and Oxford, also came from a broken home, and when they first met it may not have been love at first sight, but there was an immediate attraction. Sarah was in India with her father, who was working as production stills photographer on the movie *Heat and Dust*, and Daniel was acting in the film. The relationship developed cautiously, with holidays abroad taken together and Daniel being introduced to Sarah's royal relations gradually. Eventually after several years together, they decided to get married, and the Queen gave her consent, as she had to under the Royal Marriages Act of 1772, which states that those in the direct line of succession must receive permission to marry from the Sovereign. If that permission had been withheld, the couple would have had to petition parliament in order to reverse the Sovereign's decision. However, all was well, and the wedding was arranged.

Because Snowdon's elder daughter, Lady Sarah Armstrong-Jones, had enjoyed a three-year relationship with the man she was to marry, and because their lifestyle was considered to be bohemian, it was expected that their wedding would also be alternative. However, when the time came, the day turned out to be totally conventional and a genuine family wedding. In sharp contrast to her mother's wedding, when 2,000 guests crowded into Westminster Abbey, Sarah and her fiancé, Daniel Chatto, chose an intimate seventeenth-century church, St Stephen Walbrook in the City of London, and invited just 200 of their close family and friends.

The wedding may have been modest in comparison with other royal nuptials but it lacked nothing in style and preparation. The bride's grandmother, Queen Elizabeth The Queen Mother, looking as elegant as ever in an ivory silk Hartnell outfit, arrived on the arm of

Prince Charles, while his estranged wife, the late Diana, Princess of Wales, turned up wearing a navy-blue coat-dress designed for her by Catherine Walker, and sat on the other side of the Queen Mother. The royal family attended in strength, with the Queen wearing a summery floral-print dress, which she had been seen wearing at celebrations to mark the fiftieth anniversary of D-Day. Prince Philip accompanied her in his summer-weight grey morning coat, while some of the younger members of the family made fashion statements of their own.

Lady Sarah's sister-in-law, Viscountess Linley, nearly stole the scene with her eye-catching black hat by leading milliner Philip Treacy, while Lady Helen Taylor wore an Indian hand-finished dress with a crocheted hat by Giorgio Armani. Prince Edward brought his then girlfriend, Sophie Rhys-Jones (now his wife, the Countess of Wessex), and the theatre was also well represented by the actress Felicity Kendal, playwright Tom Stoppard and the actor Paul Scofield, who performed a reading during the ceremony.

A crowd 500-strong waited outside the church as the bride arrived, dead on time. Her groom had already been waiting over an hour, having turned up before anyone else so that he could greet personally all the guests as they arrived. Sarah's wedding dress of white silk georgette had been designed by Jasper Conran, and as is the case with all royal brides she wore her veil back from the crown of the head. Ancient royal custom has it that brides must always reveal their faces to the groom to make sure the right woman is being married!

Tradition was also maintained with the old practice of the bride wearing something old, something new, something borrowed, something blue. Sarah wouldn't tell what three of those were, but she did admit that when it came to something borrowed she wore a pair of her mother's favourite earrings, each with a large pearl held in place by two lines of diamonds.

She was attended by her half-sister, 14-year-old Lady Frances Armstrong-Jones, the Princess Royal's 13-year-old daughter, Zara Phillips, and a family friend, Tara Noble Singh.

Sarah and Daniel took their vows in front of one of the most un-usual altars in London, a large round piece of marble sculpted by

Henry Moore, and in keeping with most modern marriages, the bride did not promise to obey her husband, as her mother had in 1960. The couple had deliberately chosen a brief service with just three short hymns, sung by the choral group Polyphony, and in a little over half an hour they emerged from the church. In fact they were so early that their cars were not ready for them, and for once royalty was kept waiting on the steps. There was a minor jockeying for position as members of the royal family tried to find their particular vehicles, but they were all in a good mood and nothing was allowed to spoil the occasion. Even the Queen and Prince Philip joined in as they looked for their Jaguar car to arrive; they had decided not to use one of the official Rolls-Royce limousines in keeping with the bride's request for simplicity. Lord Snowdon and his ex-wife Princess Margaret talked to each other in a friendly manner as they waited and they were both delighted to acknowledge the cheers of the crowd.

Finally, the transport situation resolved itself, and they all drove off to Clarence House for the reception; except for Princess Diana, who had decided, in the interests of diplomacy, not to attend the wedding breakfast. She returned to Kensington Palace alone. Coaches brought the rest of the guests to Clarence House where a marquee had been erected on the front lawn and where an outside catering firm was waiting to serve champagne and canapés.

The wedding service and the reception that followed were both simple, dignified and exactly what the couple and their parents had wanted. It had been a splendid day with three generations of royalty enjoying what for them was a rare royal occasion, a genuine family occasion in a magnificent setting. There was to be no Royal Yacht for a honeymoon. Sarah and Daniel left London's Heathrow Airport on a scheduled flight that evening to fly to India, the country where they had first met all those years earlier. It was a romantic ending to a glamorous occasion, and no one was prouder than Lord Snowdon as he waved goodbye to his daughter and new son-in-law.

Throughout their lives, and particularly when they were younger, Lord Snowdon has always been extremely careful to protect his children from gossip and from the unwanted glare of media publicity. In this he was fully supported by Princess Margaret and, later, by his second wife, Lucy, when their daughter, Frances, was born in 1979. In fact, Frances has been kept out of the limelight far more than either David or Sarah. Lord Snowdon would be happy if none of his children or grandchildren ever appeared in the press, but naturally because of who their parents and grandparents are this is not going to be practical. Anyone even remotely connected with royalty is newsworthy, and the Armstrong-Joneses are closer than most. Indeed, when Sarah celebrated her 40th birthday in May 2004, Prince Charles gave her a surprise party and the Queen was among the royal guests.

If David and Sarah have one disappointment in their lives it is that their mother did not find lasting happiness after the bitterness of the divorce. They would have loved Princess Margaret to have been able to spend the latter years of her life with someone who really cared for her. But it wasn't to be. Princess Margaret and Lord Snowdon may have made a mess of their marriage, but no one could doubt that they achieved enormous success in raising their children.

Similarly, Tony and Lucy have had their problems, but none involves their daughter Frances. She is a credit to them both, and they share a deep affection for the young woman who has made them very proud parents. Lady Frances Armstrong-Jones is a vivacious, beautiful brunette with a dazzling smile and a friendliness that disguises her innate shyness.

Frances was born prematurely at midnight on 17 July 1979 and christened three months later, being given the courtesy title of 'Lady' as the daughter of an earl. She came as a delightful surprise to the couple, as Lucy, whose previous marriage had been childless, thought she was unable to bear children. She immediately displayed her maternal instincts even though the infant had a part-time nanny during the daytime. The nanny also helped to look after Lord Frederick Windsor, the son of Prince and Princess Michael of Kent.

Lucy was a hands-on mother. She doted on her baby daughter and, apart from the daytime help, there was no way she was going to hand over the responsibility of bringing up her child to another woman. Tony was equally besotted and so, too, were David and Sarah. They willingly accepted Frances into their family, and the three have grown to love one another even more the older they become.

Frances is artistic through and through. She spent several years living in Paris, where she worked in fashion and photography, and she has now returned to live in London. She spends a great deal of time with her parents, and when she sees her father, even though she lives just upstairs, she throws her arms around him and kisses him on both cheeks, even if she is just going out for lunch. They are both unashamedly demonstrative and love each other's company. Frances and Sarah are tremendously close, have a lot in common and couldn't be closer if they had the same mother and father and were not just half-sisters.

Tony is clearly delighted that all his children get on so well. He is still obsessively protective of them, particularly where the media is concerned. He hates answering questions about them and especially about Frances. He accepts that David and Sarah will always be targets because of who their mother was and their current place in the Line of Succession to the Throne, but with Frances it is a different matter. She is a private person with no royal connections, apart from her father being a former member of the royal family by marriage. So he sees no reason why she should be subjected to the attention of the press. Of course, it is never going to go away, and the moment she is seen with a young man or announces her engagement, it will make news. But so far he and Lucy have been successful in shielding her from the worst excesses of the tabloids and will continue to do so as long as they are able.

SEVENTEEN

Tony Today

Princess Margaret suffered years of emotional insecurity and never found the companion she had been looking for to see her comfortably into old age. Friends who knew her for most of her life said she was suffering a terminal case of marital disillusion. And as her health deteriorated, many of the little luxuries she had for so long taken for granted were denied her because of her failing health.

Tony Snowdon has been much more fortunate; a brilliant career that shows no signs of waning, children who adore him and, apart from the pain that is a legacy from his childhood polio, comparatively good health. In December 2003 he was fitted with a pacemaker to regulate his heartbeat, but says he feels no ill-effects of the operation. Certainly, it does not appear to have slowed him down too significantly.

Now in his mid-seventies, inevitably some of his oldest and closest friends have died. He is one of the few survivors of that winning 1950 Cambridge Boat Race crew, and naturally that causes him a certain amount of sadness. As he remarked: 'I seem to be going to too many funerals and memorial services lately.' But he is not in the least bit morbid about the fact that the years are catching up on him. He still enjoys a wide circle of friends and acquaintances with whom he socializes regularly, even if most of them do not date back to his youth. He lives alone, apart from his daughter Frances on the top floor, in a magnificent Regency house that is the epitome of deeply traditional elegance, and of which he says, 'I would hate to live in a modern house.'

He is still a welcome guest at Buckingham Palace and many other great houses. In the old days he would have been severely criticized after the divorce from Princess Margaret and even more so following the birth of his illegitimate child. But he has handled himself with such dignity and self-deprecating good humour that he appears to be able to do no wrong. So with all that he has going for him, is he a fulfilled man? One of his oldest friends, Quentin Crewe, who died in 1998, believed not. 'I don't think he knows quite what it is he is looking for, but he suspects there is something more and he is looking for it – and will go on doing so. He is still looking.'

Crewe, along with Jeremy Fry, was a close companion for over forty years. In that time, Crewe and Snowdon between them had five wives, four divorces, numerous lovers and nine children. To say they led interesting and eventful lives might be something of an understatement.

Crewe, whose mother, Lady Annabel, was the daughter of the Marquess of Crewe, was a distinguished author and journalist who was diagnosed as suffering from muscular dystrophy when he was just 6 years old. The condition developed over the years, and he was confined to a wheelchair for the last forty-odd years of his life. Not that this in any way prevented him carrying on his trade as one of the world's leading travel writers and restaurant critics, or stopped him from indulging his passion for travel. He undertook journeys to some of the most inhospitable regions in the world, once taking a year and a half to travel throughout the Sahara Desert. Even in his seventies, when he needed someone to help him with most everyday tasks, including dressing and eating, he was always planning on what to do next.

He shared with Tony Snowdon an insatiable curiosity, the quality of being totally honest, and the more dubious characteristic of enjoying jokes at other people's expense. They first met when both were employed by *Queen* magazine shortly before Tony married Princess Margaret. They struck up an immediate rapport. Quentin Crewe was then married to his second wife, the novelist Angela Huth, who became, and remained, one of Princess Margaret's dearest and most loyal friends. They were guests at the royal wedding of the decade in Westminster Abbey, and when Princess Margaret and her husband took up residence in Kensington Palace,

Quentin and Angela were frequent visitors. 'We used to go for dinner when Tony was a splendid host, very generous and considerate and treating me in exactly the same way as he had before he joined the royal family. I would have expected no less of him. Even though it is obviously ridiculous to claim that he hasn't changed in all the years I've known him, because we all do, his attitude to me and his other friends from those days hasn't altered. Or if it has, I haven't noticed.'

Throughout his years as a journalist Quentin Crewe became adept at summing up people, and his keen eye for detail and, perhaps, the very fact that he was confined to a wheelchair meant he was able to look behind the barricades many of us erect. I asked him for his opinion of Tony Snowdon, both as a photographer and as a person. He was unequivocal about Tony the professional: 'I think he is a very good photographer, one of the best, without any qualification.' On the question of Tony as a man he made a perceptive observation: 'Tony expects a great deal from people. He can be very demanding, very impatient at times, and I think it is sometimes difficult to be a complete professional anything, photographer, writer or whatever, and also a nice person. That doesn't mean I don't like him because I do, very much, and there is nothing I couldn't ask him or talk to him about.' Someone else who has known Tony for many years is Andrew Parker Bowles. He says 'Tony is a nice guy but he can be prickly on occasions!'

Another long-term friend, the late David Hicks, described Lord Snowdon as, 'one of the nicest people I know, gentle with a huge sense of fun, but he can appear to be cruel. He likes to be cutting about some people, either to their face, or more usually once they have gone because he is not the sort of person to hurt anyone deliberately. He is very witty, but his wit can be acerbic; it is often at the expense of someone else. It's not that he sets out to be deliberately unkind to anyone – that's not his style at all – it's just that he sees the weak spots in some people and can't avoid homing in on them.'

However, Hicks said Snowdon would go out of his way to be kind to his photographic subjects: 'Nothing is too much trouble. He came to photograph Pammie [Hicks's wife] and me, and I have this complaint which has caused an unsightly swelling on my neck. Tony said, "We'll have to do something about that." So he dressed me in an elegant silk dressing gown – à la Noel Coward – and tied a loose cravat around my neck, so disguising the swelling. It was very considerate of him, and the resulting picture is very flattering, taken in profile. He said all we needed to complete the picture was a nightcap – the sort you wear, not drink – but I didn't have one unfortunately.'

Another friend who has known him most of his adult life claims Tony is a pragmatist: 'He adapted to life as a royal with chameleon-like perfection when that appeared to be where his interest lay and then, when that failed, he mastered the role of being an ex-royal celebrity, which has also served him well.'

As he settles into the final quarter of his life, he retains an enormous enthusiasm for a diversity of projects. And he says there are still many personalities he would like to photograph – or would have if they were still alive. 'I met Frank Sinatra a couple of times but never got to photograph him, which was a pity as I think it would have been interesting. In fact his whole crowd would have made fascinating subjects. I knew Sammy Davis Junior quite well and liked him a lot. He once gave me a tiny camera, which I still have.'

Lord Snowdon is passionate about many things, his work, the plight of disabled people, the attitude of the country towards the underprivileged, the state of the streets around his London home. He is also an avid gardener who grew up in one of the most beautiful homes in Britain surrounded by hundreds of acres of landscaped grounds. Nymans, bought by his great-grandfather, Ludwig Messel, in 1890, has, in its 601 acres, a 30-acre showpiece garden which today attracts over 100,000 visitors every year. When Lord Snowdon's grandfather, Colonel Leonard Messel, died in 1954, he left the house and grounds to the National Trust on condition that his daughter, the Countess of Rosse, Lord Snowdon's mother, could live there until her death. She died, at the age of 90, in 1992, and since then the house has been open to the public.

Lord Snowdon remembers with great affection the days he spent as a child at Nymans, and one of the saddest moments of his life occurred in 1987 when the Great Storm caused utter devastation to the grounds. After nearly a hundred years, the garden was completely destroyed in just one night. Unfortunately, 80 per cent of the trees, including rare Japanese wisterias and the great monkey puzzle tree at the front of the house, were uprooted and thrown all over the grounds.

The Trust immediately set about restoring the garden, which involved replacing more than 1,500 trees and shrubs. The whole process took ten years to complete, and photographs from a 1932 copy of *Country Life* were used to ensure accuracy in re-creating the beautiful Rose Garden and Courtyard Garden. The gardeners took cuttings from fallen trees and planted them on the very spots where the original trees had stood. It was painstaking work, but eventually the project was finished, and Lord Snowdon, who had been closely involved in planning the restoration, was invited to a ceremony to mark the reopening. He said he was delighted with the result, which meant a new lease of life for the garden and house. For him it meant a return to his childhood haunts, 'where I had a tree-house high up in a beech tree'.

Strolling through the gardens, he also recalled holidays from Eton during the Second World War, when Nymans housed twenty evacuees from London's East End. 'It was wonderful for me,' he said, 'suddenly to have so many companions. I wonder what they are all doing now.' Perhaps one of the saddest moments for Snowdon was when he decided to relinquish the lease he had on Old House, the cottage in the grounds of Nymans he had spent months renovating – and which Princess Margaret hated. As he no longer drives himself, and he has given up his car, the thought of having to rely on someone else to get him to West Sussex at weekends was too much. So the much loved retreat had to go. The house was sold for more than £1 million in 2002, and the contents, including a George II desk, a James I armchair and a Charles I oak tester bed, raised over £190,000 when auctioned at Sotheby's. One item not included in the sale, however, was a special plate commissioned by Lucy to mark Tony's sixtieth birthday. Bearing the legend '60 Glorious Years', it shows him in the guise of Queen Victoria.

The Oscar-winning actor Sir Anthony Hopkins has known Lord Snowdon for years, since Snowdon first photographed him during the making of his film *The Elephant Man*. 'The make-up was fantastic, and Tony became very enthusiastic about the possibilities. That was the first occasion we met and much later he also photographed me at the National Theatre in *King Lear*. He has a genuine eye for the theatrical, which few other photographers possess. He's always interested in the context of the picture, the whole story, and not just the subject itself, which I find very reassuring.'

The last memorable occasion when the two met was over five years ago at a party to celebrate Hopkins's sixtieth birthday – described by Sir Anthony as 'a real gathering of the Welsh clan as Harry Secombe, Tony and I got together'. Lady Secombe recalls saying to Snowdon how well he was looking and how slim. He replied by showing her the label inside his jacket and asking her to read the date. It was 1969. 'Not bad to be able to wear something nearly thirty years old,' said Snowdon.

Sir Anthony said: 'Tony is one of the easiest people to get along with – there's no trading on his position as a former member of the royal family. As a matter of fact it's difficult to remember sometimes just how close to the royal family he is.' Sir Anthony joined Sir Harry Secombe and Lord Snowdon in Caernarvon Castle in 1994, when they celebrated the twenty-fifth anniversary of the Investiture of the Prince of Wales. Unfortunately, now that he lives permanently in the USA, they no longer see each other as often as they used to, but they still keep in touch.

Graham Stark says he admires the way in which Tony Snowdon has managed to live his life in the full glare of public and media attention without losing his independence or good humour.

When you live your life in a goldfish bowl, it places you in a very vulnerable position. And when you become part of royalty it's even more difficult. Tony was brilliant at warding off questions about the royal family. In all the years I've known him, he has never once been indiscreet about the Queen or any other member of the royal family. He was extremely guarded whenever the subject looked like cropping up and always steered you away in the nicest possible way. He did this without being offensive, but he left you in no doubt that he wasn't going to be manipulated into saying something he might regret later. And let's face it, he could just as easily have sat back and enjoyed the privileges of royalty without any of the responsibilities. No one forced him to go back to work; it was his decision alone. He wasn't prepared to 'ponce' off society like some others I could name.

Tony Snowdon is at heart a romantic. He has loved, and been loved by, many women, the most famous, of course, being Princess Margaret. And apart from any physical attraction there may have been between him and his legion of female conquests, he also has a great liking for women. He enjoys their company and, in turn, they seem to like being with him. On the whole, he has been fortunate in his relationships, and most of his women companions have had nothing but good to say of the time they spent together. Melanie Cable-Alexander, with whom he had his last serious affair and which resulted in the birth of his second son, Jasper, did make a few not altogether complimentary remarks about Tony when they split up, but generally speaking his girlfriends have been the soul of discretion, both during and after the liaisons.

Everyone who meets him, men and women alike, are agreed on one thing: Snowdon has charm by the bucketful; it simply oozes out of him. He cannot help but be charming, to waiters in restaurants, the postman who delivers his mail, even newspaper reporters who arrive to interview him, determined to get him to reveal some indiscretion about his former royal in-laws. They are never successful, but they all leave mesmerized by his immense charm, which, coupled with an air of vulnerability, combines to make him as attractive today as he was when he first arrived on the royal scene. Whatever his secret is, if he could bottle it, he would be a multimillionaire.

During the reform of the House of Lords in 1999, the first Earl of Snowdon surprised a great many people when he accepted a life peerage from the Labour government. It was expected that, as with every other member of the royal family who was entitled to sit in the

Lords, he would politely decline the offer. He explained why he accepted: 'I didn't know whether to accept it, but they [the Queen and Tony Blair] said it would be rude not to.' Also the life peerage gives him the continued opportunity to use the House of Lords as a platform from which to air his views about the problems of disability. He retains his hereditary earldom, which will eventually pass to his son, David, but David will not inherit the right to sit in the House of Lords. That privilege dies with the death of the recipient.

Tony rarely uses the social facilities of the Lords these days, preferring to dine with friends and family in a small number of favourite restaurants. He likes few things better than a long, leisurely meal combined with plenty of good wine and sparkling company. And he gives the impression that he is enjoying life as much today as ever, in spite of the effects of polio that have recurred in recent years.

EIGHTEEN

Two Royal Deaths

Princess Margaret died in her sleep on Saturday 9 February 2002. Her two children David and Sarah were by her side. She had suffered a massive stroke at home in Kensington Palace and never recovered. Buckingham Palace issued the following statement:

The Queen, with great sadness, has asked for the following announcement to be made immediately. Her beloved sister, Princess Margaret, died peacefully in her sleep this morning at 6.30 a.m. in the King Edward VII Hospital. Her children, Viscount Linley and Lady Sarah Chatto, were at her side.

Princess Margaret had suffered another stroke during the evening before she died and, as her condition worsened, her doctors called an ambulance to take her to the hospital at 2.30 in the morning. They knew that little could be done for her at this stage, and her two children stayed at her bedside until the end. Princess Margaret had also had two previous strokes in recent years. In February 1998 she suffered what was described as a 'mild stroke' while on holiday at her home on the island of Mustique and was flown back to the United Kingdom for treatment.

Dubbed the 'royal rebel', Margaret was 71 when she died, though she had virtually retired from public life many years before and her days at the centre of the decade's glamorous social scene of the fifties and sixties were long gone. Onlookers were shocked when she appeared with other members of the royal family at Clarence House on the occasion of the Queen Mother's 101st birthday on 4 August 2001. Margaret was being pushed in a wheelchair by William

Tallon, Queen Elizabeth's famous page, known affectionately as 'Backstairs Billy'; her face was badly puffed although partly hidden by heavy sunglasses, and her left arm was in a sling. William was heavily criticized for allowing her to be seen in that condition, but as he later said, 'Do you think I would have dared to push her as I did unless I had been ordered to do so.' It was one of the last times she was seen in public and not one she would have wished to be remembered for. Her appearance came as a shock to everyone, especially to those who had last seen her only two months earlier when she attended Prince Philip's eightieth birthday celebrations at Windsor Castle. She had been determined to be present at both the service in St George's Chapel and the reception that followed in St George's Hall.

The Princess also insisted on attending the 100th birthday party of her only surviving aunt, Princess Alice, Duchess of Gloucester in December. The actual birthday was not until Christmas Day (a birthday she shared with Princess Alexandra), but the party was held two weeks earlier on 12 December in Kensington Palace (Princess Alice died aged 102 in October 2004). The following week Margaret and her mother were flown by helicopter to Sandringham to spend the Christmas holidays with the Queen. The Princess returned alone to London on 6 January as she had several engagements in her diary. Being confined to a wheelchair did not mean she intended to spend her days isolated in her apartment at Kensington Palace. She went to see the new British Galleries at the Victoria and Albert Museum, where other visitors described her as being 'remarkably cheerful'. Then on 5 February came her final outing, and one she would not have missed if they had had to carry her there on a stretcher. It was the third birthday party of her and Lord Snowdon's grandson, Arthur Chatto, where, again, she appeared to be in good spirits. Three days later she was dead. As soon as her death had been confirmed by the doctors at the hospital, David Linley informed the Queen at Sandringham and then telephoned his father to give him the sad news. Prince Philip gently broke the news to the Queen Mother. The royal communications machine then swung into action, with Prince Charles, who was staying with his friends the Duke and Duchess of Devonshire at Chatsworth in Derbyshire, being next on the list. The Prince immediately left for Sandringham to comfort his grandmother, while the Queen cut short her New Year's holiday in Norfolk to travel straight to Windsor. The 101-year-old Queen Mother, who had a chest cold, remained at Sandringham. The Prime Minister, Tony Blair, was en route to Sierra Leone when he was given the news. Speaking from his aircraft he said: 'I am deeply saddened to hear of the death of Princess Margaret. My thoughts are with the Queen, Queen Elizabeth The Queen Mother and the rest of the royal family at this time.'

Princess Margaret had left instructions about who was to be informed of her death and the order of precedence. First was to be the Queen, followed by her mother, then her ex-husband. As it happened, it was Prince Philip who was asked by the Queen to tell her mother in person, and Lord Linley made a private telephone call to his father.

For Lord Snowdon, the news did not come as a surprise. He had been kept informed of his former wife's condition ever since her first stroke four years earlier. So he knew when she was admitted to King Edward VII's Hospital for Officers (known locally as Sister Agnes's), she was near the end. In the latter days of her life they had become closer than they had been for decades, exchanging Christmas and New Year's cards and gifts. Any ill feeling there might have been twenty years earlier had long disappeared. They were comfortable with each other, and he took no pleasure in seeing her lose her looks and her health, while he remained comparatively healthy and youthful looking.

Among the royal household, where gossip is always rife, there were even rumours that they might get back together in her final years. While the Queen Mother would probably have welcomed the idea, there was never any realistic prospect of it coming true, but it made a fascinating talking point below stairs at the Palace.

Princess Margaret's coffin, draped in her personal standard, was taken back to Kensington Palace, where it was placed in her bedroom and where Lord Snowdon paid his personal respects.

One could only imagine his thoughts as he stood there alone in the home he had shared for eighteen years with the woman whose body now lay in an oak coffin.

Later the Princess was transferred to St James's Palace where she rested in the Queen's Chapel at Marlborough House, the church where, in December 1999, she had witnessed the christening of her youngest grandson, Charles Armstrong-Jones.

The day of Princess Margaret's funeral, Friday 16 February 2002, was doubly painful for Queen Elizabeth The Queen Mother. Not only was she suffering the worst bereavement any parent can endure, that their child should die before them, but the funeral took place exactly fifty years to the day after her husband, King George VI, had been buried. That service also took place in St George's Chapel at Windsor Castle, but Princess Margaret's funeral was without any of the pomp and ceremony that had accompanied His Majesty's interment. The King, of course, had been accorded a full State funeral, after lying in state at Westminster Hall for four days so that his people could file past. His younger daughter, by contrast, had given specific instructions that she wanted no fuss, just a simple funeral attended by family and close friends. Eventually some 400 of these, including representatives of her many organizations, were invited to the funeral service. Outside Windsor Castle over 3,000 mourners waited silently to see the funeral procession.

The Queen Mother, at 101, was not really fit enough to attend, having been confined to her room at Sandringham for almost two months with a severe cold, but despite her frailty, she insisted that she would say her final farewells, even submitting to a 45-minute helicopter flight from Norfolk to be there. And as Princess Margaret was brought into St George's Chapel for the last time, a simple wreath of pink tulips and white roses from her mother was seen resting on her coffin.

Lord Snowdon was not involved in the practical arrangements for the funeral, which were all handled by the Palace in conjunction with Princess Margaret's children, but he was kept aware of what was happening throughout and the form the funeral service would take. As an ex-husband, there was no specific role for him, which he was fully aware of, of course, but both the Queen and the Queen Mother, knowing his feelings, felt it perfectly natural to include him. As he entered St George's Chapel to say goodbye to his former wife, no one seeing the sadness deeply etched on his face could doubt the effect her death had had on him.

After the service, the chief mourners, Viscount Linley and his sister Lady Sarah Chatto, together with their spouses, walked slowly behind the Princess's coffin as it was placed into the hearse for its final short journey to Slough Municipal Crematorium. Behind them came the Queen and Prince Philip with the other members of the royal family but not the Queen Mother, who was too frail to negotiate the steep steps outside the West Door of St George's. She left quietly through a side door.

In a major break with royal tradition, Princess Margaret had left instructions that her body was to be cremated and not interred in the royal burial ground at Frogmore. There hadn't been a royal cremation since December 1939, when Princess Louise, a daughter of Queen Victoria, had been cremated. One of Margaret's oldest friends and a former lady-in-waiting, Lady Glenconner, whose husband had given Princess Margaret the land on Mustique where she built her famous holiday home, said that Margaret preferred cremation to burial because she found Frogmore to be too 'gloomy'. Another reason, and perhaps the real one, was that she wanted to be placed near her beloved father in the royal vault at St George's Chapel and she realized there simply was not enough room for her. However, there was room for her ashes, and following the cremation that is what happened. The urn was carried, without ceremony, back to St George's where it was placed alongside her father's tomb.

Lord Snowdon had known all along that his ex-wife wanted to be cremated, and he was in full agreement with the arrangement. It was practical, inexpensive and could be carried out with the minimum of fuss, something of which he was bound to approve.

Throughout her life, Princess Margaret had enjoyed the best of everything that money could buy. She unashamedly wallowed in luxury – clothes, food, wine and holidays. She was never interested in the price of anything because she had never had to be. If she wanted something, it was provided. Friends fought to bestow expensive gifts on her, and throughout Britain the best doors in the land were always open to her. She accepted it all as her right. Yet her funeral could not have been more simple – or less expensive. The cremation cost the standard fee of £280 and was one of six carried out on the same day. Neither the Queen nor any other member of the royal family attended the cremation – again at the wishes of the Princess – and apart from David Linley and his wife Serena, and Lady Sarah Chatto and her husband Daniel, the only witnesses were former members of her household and representatives of the Lord Chamberlain's Office at Buckingham Palace.

For Lord Snowdon it had been a traumatic day, physically demanding and emotionally draining. His children had been his strength. But in a few short weeks another event was to occur that would bring more grief and sadness, not only to him but to the entire nation.

The Queen Mother's death was, of course, not unexpected. She was, after all, 101 years old. But to many people she was indestructible. They thought she would go on for ever. But her health had been fading for months, and the death of her younger daughter Princess Margaret caused her the deepest sadness any mother can be asked to bear.

Just seven weeks after Princess Margaret died, Queen Elizabeth was staying at Royal Lodge in Windsor Great Park, the weekend home she had occupied for over half a century. Physically, she was obviously failing and getting very frail. Yet until the final hours she remained mentally alert, and just a fortnight before she died she watched the racing from Cheltenham on television. On the evening before she died, she became weaker and one of her ladies-in-waiting, the Hon. Margaret Rhodes, who also happened to be her niece – her mother, Lady Mary Bowes-Lyon, was the elder sister of the Queen Mother – called the doctors. Mrs Rhodes said later: 'It was clear she was going to die. The Queen was out riding. She was called. She came at once. In the morning I rang our local clergyman who came before she died and said some prayers. . . . It was wonderfully peaceful.' Then the Queen returned after changing out of her riding clothes, and both Sarah Chatto and David Linley were there at the end. As Mrs Rhodes explained about the actual moment of death, 'She just slipped away.'

For Lord Snowdon the death of his former mother-in-law came as a double blow, following as it did his ex-wife's death in such a short period. And Queen Elizabeth had been no ordinary mother-in-law. From the moment she first set eyes on Tony, she liked him, and the longer they knew each other the greater the affection and mutual respect. Neither could do any wrong in the other's eyes, and throughout the eighteen years he was married to Princess Margaret and the twenty-four years afterwards when they were divorced, Tony was always welcome at Clarence House. The Queen Mother was completely non-judgemental, and the fact that Tony had done nothing to adversely affect the image of the royal family or, more importantly, the monarchy, even with an acrimonious divorce, kept him in her good books.

Of course, Princess Margaret was well down the list in the Line of Succession by then; at one time she had been fourth. By contrast, when the Prince and Princess of Wales were divorced, followed by the scandals surrounding the Duke and Duchess of York, the potential constitutional problems that arose caused the Queen Mother immense concern. She was the self-appointed guardian of royalty, and if anyone – of whatever rank – threatened the good name of the family they immediately became her enemy – and she was not a woman to cross.

Another reason why she was so fond of Tony was because she loved his artistic temperament and his knowledge of the theatre and film world. He could regale her with all the latest gossip about which stars were doing what with whom, and she would listen for hours enthralled. Tony has always been a wonderful storyteller, and she encouraged him to tell all and hold nothing back. They also had this strong blood connection through David and Sarah. Queen Elizabeth adored all her grandchildren, and the relationship between her and Prince Charles has been well documented. No one was more devastated than Charles, even the Queen, when his beloved grandmother died. But there was also a very special bond between her and Tony and Margaret's children, and there was no more poignant sight than when David Linley joined his royal cousins, the Prince of Wales, the Duke of York and the Earl of Wessex, to stand guard over their grandmother's catafalque as she lay in state in Westminster Hall, in a repeat of the moving tribute last paid to King George V by his sons in 1936. The Queen Mother was only the second royal consort to be accorded the honour of a lying-in-state. The first was her mother-in-law, Queen Mary, who died in 1953. Before the official lying-in-state, the Queen Mother's body was taken to the Queen's Chapel in the precincts of Marlborough House to rest at the same spot as Princess Margaret's had seven weeks earlier. The Chapel Royal could not be used because it was undergoing refurbishment. It was in the Queen's Chapel that members of the royal family and certain other VIPs, including Lord Snowdon, paid their private tributes.

The arrangements for the funeral had been in place for many years, as they are for all members of the royal family. Even today, the Palace holds regular meetings to update the details for the funerals of even the youngest members such as Princes William and Harry, and they are all given special code names; the Queen Mother's was Tay Bridge (Princess Margaret's was Chelsea Bridge). So the lists of who was to be invited to the service in Westminster Abbey on 9 April had been circulated to everyone concerned within hours of Queen Elizabeth's death. Not only was it necessary to include those who would automatically be included, such as government officials, Commonwealth leaders and other VIPs, but also representatives of the many organizations, both military and civil, she patronized.

Queen Elizabeth had also left instructions regarding her own personal wishes. High on this list was the name of her former son-in-law Lord Snowdon. She knew that he would want to be present, and of course his children David and Sarah were going to be there. The Queen is consulted on all such matters, and she, too, knew that it was her mother's wish for Tony to be in the abbey.

In total, 1,700 troops accompanied the horse-drawn carriage carrying the coffin, and a further 1,000 lined the route from St James's Palace to Westminster Hall for the lying-in-state. Then on the day of the funeral, a party of Irish Guardsmen acted as pall-bearers for the short procession of the cortège from Westminster Hall across the road to the abbey.

Following the State funeral service, the Queen Mother's body was taken by car to Windsor, where after a brief service it was interred in the royal vault in St George's Chapel alongside that of her husband, King George VI, who had died fifty years before.

Just ten days after the funeral the royals returned to Westminster Abbey to attend a memorial service for Princess Margaret. And, as with her funeral, the Princess had left specific instructions about the form the service was to take and who was to be invited. The fifty-minute service was sung by the choirs of Westminster Abbey, King's College Cambridge, St George's Chapel, Windsor, and the Academy of St Martin in the Fields. The soloists were international opera stars Bryn Terfel and Dame Felicity Lott who sang arias from Faure's *Requiem*, again at the Princess's request.

Lord Snowdon had been invited along with 25 members of the royal family, together with 600 of Princess Margaret's friends and a further 600 from the charities and other organizations she had been associated with. So many members of the public wanted to attend that a ballot had to be organized and 580 were chosen to be inside the abbey. The actress Felicity Kendal, one of Margaret's friends, gave a reading, as did David Linley. Princess Margaret would have loved every minute of it.

For Lord Snowdon this was truly the end of an era. In the space of seven weeks he had lost the woman with whom he had once been madly in love, and who had given him two wonderful children, and then a former mother-in-law whom he clearly adored.

The year 2002 was supposed to be a year of nothing but celebration as the Queen's Golden Jubilee year. With two royal deaths in the first two months it wasn't an auspicious start, but once Court mourning had ended the festivities began and gathered momentum as the year progressed. Lord Snowdon once again found himself on the Queen's guest list and, with David and Sarah and their spouses, enjoyed a touch of royal hospitality. Though he must have found it strange to be in the company of the royal family without the presence of the two women to whom he had once been so close.

NINETEEN

Still Searching for Happiness?

The royal family is notorious for its ruthlessness towards those it feels has stepped out of line, as Diana, Princess of Wales and Sarah, Duchess of York found out to their cost. Yet Lord Snowdon, who some might feel, has given them plenty of reasons to exclude him from their midst, has remained a welcome guest at practically every important royal occasion, on the express orders of no less a figure than the Queen herself.

He was invited to the service celebrating Her Majesty's Golden Jubilee year in 2002 and was on the guest list at the wedding of the Earl and Countess of Wessex – and included prominently in the wedding photographs. Earlier, in 1996, his was the first name on the list when the Queen and Prince Philip were looking for someone to take the official photographs of Prince Harry on his sixteenth birthday. Of course, Diana also had a great deal of say in that decision, and she had never hidden her affection for and admiration of Tony.

But where the royal family is concerned, the surprise is that they kept him in the fold even after the bitter divorce from Princess Margaret. He had done the gentlemanly thing and allowed her to divorce him, in spite of the fact that it was her very public affair with Roddy Llewellyn, a man seventeen years her junior, that provoked Tony into deciding to end the marriage. Yet even within the family, much of the blame for the break-up was heaped on Margaret and, while any other man might have expected to be publicly castigated for his tangled love life, he escaped with his reputation relatively unscathed. Perhaps it was because Margaret had always been seen as a spoilt young woman with an insufferable air of arrogance who did little to justify her privileged lifestyle, while

223

Tony, throughout their eighteen-year marriage, kept working at his profession and did not appear to trade on his royal connections or just sit back and enjoy what could have been an easy and idle existence. Whatever the reason, it was Margaret who received most of the blame both at the time of the divorce and later, while he continued to work and also to enjoy several relationships all carried out in the public eye. Even when it emerged that he had fathered an illegitimate child by a woman young enough to be his daughter, not many people condemned him outright. True, his second wife, Lucy, sued for divorce in September 2000 and was granted a decree nisi, but four years later, neither has applied for a decree absolute, which means that, as stated earlier, legally they are still married.

And Lucy remains on excellent terms with Tony. She lives very near him and they frequently meet and attend functions and social gatherings together, and they share a great affection for their daughter, Frances. So whatever his particular brand of charm is, it obviously still works. His private life may have been turbulent in the extreme, but if it is then there are few physical signs that this distresses him. But he is such a private person, with amazing self-control, that even if he were suffering the most agonizing inner turmoil somehow I don't believe anyone would ever know. He has been described as a 'great ladies' man', and even in his seventies remains attractive to women of all ages. But with men and women alike he has mastered the art of making the person he is with at the time feel they are the most important people around and there is no one he would rather be with.

His warm relationship with the royal family and in particular with the late Queen Mother, who would never hear a word said against her former son-in-law, has lasted not simply because of his pleasant personality and perfect manners, but because he has obeyed the cardinal rule – silence. Tony has never once spoken out of turn about any member of the family, and he was discretion itself when it came to Princess Margaret. They may have had stand-up rows for years when they were together, but once they had split up (and they had been divorced for twenty-four years by the time she died), no one heard him speak disparagingly about her even in private. Several of his closest friends told me that not only would he never talk badly about her but neither he would allow anyone else to do so. It is an admirable trait that has proved he is above all a gentleman of the old school. Even Prince Philip, not one of Tony's greatest admirers, has to admit that he 'knows the form' and has kept to the rules. If he hadn't there is no doubt that he would have been ostracized in precisely the same way as Sarah, Duchess of York, who, in spite of her efforts to regain the confidence of the royal family, still finds herself completely shut out. Her ex-husband Prince Andrew has apparently forgiven her for her indiscretions, and they are seen together – often with their daughters, Princesses Beatrice and Eugenie – on many occasions. But Sarah has discovered to her cost that where royalty is concerned loyalty is a one-way street; they demand it from everyone else, but are not so quick to give it themselves.

When the Queen decided to confer an earldom on her brother-in-law, it wasn't because he had lobbied in any way, and there is no truth in the rumour that Princess Margaret was furious because he was not made a duke as Prince Philip was when he married Princess Elizabeth. Margaret may have secretly wanted her husband to hold the same rank as her brother-in-law, but she was wise enough not to try to exert any pressure on her elder sister. It wouldn't have made the slightest difference if she had. The Queen makes her own decisions and even to accommodate her sister, for whom she had enormous affection, she would not have changed her mind. And Tony would probably have been highly embarrassed at being promoted from being a mere Mr to a duke overnight. Not that he dislikes his own title, but he tends to use it to promote his causes rather than for his own benefit. Because of his fame and reputation, he can still obtain the best tables in any restaurant in London. So, while being an earl is certainly no handicap, he doesn't exactly need it to enhance his lifestyle.

Snowdon has achieved much in his life. He is acclaimed as one of the world's top photographers as well as being a multi-talented designer, award-winning film-maker and arts administrator, while his efforts to improve the plight of the disabled have been applauded throughout Britain. But it has taken years for him to be recognized for his professional accomplishments rather than just as the ex-husband of the Queen's sister. By most ordinary standards he is well off but nowhere near as rich as his two elder children, David and Sarah, who are both multimillionaires in their own right (each is said to be worth over £14 million). They received the bulk of the fortune left by their mother and also substantial amounts from their maternal grandmother, Queen Elizabeth. In addition, David has run a successful bespoke furniture business for many years, with his handcrafted tables and chairs selling for thousands of pounds to buyers at home and abroad. In 2003 Sarah held a one-woman art show in London where she sold forty-two oil paintings and pencil drawings, with the cheapest costing £700 and the most expensive £8,000, the entire show realizing over £200,000. Snowdon's younger daughter, Frances, by his second wife Lucy, is also an astute businesswoman and accomplished artist who is making a name for herself. And when Serena Linley gave birth to a baby boy in 1999, making Tony a grandfather – he has since had several more grand-children – no one could have been more delighted. He said at the time, 'It's wonderful news. I am very proud.'

Being a grandparent is something he is enjoying tremendously. Or as he puts it, 'It's the best of both worlds, all the pleasure and none of the responsibility.' His paternal feelings have been aroused with the new arrivals, and he is always experimenting with new toys and inventions to amuse his grandchildren. They have a fascinating few years ahead of them with a grandfather who possesses magic fingers and a fertile imagination.

Tony has often described himself as 'lucky' and to some people it might seem that he is – with his good looks, comfortable lifestyle and ready access to royalty. But he has also had to overcome handi-caps that could easily have turned him into a sour, frustrated young man. Suffering polio at such an early age, when other boys were all playing sport and enjoying the normal pursuits of teenagers everywhere, he fought back. And perhaps coxing the winning Cambridge boat could be regarded as his greatest achievement – it certainly would be by his Oxbridge contemporaries. His marriage to Princess Margaret was seen by millions on television throughout the world. He and his new wife were the first couple to have their honeymoon on the Royal Yacht. He moved into a palace; both his mother-in-law and sister-in-law were queens, while his brother-in-law was a prince. He was invited to the most prestigious homes in the country, and dukes and duchesses fought for his friendship. Throughout it all he retained a sense of proportion and, more importantly, a sense of humour. He is self-deprecating to a fault, but woe betide anyone who is rash enough to take liberties. Tony is fiercely protective of his own family and of the royal family, particularly the Queen. She has remained loyal to him, and he returns the feelings 100 per cent. Her Majesty appreciates this, especially in an age when so many of her subjects seem to be of the opinion that loyalty is an outmoded and highly overrated virtue.

When Tony married Princess Margaret it was because he was in love with her, not because he thought marrying royalty would be beneficial to his career. He has always been ambitious to a degree, but not socially. He was determined to reach the top in his chosen profession but that did not mean spending the early years of his marriage simply as an appendage to his royal wife. The idea of years spent undertaking public duties just because of the woman to whom he was married never appealed to him in the slightest. He had already seen the way in which Prince Philip was perceived, before he managed to establish a niche for himself in the nation's life – and that took years to accomplish. And he wasn't prepared to follow suit. Tony needed to work. He was and is one of the world's leading professional photographers, and perhaps that was one of the reasons why his marriage to Princess Margaret was doomed to failure. She could not understand why palace life was never going to be enough, and he failed to convince her that they could still have a happy life together if only she would stop being so possessive. With all his relationships and both marriages, the one thing that comes first in his life in his work. Even his children and grandchildren, whom he adores, know that they, occasionally, have to take second place.

People who have worked for and with him say he is a hard taskmaster. He doesn't suffer fools gladly, and even if he manages to make all his instructions sound like the most reasonable requests, they know he wants it done yesterday. Instant obedience is the order of the day in the Snowdon household. He is obsessively tidy and knows where everything is in his office, home and studio, and he hates anyone to move things without his permission. He notices if a lamp has been moved or a chair's position altered the moment he enters a room. And while he is normally very quietly spoken, when necessary, he can make himself heard three streets away; a legacy of his training as cox of the winning Cambridge boat.

I have never met anyone who is more interested in everything. He loves to talk to workers in the street – bricklayers, carpenters, plumbers and electricians – and there is nothing patronizing about it. He is genuinely fascinated by what goes on around him and will stop and chat with all and sundry. He is anxious to learn and says that some of the artisans he meets talk more sense than many far better educated men he knows.

He still manages to make news, even sometimes by default. In January 2004 a car dealer was fined £2,500 for selling a Rolls-Royce Silver Spirit after falsely claiming it had once belonged to Lord Snowdon.

He lives in a grand house in Kensington, which will one day belong to his two older children, David and Sarah, as it was put in trust for them at the time of his divorce from Princess Margaret. There are some things about modern life that appal him such as mobile phones, particularly if people use them in restaurants. He deplores the lack of good manners prevalent in modern society, the way some drivers park their vehicles on the pavement obstructing the passage of wheelchairs and young mothers with prams. If he doesn't see his children every day, they invariably talk on the telephone, but he wouldn't dream of inflicting himself on them for family holidays. He believes they need a little time to themselves – and so does he.

Tony Snowdon is not the easiest man to get to know. It takes time and patience. Although for much of his life he has lived in a welter of publicity, he is, basically, a shy man with a reserve he disguises by appearing to be outgoing and gregarious. His very friendliness is a cover, I feel, for a nature that has become suspicious after nearly half a century of living in the public eye and always having to watch what he is saying and doing. It cannot be easy knowing that your every word or gesture might be reported in a manner that will put you in the wrong. It doesn't happen all that often now, but twenty years ago he could barely make a move without offending someone. He gives the impression of a man who has always felt the need to prove himself – and it is still the case today.

It is rare to meet someone of his age who still thrives so obviously on activity. It is as if he believes that if he stands still, it will all come to an end. He loves to be busy and to have a range of projects on the go at the same time. His enthusiasm is infectious, if a little over-powering at times. He is not the most patient of men; not always waiting for his secretary to open the mail in the morning. If he is up and about before she arrives, he goes through the post, quickly discarding anything that doesn't catch his interest and working on his replies to those he likes straight away, often writing letters himself in a scrawl that would do justice to a doctor. Most of the letters he writes take longer to read than they do to write.

Try talking to him about anything personal and he immediately goes off at a tangent, forcing the conversation away from himself while at the same time giving the appearance of being frank and open. He has a disarming manner that makes it hard for anyone to take offence, and he has become a master at building layers of protective fudge between himself and would-be interrogators. It's not that he sets out to be deliberately obstructive; it is just that he cannot answer private questions frankly without seeing the hidden traps. After a lifetime spent trying to avoid giving offence and guarding against saying anything that might reflect badly on his late ex-wife and former in-laws, it has become second nature to him to steer clear of all conversation that even looks like being dangerous. Yet he loves gossip and enjoys few things more than to sit with friends and acquaintances over a good meal, with a glass or two of wine, and listen to the latest scandals, the more salacious the better. He is a very good listener but very careful about what he says and to whom.

His old friend, the late David Hicks, said of him, 'Tony has spent so long looking over his shoulder it's a wonder he hasn't got a

229

permanent crick in the neck. He's had to be so careful of what he has said that privacy has become almost an obsession with him. It's not that he doesn't trust people, I think he doesn't trust himself. He's afraid that if he opens up just a little then the floodgates will open and it will all come out.'

As he looks back at his life, particularly the forty-five years since he married Princess Margaret, he must wonder if it has all been worthwhile. Should he have married her in the first place and, if so, should he have remained with her in spite of the unhappiness? Would it have been better if he had remained what he was, a successful photographer with the world at his feet and an independence no one would try to change? Recently he was taken to see their old apartment in Kensington Palace. He said it was very sad, but he remembered not the stand-up rows that led to an acrimonious divorce, but the great joy they shared in those rooms. As he put it, 'We really did have an enormous amount of fun here.' And recently, when talking to the author about Princess Margaret, he said, 'She was wonderful.'

When Snowdon's obituary comes to be written, there is one description that will fit him perfectly. He was truly the first royal rebel.

Appendix I: Snowdon the Craftsman

L ord Snowdon has often been asked to reveal the secrets of his craft (he refuses to call it an art), and he has always claimed there is no secret, no magic formula, that it's simply a matter of application. If that is true then he has become the master of applying himself and the results have been truly spectacular.

He once decided to write down his thoughts on taking photographs or snapshots as he prefers to call them in the studio. These are his own words:

The word studio to most people means a huge, high-ceilinged white-washed space with a north light. If it is used by a photographer it is usually filled with spotlights, floods and electronic flash.

My first studio in Pimlico, where I worked throughout the fifties, was a converted ironmonger's shop with no daylight. I tried to simulate natural light by building a large aluminium box filled with about sixty electric light bulbs covered with tissue paper. My studio today is even smaller; it's the size of a lean-to greenhouse: 10ft wide, 14ft long and only 7ft high, not by desire, but because of building regulations.

There is something to be said for the studio not being very impressive; sitters are not too intimidated. And if everything was ideal I might settle into a formula and every picture would be lit in exactly the same way. It faces west, completely the wrong direction for constant light. There's ordinary greenhouse glass on the roof, but I've pinned two layers of frosted plastic to diffuse the daylight. I use polystyrene reflector boards, white on one side and black on the other, putting some in the garden to boost the light from the side.

I have dozens of different backgrounds, all of which look almost the same. A background has to be just on this side of being something, and just on that side of being nothing: you can only use it until it becomes recognizable, then it's past its usefulness. Within the emptiness and terror of a plain background I try to capture something which is not only a likeness of a person but says something about them. I want my sitters to be recognized, not my work.

There are usually no lights in the studio because I infinitely prefer daylight. Black velvet curtains down one side cover the windowless wall, and I use black blinds on rails to change the direction and the amount of light. Every surface in the studio that is not glass is painted black. I find it easier to add light than subtract it.

All photography is about really is snapshots. Its capturing a moment that is typical. The photographer is essentially unimportant. It is the subject that is being recorded that is all-important. Great photographs that are remembered and illustrate a moment of history are those which have frozen a moment of emotion, of sadness, of happiness, photographs that stimulate an emotion in the viewer. Portraits of people taken in a studio seldom do that; they are purely a record of the sitter and will only be interesting to future generations because of the face and expression of the sitter. Their only lasting quality is likely to be that they serve as a record of the people whom other people wanted to see at a particular time. That is partly why I prefer to work for magazines rather than private commissions. I don't want the sitters to choose the pictures because they are seldom the best judges.

Being photographed is a bit like being in the electric chair; nobody likes it. I think the only way you can learn about taking photographs is to be photographed yourself so you can see what an awful experience it is. Nothing is more nerve-racking than a stream of ludicrous small talk from behind the lens. The whole process is embarrassing and can often tell truths that people want to hide.

Most of the time my eye is close to the viewfinder; I am seeing the sitter through the ground glass screen. There is no direct eye contact; it is like seeing them on a television screen. I nearly always want their eyes looking directly into the lens. A lens is a frightful,

232

powerful, horrible device, and the people who are being photographed usually want to escape from it. And because they are shy or embarrassed, or at a disadvantage and trapped, sitters will try to escape by making eye contact with anyone else who is in the studio. That is why I need absolute silence, rubber soles for me and my assistant, whom I expect to be even more inconspicuous than I am. I never want an assistant to talk technical jargon or catch an eye line. The relationship between myself and an assistant is schizophrenic. During the session I expect him to be anonymous and then at lunch or supper afterwards I like him to be an extremely firm critic, an amusing companion and a fund of technical data mixed with spicy gossip.

I always start by taking Polaroids for three reasons: first to let me know the shutter is working; second to show the effect of the lighting; third to check on composition. The expression on the Polaroid isn't important; that comes later. I never like to prepare the studio before a sitting. All the manuals say you should have everything ready before your sitters come, so that they will not get nervous hanging about. They also suggest that you should talk like mad to make a relaxed atmosphere. I find I don't do this. I don't want things to be too relaxed. I think it's important to have nothing prepared but rather to start off with an empty box and build it up from nothing each time. That is why I find that perhaps the most important aspect of taking photographs of people is to find out as much as possible about the sitter. On location I nearly always find the background too busy, and end up rearranging a room, and taking out anything distracting. I prefer to find a plain space which I use like an improvised studio. The limitations sometimes work to my benefit. I often end up in an attic using the light from a skylight or in a garage with the doors open.

I like to direct my subjects and tell them exactly what to do. It is not always a matter of making people feel totally at ease. Often the only way that one can break through someone's prepared face is to make them slightly uncomfortable, physically or mentally. Sometimes people can be awkward or ill at ease in a way that expresses themselves better than when they are relaxed. I may,

233

perhaps, ask them to hold a pose for longer than is natural, or I make a remark about the sitter or their work which surprises them, and then watch for their immediate reaction. On the other hand, I sometimes ask someone to move fractionally, not because I know what I want them to do, but simply because I do not like what I am seeing and if the person moved I might like it more. Only when things are going badly do I use the tactic of talking; it is a conscious and artificial device, and I only listen to what is said in the hope that an idea will come out of it; sometimes I leave the sitter alone for a few minutes to change the mood. Often when people are told exactly what to do they become more themselves than they know. In contrast, of course, it is crucial with children and the old, who tire quickly, to work fast and get the shot before they shut down like a machine that is turned off. One of my worries comes when the eyes go dead and people go blank. If this happens we have coffee or change the location and start again. The collaboration between the sitter and the photographer gives the photographs whatever spark of life they might have; it is the coming together of the way the sitters choose to show themselves and the way I choose to show them.

Some people are very concerned about their appearance and arrive in their Sunday best so they can be recorded for posterity as they think they ought to appear. Their choice of clothes is often too formal. A dark suit, white shirt and tie is my least favourite, along with stridently patterned dresses or blouses. I prefer overcoats, open-necked shirts and plain colours. I want the viewer to be unaware of clothes unless they tell me something about the person. That is why I'm such a bad fashion photographer.

For me photography is a way of recording things because I can't draw. I think 'portrait' is a tiresome word and makes a false analogy between photography and painting. The biggest insult, as far as I'm concerned, is if someone says, meaning well, one of my photographs is like a painting. I suppose it's as insulting as it would be to a painter if he was told his painting was just like a photograph. Work has to be fun. It's a difficult and curious balance. It's all games. I need to play games but professionally. The game is up when your work is published. . . . After taking photographs for forty years I suppose I should have gained more confidence or got better at it, but I find neither has happened – the dread of starting is just as bad, the disappointment on seeing the results is even worse.

Appendix II: Snowdon Family Tree

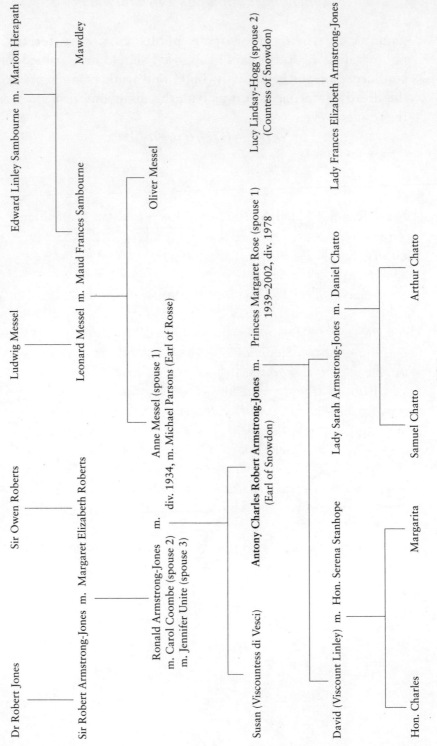

Dr Robert Jones

Sir Owen Roberts

Edward Linley Sambourne m. Marion Herapath

Mawdley

Ludwig Messel

Sir Robert Armstrong-Jones m. Margaret Elizabeth Roberts

Leonard Messel m. Maud Frances Sambourne

Oliver Messel

Ronald Armstrong-Jones m.
m. Carol Coombe (spouse 2)
m. Jennifer Unite (spouse 3)

Anne Messel (spouse 1)
div. 1934, m. Michael Parsons (Earl of Rosse)

Antony Charles Robert Armstrong-Jones m.
(Earl of Snowdon)

Princess Margaret Rose (spouse 1)
1939–2002, div. 1978

Lucy Lindsay-Hogg (spouse 2)
(Countess of Snowdon)

Lady Frances Elizabeth Armstrong-Jones

Susan (Viscountess di Vesci)

David (Viscount Linley) m. Hon. Serena Stanhope

Lady Sarah Armstrong-Jones m. Daniel Chatto

Hon. Charles

Margarita

Samuel Chatto

Arthur Chatto

Select Bibliography

Allison, R. and Riddell, S. *The Royal Encyclopedia*, Macmillan, 1991

Bradford, Sarah. *Elizabeth: A Biography of HM The Queen*, Heinemann, 1996

Dempster, Nigel. *HRH The Princess Margaret*, Quartet, 1981

Dimbleby, Jonathan. *The Prince of Wales*, Little, Brown, 1994

Hoey, Brian. *Her Majesty*, HarperCollins, 2002

——. *Mountbatten*, Sidgwick & Jackson, 1994

Judd, Denis. *Prince Philip*, Michael Joseph, 1980

Lacey, Robert. *Majesty*, Hutchinson, 1977

Lewis, Roger. *The Life and Death of Peter Sellers*, Century, 1994

Longford, Elizabeth. *Elizabeth R*, Weidenfeld & Nicolson, 1983

Pimlott, Ben. *The Queen*, HarperCollins, 1996

Snowdon, Earl of. *Snowdon on Stage*, Pavilion Books, 1997

Townsend, Peter. *Time and Chance*, Collins, 1978

Warwick, Christopher. *Princess Margaret*, Weidenfeld & Nicolson, 1983

——. *Princess Margaret: A Life of Contrasts*, Andre Deutsch, 2002

Index

Aberfan disaster 13–15
actors
    photographs by Snowdon 50–2
    Snowdon friends 6, 20, 23,
      103–6, 219
    see also film stars
Aga Khan 98
Alice, Princess, Duchess of
    Gloucester 155, 214
Allison, Ronald 152–3, 154
Andrew, Prince, Duke of York 71,
    166, 169, 225
Anne, Princess Royal 67, 83, 84
    marriage to Mark Phillips 166,
    169
    royal titles 13, 183
    and Tim Laurence 63, 156
Archbishop of Canterbury *see*
    Fisher, Geoffrey, Archibishop
    of Canterbury
Armstrong-Jones, Anne *see* Rosse,
    Anne, Countess of
Armstrong-Jones, Antony *see*
    Snowdon, Antony,
    1st Earl of
Armstrong-Jones, Carol (*née*
    Coombe) 35, 77

Armstrong-Jones, Frances 1, 181,
    226
    birth 183, 203
    personality 173, 191
    relationship with father 9, 201,
    204
Armstrong-Jones, Jennifer (*née*
    Unite) 31, 35, 77
Armstrong-Jones, Peregrine 31, 32
Armstrong-Jones, Robert 2, 31,
    32–3
Armstrong-Jones, Ronald 12, 17,
    31, 41, 42
    career at the Bar 27, 41
    divorces 29, 35
    financial help to Snowdon 48,
    49
    relationship with Snowdon 33,
    42
    on the royal engagement
    72–3
    success and lifestyle 27–8
    at the wedding 77–8, 86
Armstrong-Jones, Sarah *see* Chatto,
    Sarah
Armstrong-Jones, Susan *see* Vesey,
    Susan

Armstrong-Jones family 33, 190
arts 23, 108
    family influence 30–1
    see also actors; film stars
Astor, David 126

Baron (Sterling Nahum) 48–9
Barton, Anthony 43, 131, 189
Beaton, Cecil 47, 85
Bedales School 190, 192
Birr Castle 33–5
Bliss, Arthur 84, 141
Born to be Small 54, 151
Boxer, Mark 125
Brabourne, John 52, 53, 199
Brinson, Gunn 126, 128, 129
Britannia 89–92, 140
Bruno, Frank 7
Butcher, David 192

Cable-Alexander, Jasper and
    Melanie 186–7, 211
Cambridge University 17–18, 41–2,
    44–5
Cavendish, Elizabeth 61, 189
Charles, Prince of Wales 104, 168,
    172
    on death of Queen Mother
        219–20
    Investiture of 16, 83, 133–43
Chatto, Sarah (*née* Armstrong-
    Jones) 9, 123, 169, 189
    death of Margaret 213, 217,
        218
    godmother to Harry 176
    painting 190, 192, 199, 226

personality 173, 198–200
relationship with parents
    191–3, 198
wealth 226
wedding 200–2
Chatto family 190, 200–2, 214, 218
Churchill, Winston 58, 79
Clarence House 62, 71, 78
Coombe, Carol 35, 77
Coronation of Queen Elizabeth
    133–4
Coward, Noel 20, 79, 103
Crewe, Quentin 108, 174–5, 180,
    206–7
Cronin, Thomas 114–16

Davies, Lucy *see* Snowdon, Lucy
Diana, Princess of Wales 166,
    172–4
    mishandling of 13, 24, 168
    Royal Family and 163–4,
        168–9, 170–1
    Sarah Chatto and 200, 201,
        202
    similarities to Snowdon 163–5,
        166–8, 171–3, 176
    warmth of 15, 91, 167
Don't Count the Candles 54, 151
Douglas-Home, Robin 146–7
Duff, Michael 32

Eades, William 34–5
Edward, Duke of Windsor 27, 77,
    117, 135
Edward, Prince 161, 201, 223
Ekland, Britt 106, 107, 108, 109

Elizabeth, the Queen Mother 67,
    69, 79, 166
    death 218–19, 221
    death of Margaret 215, 216
    Snowdon and 19, 62, 101–2,
        146, 157, 219–21
Elizabeth II, Queen 69, 71, 154
    Coronation 133–4
    death of her mother 218–19,
        220
    on divorce 155, 156, 169
    Investiture of Charles 133,
        139, 141
    personality 69, 172
    and Snowdon 125, 157, 168,
        182, 225
    and the Townsend affair 19, 58
Emmy awards 22, 54
Eton college 17, 35–6, 38, 40, 173
European royalty 75, 78, 97, 165

Ferguson, Sarah *see* Sarah, Duchess
    of York
film stars
    photographs of 52–3, 124–5,
        200, 210
    socialising with 97, 219
    see also actors
Fisher, Geoffrey, Archibishop of
    Canterbury 11, 75, 84, 86
Fry, Jeremy 78, 180

George VI, King of England 100,
    122, 221
Gilliatt, Roger 78
Glenton, William 63, 101–2

Golden Jubilee Year 221–2, 223
Goodwin, Richard 52, 53
Goon Show 103, 105
Gordon, Ruby 113, 114
Griffin, John 152
Guinness, Alec 51, 52
Gunner, Laura 28

Harewood, George, 7th Earl
    155–6
Harry, Prince 173, 176
Hart, Derek 22, 53–4, 151
Hartnell, Norman 79, 82, 83
Herapath, Maud 30–1, 149–50
Hicks, David 70, 75–6, 114–15
    on Snowdon 21, 56, 207–8,
        230
Hicks, Pamela (*née* Mountbatten)
    75–6, 149, 208
Hills, Ann 184–6
Hopkins, Anthony 210
horse riding 163, 190–1,
        218–19
Huth, Angela 108, 174, 206–7

Ingrid, Queen of Denmark 76, 78
Investiture of Prince of Wales 16,
        83, 133–43
    Ball 104
    chairs 1, 2, 137–8
Issigonis, Alec 4

Kensington Palace
    marriage home 23, 101, 107–8,
        113–18
    moving from 122–3, 154

Launceston Place 1–3, 8–9, 169, 180, 228
Laurence, Tim 63, 156
Legh, Francis 82, 91
Lindsay-Hogg, Lucy *see* Snowdon, Lucy
Lindsay-Hogg, Michael 151, 182
Linley, David 173, 180
    birth 123, 189
    death of Margaret 213, 214, 217, 218
    furniture maker 190, 191, 194–5, 226
    inheritance 94, 169, 183, 226
    personality 194, 195, 196–7
    relationship with father 3, 9, 124, 177, 190–3
    relationship with mother 177, 191–2
    resemblance to father 189, 191, 193
Linley, Serena (*née* Stanhope) 190–1, 197, 226
Llewellyn, Roddy 150–1, 159, 172
London Zoo aviary 23, 45
Lord Chamberlain 76, 77–8, 113, 118

McBride, Bernard 100
McDonald, 'Bobo' 113–14
Macmillan, Harold 134
Margaret, Princess
    affairs 131, 146–7
    death 213, 214
    extravagance of 59, 90, 92, 99, 123, 158, 217–18

on family image 170
funeral 216–18
ill-humour 66, 75–6, 91, 99–100, 100, 121
later life 159–60, 183–4, 203, 205, 214
love of actors 20, 23, 61, 110
media and 120
motherhood 177, 191–2, 198
Peter Sellers and 106, 109–11, 148, 150
Peter Townsend and 12, 19, 57–8, 69–70
protocol, stickler for 22, 57, 108–9, 160
public dislike of 158–9, 223–4
retention of Snowdon title 182–3
Roddy Llewellyn and 150–1, 159, 172
Snowdon and
    at Balmoral 67–70
    courtship 19, 57, 62–6
    engagement 70–3
    first meeting 60–1
    post-divorce 157–60, 215
    wedding 11–12, 19–21, 75–87
    see also marriage; wedding
    suitors 59–60
    upbringing 22, 65, 124
marriage
    cracks in 129–31
    divorce 12, 23, 29–30, 147, 148, 154–5
    divorce settlement 169

doomed from start 21, 149,
150
early married life 97–111
honeymoon 89–95
married life 119–31
rumours of rift 100–1
separation 152–4
see also wedding
media
Diana and 13
marriage rift and separation
147, 148, 151–4
Peter Townsend affair 58
royal couple and 72, 92–3, 97,
99, 100, 101
royal household moles 64,
115–16
Rufus-Isaacs affair 148–9
Snowdon and 13, 15–16, 63,
117, 120, 125, 126
Snowdon children and 197–8,
202–3, 204
Snowdon's divorce 158
Snowdon's second marriage
178–9, 181
see also television
Marina, Princess, Duchess of Kent
56, 73
Messel, Anne *see* Rosse, Anne,
Countess of
Messel, Leonard 27, 145, 208
Messel, Oliver
favourite uncle 39
influence on Snowdon 17, 31,
37, 50
in Mustique 109

Messel family 30–1
Milligan, Spike 105, 106
monarchy *see* royal family
Mountbatten, Louis, 1st Earl of 21,
76, 133
Mountbatten, Pamela 75–6, 149,
208
Mustique, island 60, 93–4, 109,
150

Nahum, Sterling 'Baron' 48–9
National Service 40–1, 142
newspapers *see* media
Norfolk, Duke, Earl Marshal
133–4, 139
Nymans, country house 30, 145,
208–9

Ogilivy, Angus 119, 166, 184
Old House at Nymans 145–6, 209
Olivier, Laurence 51–2

Philip, Prince, Duke of Edinburgh
14, 48, 122, 168–9
giving away Margaret 80–1
personality 5, 15, 68–9, 157
prejudice against 165, 168
Snowdon and 68–9, 120–1,
137, 150, 225
Phillips, Mark 166, 169, 184
photographs 2, 9, 10, 54–5
actors 50–2
film stars 52–3, 107, 124–5,
200, 210
in print 51, 54, 56
royalty 56, 164, 223

photography
  beginnings of 18, 37, 47–56, 56
  income from 8, 10, 22, 126
  perfectionism 126–7, 128, 129, 207
  during royal marriage 99, 124–30, 149, 227
  Snowdon's process of 231–5
  studio 2–3
Plas Dinas 31–3, 38
Pound, John 136, 142, 143

Queen magazine 55, 206

Rhodes, Margaret 218–19
Rosse, Anne, Countess of 12, 17, 39, 208
  beauty of 27, 33, 167
  married life 28, 29, 30, 33
  and Snowdon 27–8, 37, 47–8, 77–8, 86
Rosse, Michael, Earl of 33–4, 39, 77
Rotherhithe 63–4, 101–3, 146
royal family
  aloofness 24, 172
  deception and 64, 147
  democratization of 20–1, 72
  on divorce 12, 155–6
  expenditure 87
  protocol 57, 77, 130, 160–1
  public attitude to 12–13, 19
  Snowdon and 119–22, 124, 130, 157, 163, 169, 223
  see also European royalty

royal household 156, 171
  media moles 64, 115–16
  Snowdon and 34, 63, 100, 113–18, 124, 171
Rufus-Isaacs, Jackie 148–9

Sambourne family 30–1, 122
Sandroyd preparatory school 35
Sarah, Duchess of York 166, 169, 184, 225
Sardinia 98–9
Secombe, Sir, Harry and his wife Myra 103–6, 109, 210
Sellers, Peter 3, 103, 105–6, 108
  and Margaret 106, 109–11, 148, 150
Snowdon, Antony, 1st Earl of
  affairs 148–9, 184–7
  appearance 103, 117–18, 142, 159, 194
  birth 27–8
  boxing 7, 17, 38, 40
  cars 3, 16, 43–4, 141, 196
  celebrity friendships 103–6, 109–11
  charm 211, 224
  childhood 28–30, 32–3
  children 3, 9, 124, 177, 190–3, 201, 204
  courtesy 6, 164, 181, 186
  craftsman 1, 2, 3, 34–5, 36–7, 191, 193
  Diana and 163–5, 166–8, 171–3, 176
  disabled and 174–5
  discretion 177–8, 179, 180, 224–5

education 17–18, 35–6, 38, 40,
    41–2, 44–5, 173
Elizabeth and 69, 71, 125, 157,
    168
family background 17, 29, 33,
    35
financial acumen 49, 126, 127,
    128, 129
friendliness 65, 99, 104
friendships 41, 45–6, 125,
    206–8, 210–11
kindness 7–8, 14–15
lack of fulfillment 206, 223–30
in later years 1–10, 205–35
Lucy and
    courtship 177–8
    marriage 182–4
    separation 186–7, 224
    start of relationship 131, 151
    wedding 179–80
Margaret and
    death of 217, 218
    early relationship 60–1, 62–6
    engagement 70–3
    post-divorce 157, 183–4,
    215
    see also marriage; wedding
media and 13, 15–16, 63, 117,
    120, 125, 126
motorbikes 3, 22, 37–8, 43,
    116, 141
peerage 122, 182, 211–12, 225
polio 3, 7, 17, 38–40, 174
practical side 49, 174–5
Prince Philip and 68–9, 120–1,
    168–9, 225

public goodwill 223–4
Queen Mother and 19, 62,
    101–2, 146, 157, 219–21
reserve 185, 210–11, 228–30
rowing 17–18, 27, 32, 40,
    44–5
Royal Family and 119–22,
    124, 130, 157, 163, 169,
    223
royal household and 34, 100,
    113–18, 171
royal role and 13, 22, 24,
    119–31, 149, 170–1
welshness 13, 31, 32, 33, 104
women and 50, 130, 211, 224
see also photographs;
    photography
Snowdon, Lucy (*née* Davies) 164, 176
    courtship 177–8
    marriage to Tony 182, 183,
    184
    motherhood 183, 203
    personality 180, 181
    separation 186–7, 224
    start of relationship 131,
    151
    wedding 179–80
Snowdon Award Scheme 175
Snowdon on Stage 52
Stanhope, Serena *see* Linley, Serena
Stanhope family 190–1
Stark, Graham 106, 109–11,
    210–11
Stevens, Jocelyn 55, 72, 107, 117
Sunday Times, Snowdon's work on
    101, 124–9, 147

Tallon, William, 'Backstairs Billy'
　7–8, 213–14
television
　at Investiture ceremony 16,
　　133, 135–6, 137, 139–40
　at Snowdon's wedding 78–9,
　　81
　Snowdon's work on 22–3, 54,
　　151, 182
　see also media
Tennant, Colin 60, 93–4
theatre *see* actors
Thomas, George 15
Toms, Carl 83, 136, 137, 140, 142,
　143
Townsend, Peter 12, 19, 57–8,
　69–70

Unite, Jennifer 31, 35, 77
University Boat Race 17, 44–5

Vesey, Susan (*née* Armstrong-Jones)
　28, 29, 32, 33, 77

Wagner, Anthony 138–9
Wallace, Billy 59–60
waterskiing 117, 138
wedding 11–12, 19–21, 75–87
　breakfast 77, 85–7
　dress 82–3
　presents 95
　see also marriage
Wessex, Earl of 161, 201, 223
Weston, Simon 175
William, Prince 173